LYIT
LIBRARY
LETTERKENNY

ALL THE BEST PEOPLE...

the pick of **PETERBOROUGH**

1929-1945

ALL THE BEST PEOPLE...

the pick of PETERBOROUGH 1929-1945

chosen by
Alex Faulkner and Tom Hartman

with résumés of each year's events by
Tom Hartman

introduced by
Michael Hogg
Editor of Peterborough 1971-1979

illustrated by
Timothy Jaques

London
GEORGE ALLEN & UNWIN
Boston Sydney

First published in 1981

GEORGE ALLEN & UNWIN LTD
40 Museum Street, London WC1A 1LU

British Library Cataloguing in Publication Data

All the Best People . . . The Pick of Peterborough
1929–1945
1. Great Britain – History – George V, 1910–1936
2. Great Britain – History – Edward VIII, 1936
3. Great Britain – History – George VI, 1936–1952
I. Faulkner, Alex II. Hartman, Tom
941.083 DA566

ISBN 0–04–808029–2

Typeset in 10 on 11 point Imprint by Bedford Typesetters Ltd
Printed in Great Britain
by Hazell Watson & Viney Ltd, Aylesbury, Bucks.

Contents

Introduction

by Michael Hogg
Editor of "Peterborough" 1971–9

"*The Daily Telegraph* may have broken records," wrote its former managing director, the late Lord Burnham, in his book *Peterborough Court*, "certainly it kept none." Like any recorder of other people's history, it is reticent, not to say incompetent, about its own.

Nevertheless it is possible to claim firmly for the Peterborough column that it has the distinction of surviving more than fifty years —something remarkable in itself in the evanescent world of journalism—and the still more remarkable distinction of having only five editors in its first half-century.

More remarkable again, perhaps, is that one man, the legendary Hugo Wortham, spanned half the fifty years editing the column, from 1934 to his death at the age of 75 in 1959. A totally Edwardian character, he was perhaps the ideal diarist for his time. He joined *The Morning Post* as a leader writer, and was a music critic for *The Daily Telegraph* before taking on "London Day by Day" for his quarter-century stint. His erudition was as wide-ranging as his conversation; his interest in every field of life never flagged.

It was he who coined the classic definition of a Peterborough paragraph—that "it should contain a fact, a generalisation and preferably a very slight inaccuracy." This is a tradition his successors have tried to maintain, only too successfully, alas, as far as the last condition is concerned. Nevertheless the inaccuracies, inevitable as they are, fulfil an involuntary purpose in providing another paragraph a day or so later, and also in establishing a kind of continuity which helps, I hope, to maintain a rapport between the column and its readers.

Of course, one depends on the readers for opinions and information, far more, I would almost say, than on the staff of the column themselves. After all, it is their interests that one tries to cater for, and nothing has worried me more in the last few years than the effect that increasing postage rates and the general decline in letter-writing seemed to have on the vital two-way communication between the column and its readers. Peterborough still tries, though, as it always has, to mirror the age it lives in by illuminating the odder corners of the news, the people behind the news, and sometimes news stories that just seem worthy, if that is not too pompous a word. Readers of this book must judge for themselves how well the founding fathers of the column achieved this aim.

To revert to history, Wortham's predecessors were the late Victor Gordon-Lennox, who started the column in 1929 and ran it until 1932 before becoming the paper's diplomatic correspondent, and the late E. D. "Toby" O'Brien (1932–4), who went on to become Director of Information Services for the Conservative Party after the war and then a well-known and successful public relations man in his own right. His successor was Fred Salfeld (1959–70), a character far too modest to describe himself as something in the Wortham mould (which nevertheless he was), who taught me, in five years as his deputy, all I knew about the job. To succeed such men was an honour—which gained agreeable savour from the coincidence that Gordon-Lennox was a family connection of my wife's (from such things diary-writers gain their stock in trade)—a feeling shared, I hope, by my own successor, Michael Green, the sixth and present "Peterborough."

That pseudonym, often asked about by readers, comes simply from the fact that the site of the paper's office, 135 Fleet Street, used to be Peterborough Court, once the site of the London hostel of the Abbots of Peterborough. But the column in fact started without a signature—headed, as it still is, "London Day by Day." This was actually a revived title. A column under that heading was started in 1888 and ran on until the First World War. In its present form it first appeared on February 17, 1929: the signature "Peterborough" was added without any explanation on November 2 that year, and has provided a cloak of anonymity for the column's editors ever since.

Anonymity, though, is a pretty subjective term. Prejudices and special interests keep showing through, and the world as a whole, of course, is what really conditions the whole. One of the things that struck me most over the years was that all newspaper diaries were dull when the world was dull and livelier when the world was livelier. It seems to hold good no matter how different the targets of Peterborough might be from those of the *Daily Express*'s William

Hickey, from the *Evening Standard*'s Londoner's Diary or Nigel Dempster's diary in the *Daily Mail*. Often I felt that a disastrously dull Peterborough had been sent to bed the night before, only to find that every other diary the next day was disastrously dull too. Mercifully, though, the result more often than not looked better in print than it had in typescript.

But such coincidences play a major part in diary-writing too. It is astonishing how often one finds oneself confronted by three, say, out of the day's ten paragraphs dealing with people celebrating their eightieth birthday, or four mentioning flowers of one sort or another, or five covering Service reunions.

This is perhaps inevitable in what is after all a corporate effort—a column produced partly by its own staff, partly by the newspaper's own specialists, and partly with the help of readers. The editor's function in the last resort is to construct the best he can out of the material that lands on his desk. His prejudices, inevitably, show through. However anonymous he may appear to be, the column finally reveals a great deal about its editor—more, I have often felt, than I would really care to have revealed.

This perhaps is why, as other ex-columnists agree, when one stops being a columnist one feels a peculiarly vast sense of relief. Terrified as I was when I first took charge of Peterborough—facing what Stephen Leacock called "the fear of the blank page"—it has been a marvellous miniature empire to command and to enjoy. Not to command it is to have a weight lifted from one's shoulders. But, goodness, it was fun while it lasted. I hope readers of this book get some sense of this fun as it was in the past, as well as of the times in which it was written.

MICHAEL HOGG

1929

1929 will always be remembered as the year of the Wall Street Crash, which, although it did not begin until October, totally eclipsed all other events of that year and certainly had the most far-reaching effects. Nevertheless, a brief résumé of some of those other events and the background against which they occurred may help the reader to appreciate more fully the paragraphs which follow.

In Britain Stanley Baldwin's Conservative Ministry had begun its fifth year in office at the end of 1928, so 1929 opened under the shadow of a General Election. The state of the country was not such as to make the bulk of the people enamoured of Mr. Baldwin's Government. Industry was still suffering from severe depression and the number of unemployed stood at nearly 1,500,000. In the General Election held in May the Labour Party was returned to power, although without an absolute majority, and Ramsay MacDonald was appointed Prime Minister for the second time. Miss Margaret Bondfield, appointed Minister of Labour, became the first woman to attain Cabinet rank and a place in the Privy Council.

Other events which caught the public eye in Britain during the year included the recovery of King George V from a serious illness, which had necessitated the precipitate return of the Prince of Wales from a visit to East Africa; the aeronautical exploits of such intrepid pioneers as Lady Bailey and the Duchess of Bedford; the unedifying squabble which arose out of the Salvation Army's decision to relieve General Booth, the founder's son, of his post, and the sentence of fifteen months' hard labour on Mrs Kate Meyrick for "corruptly receiving and giving money in connection with night-clubs". All in all 1929 cannot be described as a momentous year in the history of Great Britain.

In the United States Herbert Hoover succeeded Calvin Coolidge as President, having been elected by a record majority; Franklin D. Roosevelt became Governor of New York State, and a year which had started with such high promise ended, as already mentioned, in the chaos of the Wall Street Crash. This was the era of prohibition, the heyday of Al Capone and the year of the famous St. Valentine's Day massacre.

In Europe the aftermath of the First World War was changing gradually into the prelude to the Second. The post-war collapse of the German economy, caused mainly by the reparations imposed by the Treaty of Versailles, had been followed by four years of prosperity brought about by massive injections of American capital. Inevitably the Wall Street Crash was to have catastrophic results, leading directly to the supremacy of the Nazi party four years later.

France, too, under the able leadership of Raymond Poincaré, enjoyed a level of prosperity and world respect in the late 'twenties that few could have thought possible when he came to power in 1926. Poincaré resigned in July, 1929, leaving his successors to cope with the consequences of the Wall Street Crash, which, owing to her traditional policy of trade protection, actually hit France less severely than most other countries. The complacency brought about by economic stability was not, however, shared by the War Ministry, who, in 1929, started building the Maginot Line, ironically itself to become that symbol of complacency par excellence—a supposedly infallible defence.

Italy also appeared outwardly stable under the virtual dictatorship of Mussolini, who had come to power in 1922 as leader of the Fascist Party. In February, 1929, he settled his differences with Pope Pius XI through the Lateran Treaty, by which the Pope recognized the Kingdom of Italy under the House of Savoy, although Victor Emmanuel was King in name alone, and Italy recognized the independence of the Holy See.

Russia, isolated from and largely ignored by the Western world during the 'twenties, suffered under the increasingly barbarous tyranny of Stalin who, in 1929, banished his only surviving vocal critic, Leon Trotsky.

Spain, though still nominally ruled by King Alfonso XIII, was actually under the yoke of a military dictatorship headed by the unpopular General Primo de Rivera.

To return to the theme of this book: as the reader will often have occasion to remark, many of the topics touched upon by Peterborough have lost none of their appeal to the Press during the passage of fifty years. We find, for instance, Peterborough giving his views on the Channel Tunnel project, discussing the possibility of a rise in the price of petrol and sympathizing with the Duke of

Portland on being obliged to sell his Vase to meet the demands of the taxman. It may also come as a surprise to younger readers to learn that names such as Yehudi Menuhin, Quintin Hogg (junior) and Evelyn Waugh were already "newsworthy" over fifty years ago.

Story of Rodin and the Kaiser

Mademoiselle Judith Chadel, for many years secretary to Rodin, has some good stories to tell of the off-hand way in which the famous artist treated commissions, even from crowned heads.

She recalls how, on returning from a visit to Scotland at the end of the war, Rodin received a message from the King, asking him to visit Buckingham Palace. But Rodin would not go. "The King will understand that I am homesick for my Paris," he said, and back he went.

Because in the days before he became famous the Kaiser did not appreciate his art, Rodin later in his career refused to execute a bust of the Emperor, though a special envoy was sent from Germany to make the arrangements.

Rodin pleaded illness as an excuse, and later when war was declared he feared that the Kaiser would, if he were able, wreak vengeance on him for the slight. So he asked the American Ambassador in Paris to take his studio and museum under the protection of the then neutral United States. *February 25*

Henry Lamb's Pictures

There will undoubtedly be a great crowd of notabilities at the Leicester Galleries on Saturday for the private view of Henry Lamb's exhibition.

No one who has seen it could ever forget the wit and strength of his portrait of Lytton Strachey some years ago, and this time he has caught triumphantly not only the shy, eager look of young Evelyn Waugh, but his impeccable taste in clothes.

This symphony in blue brings out amazingly well those qualities which have made the young man, already an accomplished novelist, an astute critic and an artist of no little promise.

Lamb, who fought with distinction in the war, married Lord Longford's daughter, who under her maiden name of Pansy Pakenham wrote a fantastic novel last year of great charm and originality.

This exhibition will undoubtedly ratify the impression given by his earlier work, that both in his portraits and landscape Lamb is one of the most considerable artists of our time. *February 27*

Some Morris Secrets

In no quarter has the recognition of public service been received with greater satisfaction than in the workshops of Morris Motors, when it was learned yesterday morning that a baronetcy had been conferred upon the head of the firm.

True, it will be a little time before the hands in the continually expanding workshops become accustomed to addressing the boss on his daily visits as "Sir William." But there can be few factories in which closer bonds unite the employer and his workpeople.

The honour is one which Sir William might have received long since, but it is no breach of confidence to say that he has declined it on more than one occasion.

Similarly nearly two years before Morris Motors Ltd. was floated as a public company, with a capital of £5,000,000, Mr. Morris refused an offer of more than that amount to sell the business.

In each case the explanation was the same. Creation of the business has been his life's work. A six-day week at the works continues to be his greatest pleasure. To the terms on which he stands with his men Sir William proudly attributes the fact that he has never had a strike or lock-out in any of his concerns. *March 2*

Tragedy of a Changed Name

An Honours List has just been published, and in consequence a number of people are entitled to be known in future by a new style. In some cases—on this occasion the number is small—those who have long been identified by a certain name may elect to be known by a title at first wholly unfamiliar to their friends and acquaintances.

It is important to keep track of these changes, for failure to do so may lead to unfortunate consequences. Take the well-authenticated instance of a young man who was the luncheon guest of a certain Mr. So-and-so, now Lord Blankburgh, at a sporting club whose name is a household word.

"You ought to be a member here," said the kindly host. "If you will allow me to propose you your immediate election is assured." The guest murmured his thanks and departed.

A few days later came a letter conveying a similar suggestion, signed "Blankburgh." The name was unfamiliar, but, anxious to avoid revealing this fact, the young man replied in friendly terms.

"Dear Lord Blankburgh," he wrote, "it is really most kind of you, but unfortunately that crashing old bore George So-and-so has already promised to propose me."

History does not relate what followed, but clearly a closer familiarity with the affairs of the day might have saved the gentleman in question from a gaffe of no ordinary magnitude. *March 4*

Why the Portland Vase Must be Sold

A tragic commentary on the effect of burdensome taxation on great properties can be found in the decision of the Duke of Portland that he must sell the famous Portland Vase, regarded by the authorities of the British Museum, where it is housed, as one of the artistic wonders of the world.

Similar decisions are continually being forced upon the owners of great estates, who must choose between contraction of the properties which they hold in trust for those that are to come after them, and parting with some valued work of art.

Only quite recently the Duke of Richmond and Gordon chose in favour of selling a magnificent collection of Goodwood race cups. The sum which they realised must have seemed a very meagre recompense for the loss of trophies so intimately connected with the family history. *March 9*

Canvassing the Flappers

An M.P., canvassing some new women voters, suggested that a young maidservant should give him her vote, but was met with a firm refusal. The conversation ran as follows:

M.P.: I hope you are not going to give it to the other side.

Maid: I'm not going to give it to anybody.

M.P.: Pity—that. What's the reason?

Maid: Well, I've only just had it given to me and I'm not going to give it away again.

Collapse of M.P. *March 11*

Professor Einstein 50

Birthdays are probably of little interest to Professor Albert Einstein, who is 50 tomorrow, for his theory of relativity leaves little scope for such arbitrary markings of the passage of time.

"Time," according to this ex-engineer in a patent office, and professor in turn at Prague, Zurich, and Berlin, "is measured by the interval between two events, and this interval will be shortened if we move towards one of the events."

The Professor would appear to be moving towards his 50th birthday mark, but whether the interval between this event and his birth is shorter than fifty years probably nobody can say with certainty—unless Sir Oliver Lodge or Professor Eddington can solve the problem. *March 13*

Experts and the Tunnel

Since the Channel Tunnel project was revived some weeks ago there has been growing in the public mind a conviction that the new link between England and the Continent is virtually an accomplished fact.

Already in imagination week-enders are planning trips to the French coast resorts and to Paris, free from the harassing fears of a rough crossing, and with a reduced travelling time.

But it is to be feared that such plans are doomed to disappointment. Experts who have been giving the subject close attention are convinced that the project is not economically sound.

Apart from the damage that might well be done to the English south coast resorts, which cannot offer the casino attractions available across the Channel, grave doubts are expressed as to whether the traffic through the tunnel would be sufficient to show a profit on the huge capital outlay. At a time when new capital is urgently needed for other works of development, the Government is not disposed to give its approval and blessing to a project which, in its opinion, would result only in the total waste of at least half the expenditure involved. *March 21*

Petrol Price Rumour

Since the announced increase in the price of petrol rumour has been busy with a story that the oil companies are planning to fix a further advance in the near future.

Motorists will be relieved to learn that there is no foundation in fact for these stories, at any rate, for the present. No such proposal has been considered by the companies, as a whole, up to the present time.

It is probably true, however, that the recent price advance has greatly complicated the problems of the Chancellor of the Exchequer, who was anxious to give some measure of relief to motorists in the forthcoming Budget. *March 21*

Mr. Bernard Shaw's American Vogue

A remarkable vogue for the works and sayings of Mr. George Bernard Shaw is developing in the United States at the present time.

His every public utterance is cabled to America in full—a distinction which he shares with few Englishmen (or Irishmen), except the Prince of Wales.

Englishmen in New York find it difficult to account for this state of affairs, unless it be attributable in part to Mr. Shaw's persistent and vigorous refusal of all invitations to cross the Atlantic.

Fantastic prices are being paid for autograph copies of his first editions. A copy of his "Quintessence of Ibsenism" was sold the other day for nearly £600.

Even more astonishing is the payment of nearly £300 for an uninscribed first edition copy of "An Unsocial Socialist" (1887), and an even higher sum for the galley proofs of a small booklet about him in which he had written some biographical notes.

The buyer of a copy of Locke's "Human Understanding," for which he paid more than £300 because certain marginal notes were thought to be attributable to Mr. Shaw, will be relieved that the bidding did not reach a higher figure.

One gathers that he was prepared to go to several times that sum, but Mr. Shaw now reveals that the notes were, in fact, made by his father-in-law, whose name, Horace Townsend, according to Mr. Shaw, is written in the volume. *March 25*

The Lord Chancellor's Promising Son

Mr. Quintin Hogg, President of the Oxford Union, whose thoughtful article in the *Sunday Times* on "Why I Prefer Conservatism" has attracted attention, is the elder son of the Lord Chancellor, Lord Hailsham.

He was given the Christian name of Quintin after his grandfather, the founder of the Polytechnic, an institution in whose welfare Lord Hailsham naturally takes a keen interest.

As a member of the University Conservative Association Mr. Quintin Hogg was one of a small band of Oxford undergraduates who attended the annual conference of the Conservative party at Great Yarmouth last autumn.

On that occasion he made a speech strongly tinged with idealism, but refreshing in its candour, and full of sincerity.

Those who heard it with delight registered the name of the speaker as one who, like his father, will go far in politics if he eventually chooses this sphere of activity. *April 3*

Changing Mayfair

The changes that are coming over the London of ten years ago are not confined to its outward appearance; they are essential changes of character.

Nowhere is the subtle difference more noticeable than in Mayfair, where commerce is steadily thrusting its way ever deeper into this once-sacred residential area.

Curzon Street has, of course, long since succumbed to the demand for shop accommodation in an aristocratic neighbourhood. Now Hertford Street, too, has broken with tradition. A dress shop belonging to Lady Cecil Douglas has just made its appearance.

So it goes on, while, in response to the demands of Bond Street for an alternative north to south traffic artery, plans are being considered for running an omnibus route through Berkeley Square. To lovers of London as it was the changes are tinged with sadness, inevitable though they may be. *April 4*

"The Well of Loneliness": Many Translations

While the Home Secretary has succeeded in preventing the publication here of Miss Radclyffe Hall's notorious "Well of Loneliness," his action has created a huge demand for the book in other countries.

At the moment Miss Radclyffe Hall is supervising the translation of the work into French in order that it may be published shortly in

Paris. To have had the proofs sent to her in England might have been to court trouble with the postal authorities, so she is remaining in France.

Translations are also being prepared in German, Dutch, and Danish, and offers from publishers in Italy, Czechoslovakia, Sweden and Spain are now being considered by the authoress.

Incidentally, over 60,000 copies in the English language have been sold. All of which is very depressing, and shows how difficult it is to control public morals by regulation. *April 10*

Mr. Churchill's Great Reception

The Chancellor of the Exchequer is accustomed to occupying the centre of the limelight on Budget Day. Mr. Churchill, of all Chancellors, delights in, and responds to, the sympathetic ovations of the crowd.

Small wonder that he was at the top of his form by the time he reached the House of Commons yesterday. Never had he been more crowded around than he was during his short journey on foot from No. 11, Downing Street.

His reception by his own party in the House must have given him special pleasure, for he is not insensible to the somewhat harsh things that have been said of him during the past few months by important elements of the Conservative rank and file.

Certain portions of the speech were designed specifically to remove an impression which has gained some adherents of late that his personal friendship with Mr. Lloyd George might continue to have a political significance.

The Prince of Wales, watching the Chancellor's performance from above the clock, delighted in his lighter sallies, and a little episode, noted by few, did not escape his attention.

Reference to the decline in consumption of spirits brought Mr. Churchill, not unnaturally, to a phase of his speech offering a suitable opportunity for hurried recourse to the glass of "amber-coloured fluid" which each year is placed beside him on these occasions.

The glass attracted the attention of the Prime Minister. "Brandy?" he queried of the Foreign Secretary, who was seated within reach. Sir Austen was unable off-hand to reply.

Reaching forward to the table, he removed the glass, and sniffed at the contents critically. "Brandy and soda," he confirmed, and the two leaders smiled at one another sympathetically; and perhaps, one thought, a little thirstily. *April 16*

"Corn on the Cob"

Around Paris the farmers have not been slow to realise that American visitors like to eat "corn on the cob"—that is to say, green maize boiled and served whole with hot butter.

The taste is somewhat of an acquired one, and the operation of eating the vegetable in the American fashion introduces a new style into table manners as generally understood over here.

The corn cob, dripping with butter, must be seized between the forefinger and thumb of each hand and attacked as a native would attack a slice of melon.

The American visitor to Europe frequently laments the difficulty in obtaining this dish in the average private house or restaurant, and the consequent demand in Paris has led the farmers in the surrounding districts to cultivate extensive crops. The cobs are sold at a good price to the leading hotels. *May 8*

Stockingless Tennis

A great deal of nonsense, as it seems to many people, is being talked and written anent the immodesty of girls who wish to play lawn tennis minus their stockings.

Apart altogether from the ethics of the question, it is more than doubtful whether the bulk of those who one month hence will throng round the courts at Wimbledon would be able to detect whether or not the women players were bare-legged or silk-stockinged.

For nowadays silk stockings with over-socks to reduce chafing by the shoe have almost entirely ousted the thicker stockings which women used to wear for outdoor games.

In the countries where hot summers are the rule rather than the exception—the South of France each year provides an adequate example—women go bare-legged invariably, and men play lawn tennis in bathing shorts only. *May 30*

Marvels of the New British Airship

An Air Leviathan

Not so far from Bedford stands a building which at a distance seems to be nothing more than an insignificant shed. Approach nearer, and it assumes the aspect of a pyramid in the prairie. At close quarters it looks capable of comfortably housing both the Mauretania and Nelson's Column.

That is hardly an exaggeration, for this gigantic edifice houses no less an object than the incomplete structure of the world's greatest airship, the R 101. And if all goes well, those doors will open in about eight weeks' time, and there will emerge a dirigible beside which a Zeppelin is but as a cigarette to a large cigar.

At a first glance, if one is lucky enough to enter, it is not easy to distinguish some of the uppermost framework of the airship from that of the shed itself. The girder work is a picture of symmetry, but so colossal as to be positively alarming to those who suffer from giddiness.

About its centre and inside the envelope are the most astonishing passengers' quarters that have ever promised to fly in the air. On the starboard side is a large dining-room where fifty travellers may feed. The remaining fifty (for this liner accommodates about 100 in all) will be enjoying their cocktail in the palatial lounge and will have booked for the "deuxième service."

This main lounge is worthy of something bigger than the sumptuous yacht, being lit and decorated in the most elaborate fashion. At one side a step or two takes you to a most promising balcony, from which a fine view of the world beneath can be enjoyed through a long, unsplinterable window.

Nothing is cramped or oppressive; it seems inconceivable that such an hotel should fly. The two-bunk cabins look far more comfortable than any sleeper, and will be far quieter, so they say. Moreover, the entire ship is ventilated with warm or cold air as climate demands.

This ship is a departure from convention in that the only "appendages" are the control cabin, or "bridge," which hangs underneath about 'midships, and the five "eggs," which contain five crude-oil engines of enormous size. Everything else about the ship is tucked away inside the envelope.

Crude oil has been favoured rather than petrol to obviate the possibility of fire; in fact, every precaution has been taken in that respect.

The bar-lounge, just off the main saloon, is floored with aluminium, and here one may enjoy a cigarette.

As the R 101 dwarfs in bulk every one of its predecessors, so its appearance in the air early in August may well throw most contemporary events into eclipse. *May 31*

All the Best People

Prince Bismarck, of the German Embassy, is telling a good story against himself.

It happened that recently a prominent member of the German colony in London had a mental breakdown, and Prince Bismarck went to see that he was comfortable in the home to which he had been taken.

The door was unlocked, and he was admitted, only to find himself alone in a long passage. It was some time before he could see an attendant to ask the way.

However, he found one at last, and on announcing his identity the Prince was horrified at being cut short by the attendant, who said soothingly: "That's all right, Prince Bismarck. You'll find your friends, Julius Caesar and Henry the Eighth, along there."

No one relishes the story more than the good-natured grandson of the Iron Chancellor. He and his beautiful Swedish wife are perhaps the most popular young couple in diplomatic London, as they are certainly among the handsomest. *June 18*

A Disgraceful Exhibition

Probably no greater insult has ever been offered to the London public than the exhibition at the Warren Galleries in Maddox Street of twenty-five paintings by Mr. D. H. Lawrence, whose name is better known to the public as a writer than as an artist.

So long as the exhibition remains open it must be a standing source of amazement that the authorities permit the public display of paintings of so gross and obscene a character.

To encounter a friend, particularly a friend of the opposite sex, in the Warren Galleries is, to say the least of it, highly embarrassing, and one can detect that attitude of mind in the furtive entrance of those who climb the narrow staircase.

To pretend that such subjects can be justified on any artistic grounds is sheer nonsense. Mr. Lawrence's qualifications as a painter appear, to the normal mind at least, negligible, and his subjects, lacking all sort of restraint, are of a character such as has never been seen in London before. *June 20*

A Political Intrusion

Political propaganda is the latest development on the talkies, though many might call it the latest abomination.

Thrust in among the topical news at one central place of entertainment just now is a dialogue between Mr. Lloyd George and his daughter Megan, who are "discovered" sitting on a garden seat at Churt.

It is an ingenuous performance in the old-fashioned style of Little Arthur taking his first steps in knowledge at the knee of his "dear mama". Miss Megan asks simple political questions and papa makes suitable reply.

The lesson, of course, is that if the Government are good boys and deal with the agricultural housing problem—Miss Megan sits for Anglesey—papa will support them, but if they do not treat her papa fairly and bring in the electoral reform which he demands papa will rise in just indignation and deal them a real hard knock.

The trees rustle behind the garden seat; a dog crosses the field of the camera's vision and shows for a moment a waving tail. Mr. Lloyd George talks his cigar clean out, and Miss Megan strikes the engaging pose of the adoring daughter and diligent inquirer after truth.

This may be "legitimate talkie," but it is dreary art and dismal amusement. *July 1*

Hard Lines on Mr. Burns

One of the most disappointed men in London during the past twenty-four hours has been Mr. Walter S. M. Burns, who just a month ago sold his Romney's "Blue Boy" to the Ehrich Galleries of New York.

The picture has now changed hands in America for £55,000, the new owner being an American collector living in Long Island.

Mr. Burns has confessed to his intimate friends that the sum he received for the picture was no more than £4,000, which at the time he believed to be a reasonable price. *August 16*

Hobbs's Recent Hundreds

Hobbs of late has made a series of hundreds. They have been almost consecutive, a score of 97, among others, intervening. Hobbs is 47, and this is the month of August.

W. G. Grace was 47 when he made a series of hundreds; he scored 1,000 runs in the month of May. That was in the year 1895.

Some uncanny virtue must accrue, it would seem, to a really great batsman—established as such—when he completes or approaches his 47th year. Still when "W. G." did his unprecedented scoring it was realised that he had then got beyond and below his own absolute best.

He was ever an old young man, and he early put on weight. Hobbs, on the other hand, has kept his figure and remains lithe and active.

He returns to Test Match cricket to-day, after a period of self-exclusion from it, and his performance will be watched with renewed interest. *August 17*

Chinese in the West End

The raiding of a Chinese restaurant in Oxford Street may call attention to the migration that has been going on from Chinatown during the last few years. Limehouse was always less lurid than the stories about it, and if you talk to the East End police about it nowadays, they claim to have the region completely under control. According to them the new Chinese resorts are to be found west of lower Tottenham Court Road.

But Chinese restaurants have also been multiplying in Soho and Bloomsbury. A striking change has taken place in one little street that used to be almost entirely given up to music publishers, minstrels, and jazz. This is Denmark Street, which is slowly filling up with Japanese merchants, Chinese and Japanese restaurants and cafés—so much so that one is sometimes inclined to call it the "Little Orient." *August 19*

Mr. Noel Coward's Plans

Mr. Noel Coward is not going to write another play for a considerable time. He has just been telling some intimate friends that he wishes to travel to the Far East (a tour to the Far East with his own comedies, with the author in the chief role in each case, was contemplated, but has been postponed) simply as a holiday.

He wants to rest, to broaden his mind, and to let his ideas settle and develop. He is a tremendously hard worker, and he does not want to risk writing himself out.

It is a wise scheme. Mr. Coward is still under 30, and he has made, and is making, plenty of money; his weekly royalties from "Bitter-Sweet" alone amount of nearly £300. And although he has written one or two disappointing plays, he has written many more that have been good, and some that are brilliant.

To refuse baits, however tempting, for at least a year shows that this attractive young man can couple his brilliance with shrewdness.

August 29

"A Two-strap Town"

Frinton-on-Sea seems to be finicking as well as fashionable. A young woman was the other afternoon lounging on the beach in a bathing costume of irreproachable modesty and supported by one shoulder strap. A municipal official approached with an air of grave remonstrance and the remark, "Frinton has always been a two-strap town." *September 11*

Princess Elizabeth

When Princess Elizabeth arrives back in London with her parents in October those who come in contact with her at 145, Piccadilly are likely to see a considerable change in her.

Not only has the little Princess grown, but she is beginning to show the happy effect which being with a family of children in a homely atmosphere—instead of being a rather isolated personality in a Royal nursery—has had upon her.

Always a friendly small person, she has had ample opportunity at Lady Strathmore's, where she has spent the greater part of her holiday, for development in this direction with the companionship of her cousins, Lady Elphinstone's children.

Her Grown-up Manner

That the little Princess is as quick as most children to imitate her elders is shown by a story which friends of the Duchess are telling just now.

Princess Elizabeth had been got ready for a party, and was waiting in the hall with the other children for the car which was to fetch them. The smaller ones managed to reach the doorstep and looked out to see if their conveyance was on its way, getting themselves rather blown about in the process, for it was a stormy day.

The Princess settled her frock with the slightest suspicion of a frown and then, turning to the little group, said in her best grown-up manner: "How tiresome the wind is. It blows one's skirts about terribly!" *September 19*

The Edible Snail

Snails are coming into season again. The edible snail—the "Escargot de Bourgogne" is the favourite variety—is an acquired taste, in the sense that not many people have acquired it on this side of the Channel.

But English snail-lovers are on the increase, and this delicacy is now served regularly in many London restaurants, whereas formerly it could be obtained, without difficulty, at only two—the Monico and a tiny establishment in Soho, where it has for years been a speciality.

Snails are extremely nourishing, and served very hot, with parsley butter, and garlic, are said, by those who like them, to be delicious. But, for the majority, the resemblance to a piece of fried mackintosh is rather too strong. *September 28*

The Western Drift

The progressive invasion of Mayfair by commerce is having its effect in marked degree on the rentals obtainable in Belgravia.

Shopland is rapidly advancing into that one-time dignified area, Berkeley Square, and the streets leading off it, which not long ago were regarded as the most valuable residential property in London.

For a time the great houses of Belgravia were at a discount. Few families could afford to occupy them as single residences, and their conversion into flats had not yet appealed to the speculative builder.

But there are signs of a coming change, and to-day relatively high prices are being paid in this quarter for anything from a "mansion" to a converted stable.

In Knightsbridge, shopkeepers who, for the past ninety-nine years, have paid rentals of 10s a week, are finding themselves faced with the alternatives of clearing out or renewing their leases at as many pounds per year as formerly they paid shillings.

It has often been said that civilised communities invariably extend towards the west, and that this movement in London conforms to a well-established theory.

Whether such is, in fact, the case, and whether circumstantial evidence can be advanced, is a matter upon which some reader may perhaps be able to supply information. *October 10*

"The Mews"

The growing number of well-known people who of late have taken up residence in converted mews has resulted in many applications being received by the London County Council for an official change of postal address.

To live in a mews has come, through usage, to be regarded as an indication of humble state little removed from residence in a slum, and noble lords, who are now learning the convenience of these small self-contained habitations, petition earnestly for a more high-sounding title for use in note-paper headings, the telephone directory, or the Court Guide.

But the authorities are adamant. They will hear nothing of changing the good old title—the derivation of which, by the way, is interesting and not widely known. "Mews" indicated the place where the hawks were kept, more especially the cages of the Royal hawks, and later these were used for housing the Royal horses.

So it was that all stables in London became known as mews—which, in itself, may be an indication of an earlier tendency to snobbery. *October 12*

M. Stalin

Guiding the destinies of Bolshevik Russia must be a serious strain on the health. Lenin is dead, and Trotsky had many breakdowns before his final expulsion. Now Stalin, the Soviet dictator and reputed a stronger tyrant than either of them, is reported to be in a serious condition, and is in the sanatorium in which Lenin died.

Like most of the prominent Bolsheviks, Stalin uses a false name. Since his real name is Josef Dzhooghaashvilli there is some excuse for it.

He comes of good old Georgian brigand stock, but his father renounced brigandage, became converted to the orthodox faith, and intended his son for the priesthood. He preferred, however, atheism and active revolution, and became a daring terrorist.

His courage and abilities are considerable, but he is hated, and a whole regiment, composed of ex-Georgian brigands, is necessary for his bodyguard. *October 17*

Musical Prodigies

It is strange that the invasion of London by musical prodigies should come in definite waves. For years hardly one of these uncanny little folk had appeared; yet in the last few months there have been several.

Yehudi Menuhin, a minute violinist who plays the difficult Brahms Concerto at the Queen's Hall to-night, differs from the majority of his kind in that he is not dark, but very fair; blonde prodigies are said to be as rare as white elephants or dead donkeys.

Until recently Yehudi, who has created a sensation everywhere he has played by reason of his extraordinary technique, used a small violin specially made for him, but has now been promoted to a larger instrument. He has also invariably been accompanied by his teacher, whose duty it was to tune the violin for him. *November 4*

Lady Cynthia's Red Record

The Chancellor of the Duchy of Lancaster has possibly set a new fashion in commemorative jewellery.

Sir Oswald Mosley has recently presented his wife, Lady Cynthia Mosley, the member for the Stoke Division, Stoke-on-Trent, with a brooch representing the Houses of Parliament in diamonds, the figures of her majority, 7,850, being set across it in rubies, thereby ensuring a permanent record of the fact that the majority was a "Red" one. *November 4*

G.B.S. and Ellen Terry

To-night's revival of "Captain Brassbound's Conversion" will recall to the minds of some playgoers happy memories of Ellen Terry, who played Lady Cicely, the only female part.

Except the nurse in "Romeo and Juliet," it was the last character she impersonated and her memory was already failing—an infirmity which prompted the author, Mr. Bernard Shaw, to a characteristic witticism.

Someone was asking him how the play was going. "Oh, excellently," he said; "it was a bit sticky for the first fortnight, but now that Miss Terry has improvised a perfectly charming part for herself it is doing very well indeed."

My own recollection is certainly that Lady Cicely's conversations with the brigands while she mended their coats varied surprisingly from night to night. *November 7*

The Benevolent Eye

During the recent events on Wall Street a plunger was beseeching his banker for an overdraft. The banker remained negatively adamant. Finally, in response to the urgent pleadings of his client, he smiled sardonically and said:

"One of my eyes is made of glass. If you can say which it is I will grant you the overdraft."

Unhesitatingly the client indicated an eye.

"Correct," said the banker in astonishment. "But how could you tell?"

"Because it looked the kinder," was the reply. *November 20*

The Duke of York's Birthday

It is typical of the quiet domestic life which is so much enjoyed by the Duke and Duchess of York, when not engaged on some public function, that they have arranged no special celebration of the Duke's 34th birthday to-day.

If the weather is fine the Duke will spend the day hunting, but if this is impossible he will, I gather, return to London to be with the Duchess and the little Princess.

I well remember having tea with the Duke and Lady Elizabeth

Bowes-Lyon, as she was then, in Lord and Lady Strathmore's house in Bruton Street on the day that their engagement was announced.

It is, I think, no breach of confidence now to record that at that time the Duke was as apprehensive of the great public functions which would necessarily accompany the celebration of his marriage as was his bride-to-be.

The Duke's dread of such affairs in those days was largely due to the impediment in speech of which, with the assistance of the Duchess and the advice of an expert, he has now happily cured himself completely. *December 14*

Mr. Shaw's Wedding Gift

In the list of those who had sent cheques as presents on the occasion of the wedding yesterday of Miss Peggy Leigh, daughter of the Hon. Roland Leigh, a handicapper to the Jockey Club, to Mr. Charles Graves, appeared the name of Mr. George Bernard Shaw.

That simple announcement masks a typical Shavian witticism in the form of a letter to the bridegroom, which I was allowed to read.

In excusing himself from being present at St. Margaret's, Mr. Bernard Shaw explained that (a) he never attends weddings, and (b) he had no clothes suitable to the occasion and had been informed by his tailor that the cost of an appropriate suit would be fifteen guineas.

He therefore suggested that the sum which he would have expended in order to fit himself for attending the wedding should be employed by the bridegroom in purchasing a suit for social purposes, and his cheque was made out, with typical originality, for "Fifteen guineas sterling."

I hope that the bridegroom will be able to cash it. At first sight, guineas, like doubloons, give the impression of a form of legal tender which belongs to the picturesque past. *December 18*

1930

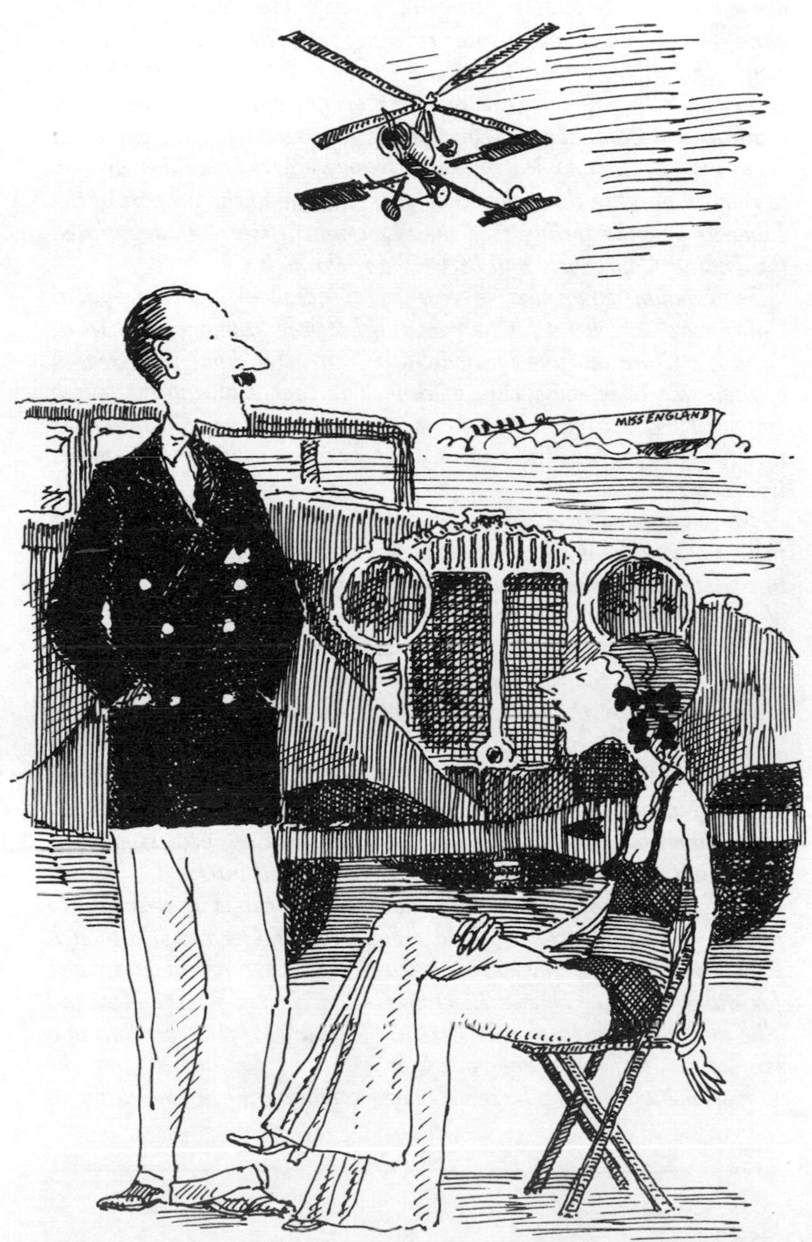

The words of one commentator, looking back on the year 1930, have a remarkably familiar ring: "Certainly no encouragement was forthcoming from anything done in Parliament. Economy seemed to be completely disregarded; expenditure, on the other hand, increased; taxation rose; revenues fell; the army of Government officials increased; and there was a notable, but possibly not surprising, accession to the numbers of unemployed." On a less familiar note, on May 1 Bank Rate was reduced to 3 per cent. However, the Labour Party, under Ramsay MacDonald, managed to remain in office throughout the year, thanks to the support of the Liberals and the feeling that the Government which had initiated the Indian Conference had better see it through.

In London 1930 was a year of conferences. At the Naval Conference, which sat for four months between January and April, Japan, Britain and the United States agreed to limit the strength of their navies in every class of ship. The year also saw the fourth Imperial Press Conference, the meeting of the Prime Ministers of the Empire for an Imperial Conference, as well as the Indian Conference.

For most countries 1930 was a difficult year. In Canada the fall in the price of wheat to little more than 50 cents a bushel led to widespread unemployment, which in turn resulted in the defeat of the Liberal Government at the General Election held in July and the return to power of the Conservatives under R. B. Bennett. For Australia, too, it was a year of increasing financial anxiety, partly caused by the fall in the prices of wool and wheat.

The Indian scene was darkened by the struggle between the Government and the Congress party. In March Gandhi set out on his famous walk from Ahmedabad to the sea to inaugurate his campaign of "non-violent" civil disobedience in protest against the Salt Laws. On May 5 he was arrested and interned.

In Europe another legacy of the First World War was laid to rest by the ending of the allied occupation of Germany, although events in that country were already giving her neighbours cause for alarm. In the General Election held in September the National Socialists, the party of Adolf Hitler, increased their representation from 12 to 107 seats, and called for a Fascist dictatorship, but the Government, under Herr Brüning, managed to maintain a majority in the Reichstag with the help of its former enemies, the Socialists.

Italy, under the firm rule of Mussolini, nevertheless suffered more than most from the economic depression; while in Spain General Primo de Rivera, who had ruled as dictator for seven years, resigned in January and his place was taken by General Berenguer, who announced his intention of restoring constitutional rule.

In Russia the year was marked by an all-out drive to "collectivize" the peasants and to exterminate the Kulaks, *whose ideas of individual effort and private property were regarded as dangerous to Communism; also by a staged trial of self-confessed "traitors" which led to vociferous protests from the British and French Governments.*

The United States remained under the shadow of the depression, business deteriorated and unemployment rose to an estimated 5 million.

Among other notable events of 1930 were the birth of Princess Margaret, the coronation of Ras Tafari as Emperor Haile Selassie I of Ethiopia, the crash of the R 101, the world's largest airship, at Beauvais in France, with the loss of 48 lives, Amy Johnson's solo flight to Australia in 19½ days and the deaths of Sir Arthur Conan Doyle, D. H. Lawrence, A. J. Balfour and Lord Birkenhead.

The death of D. H. Lawrence must have come as something of a relief to Peterborough, who shows himself to be a staunch upholder of rigid moral standards in the artistic world. It is also interesting to note that concern was already being expressed fifty years ago about the effect of the vibration caused by heavy traffic on the fabric and contents of roadside buildings, although, apparently, hansom cabs were still plying for hire in London.

The Latest Howler

That headmasters can appreciate a joke as well as their pupils was shown by the hearty laughter that greeted the latest schoolboy howler at yesterday's meeting of the Incorporated Association of Headmasters at Guildhall. Mr. A. Goodliffe, of Taunton, told of one of his pupils who translated "Pax in bello" as "Freedom from indigestion."
January 3

"Doug. and Mary" Coming to Stay

I hear that Douglas Fairbanks and Mary Pickford intend to spend a considerable time in England in the summer, and have been making inquiries about taking furnished a large house on the Thames between Henley and Maidenhead. They are very fond of this country, but of late years have seen little or nothing of it except London.

Time was, however, when "Doug." got to know the road between Liverpool and London pretty well. He landed at Liverpool without sufficient money for the train fare. So he walked it, and slept in the hedges.

But that was a long while ago.
January 11

Charlie Chaplin's Wisdom

I regarded with some degree of incredulity the statement that Mr. Charlie Chaplin was going to make a "talkie" film of "Jew Suss," and the official denial does not cause me any surprise. Although the great little comedian has (as do so many comedians) been growing more serious of late, and has been fired with an ambition to play non-comic parts, he would not be so foolish as to tackle such a part as this as his first effort in a new direction.

A more important point is that Charlie Chaplin has more than once said that he would never try "talkies" on any extensive scale. He said this to me once, adding, "Why, when I've built up a reputation in one way, trouble to build up another, when it might bring the whole thing down with a crash?"

We were both riding on the top of a 'bus in the Kennington Road. But that was when the "talkies" were not much further than the experimental stage.
February 6

The Feast of St. Valentine

St. Valentine's Day occurs this week, and there are distinct signs of a revival of the habit of sending Valentines, a habit which, a few years ago, had died out almost completely. The Christmas-card firms are issuing new and elaborate specimens, some with appropriate verses from the pens of Neo-Georgian poets, which contain, as Dr. Johnson once said, "little poetry but much affection."

At one time it was almost impossible to buy a Valentine in London, except in one street—Endell Street, off Long Acre. Here, until recently, were quaint little old-world shops which specialised in Valentines and also in "transfers," those strange and obsolete joys of one's youth. *February 10*

A Rich Father

A delightful story is told of the late Lord Rothschild. It was in the days of hansom cabs, when his sons were young men.

One night Lord Rothschild hired a cab to take him home. On alighting he paid off the driver, rewarding him with what he considered to be an ample "tip."

The cabby examined the amount, and, turning to Lord Rothschild, said, not a little reproachfully, "I often drive your lordship's son home and he always gives me a good deal more than you have done."

"I daresay he does," came the reply. "But then, you see, he has got a rich father: I haven't!" *March 3*

A Mind Diseased

Mr. D. H. Lawrence, whose death is just announced, belongs to the lost souls of literature. He had genius which might have raised him to a high place among the lesser immortals; with his vivid sense of the beauty and colour of words, he could portray live men and women as only the born novelist knows how.

His best novel, "Sons and Lovers," is an amazingly intimate picture of a boy growing up to early manhood in a Midland colliery district, where "slow rises worth by poverty oppressed," and Lawrence himself was the son of a working collier. But alas! the kink in the brain developed early, and he came to write with one hand always in the slime.

He has his apologists who find his worst and most flagrant obscenities "wonderful." So long as they are recognised for the obscenities they are, the epithet does not matter.

His later books and poems were rightly banned by the Censor, like the unspeakable pictures which were brazenly exhibited in London last summer, till the attention of the police was pointedly drawn to them in these notes and the disgusting show was closed.

Lawrence's case calls not so much for censure as for pity. The man was ill, the mind diseased, and the two maladies slowly gathered strength together. *March 4*

A "Sound" Theory

Mr. Rudyard Kipling, I hear, has written some new stories. One among them has been inspired by a very novel theory—the curing of disease by sound.

This story is based, if not on actual facts, at least on a belief held by a living doctor. Each element and metal, he holds, has somewhere in the range of sound its friendly and its hostile note. To the former it responds, while the latter shatters it by its vibrations, just as a certain note of an organ will break a window.

As an instance of what might happen in practice, it is suggested that cancer increases the lead content of the body.

Its presence would be diagnosed from its reply to the friendly note of lead, after which it would be dispersed by the application of the hostile note. A fantastic enough theory.

The story, as Mr. Kipling has written it, deals, I am told, with the illness of an eminent politician. A doctor is called in, and prescribes a somewhat unusual treatment. The treatment appears to be a failure, and the patient's life is despaired of, but a sudden and miraculous recovery follows.

The doctor is sought, to be congratulated, but is found dead by his own hand, and the secret of his treatment remains a mystery.*

March 7

*Despite considerable research, we have been unable to find any trace of such a story having appeared either in book form or in a magazine. If any reader can throw light on the matter, the editor would be delighted to hear from him.

Thrift at the Zoo

The death of one of the Zoo's ostriches usually reveals the fact that the thrifty bird had been in the habit of using his inside as a savings bank, but none has ever made so handsome a provision for his heirs as Tommy (a hen ostrich, in spite of the masculine name), who died a few days ago.

For when a post-mortem was carried out on Tommy's remains no fewer than thirty pennies were found, while other articles she had collected included a keeper's badge, several buttons, and two lucky charms.

This unfortunate bird's desire to save was even responsible for her death, because the last time she banked a penny she made the mistake of trying to swallow the coin broadside on, with the result that it stuck in her gizzard, prevented her from bending her neck, and finally choked her.

The ostrich's capacity for grinding stones in his crop seems to encourage him to try strange experiments, for many of the Zoo's ostriches die from the effects of highly indigestible meals.

March 12

Miss Megan's Début

The word "unique" should be used sparingly. Yet it may be permitted to describe the fact that Miss Megan Lloyd George makes her maiden speech in Parliament to-day.

Fathers there have been who have begun with apprehension and continued with pride the hearing of their sons' first oration in the most critical of assemblies. Now and then there has been a pause in the political conflict to admit a tribute, as from one gladiator to another, to the in-coming of the new generation.

Such an occasion occurred during the hottest stage of the Home Rule controversy when a certain young Mr. Austen Chamberlain made his début in a speech which the Grand Old Man gracefully described, with a glance at his formidable antagonist, as one that must delight a father's heart.

Filial Pride

What a pity there was no Lord Randolph to witness the Parliamentary début of young Winston. But then we have the testimony of no less an authority than Lord Birkenhead for the view that Lord Randolph died without realising what an apparition of genius had revisited the family.

So the youth was sent to Sandhurst, his future staked out as a possible colonel of cavalry.

Filial pride may well enter in to-day's advent. The visible affection between father and daughter provides a happy and wholesome interlude in our politics. The occasion is unique because never before has a father, himself the Father of the House, listened to the maiden speech of his daughter.

Politics apart, the event is one in which it would be churlish to refuse a sympathetic interest. *April 7*

Shops in Mayfair

I gathered yesterday that within a very short time practically the whole of the east side of Berkeley Square will be shops.

For many years the only shops in this square were the stationer's at the foot of Hay Hill and the famous refreshment contractor's next to it. Now the example of Berkeley Street is to be followed, and soon there will be shops in an almost unbroken line from Piccadilly to Bruton Street, which itself is becoming daily more of a trade than a residential street. *April 8*

"Scarface" Al Capone

Stories that throw a sidelight on the character of that remarkable individual, "Scarface" Al Capone, are, of course, without number.

Some American friends of mine were telling me the other day that not long ago they rented their house in Florida to Capone and his wife for the season. When the let came to an end and the owners resumed occupation, they found that the cellar had been left well stocked with excellent wines.

Various improvements had been carried out in the house, and the list of breakages was small. But the Capones insisted on paying a round figure, considerably in excess of the total for which they were liable.

The bill for telephone calls to Chicago amounted to about \$750. In discharging this debt Mrs. Capone insisted on leaving \$1,000. She said the change would pay for some damage, unnoticed, that had been done to a clock in one of the servants' bedrooms.

It is hard to identify behaviour of this kind with those infamous exploits with which Capone's name is generally associated.

April 21

The Poet Laureateship

There appears to be a general impression that the Poet Laureateship may well lapse now that Dr. Bridges is dead. It is a simple, if lamentable, fact that no one in any degree approximating to his stature remains.

But it is perhaps worth remembering that both on his appointment and long afterwards a large body of admirers of Rudyard Kipling and William Watson declared that finer, or at any rate more appropriate, candidates for the honour had been overlooked.

If the office is again to be filled, an undoubtedly popular appointment would be that of John Masefield. He is a national poet in that his love of England predominates in all his better work. Yeats and de la Mare both seem to escape from, rather than to interpret, the moods of every day, while A. E. Housman sings, alas! too rarely.

It would be an act of courage and encouragement to choose one of the younger generation on the ground of promise rather than of achievement. In that event the claims of Edmund Blunden, Alfred Noyes, one of the Sitwell trio, Humbert Wolfe, or some even younger and less well-known poet might be considered.

Undoubtedly much searching of heart would be saved if the distinction were abolished.* *April 23*

On With the Dance

A spirited attempt is being made by the London hotels and dance restaurant managers to contribute everything which lies within their power to the brightening of London this season.

During the last few months there has been something of a lull in the craze for after-dinner dancing, which may have been attributable to any one of several causes. This laziness on the part of diners-out is not, however, to be permitted to continue.

The finest and, unfortunately in many instances, the loudest

*The next Poet Laureate was John Masefield.

dance bands in the world are being brought to London with the object of compelling a dance revival.

At one of the smaller clubs in Albemarle Street a new attraction is being offered each Monday night in the form of a few bouts of after-dinner boxing.

The whole dancing floor is little larger than the ring, but to judge by the enthusiasm on Monday evening, the innovation seems likely to prove a popular one. *May 7*

The Laureate of the Hunting Field

Hunting men in particular will be delighted with the appointment of Mr. John Masefield as Poet Laureate, for "Reynard the Fox," perhaps his best known poem, besides being as English as Chaucer, is as full of the spirit of the chase as anything of Surtees.

Ordinary men and women will be pleased at the appointment, because Masefield is so much the ordinary man of action made articulate, while Oxford will be happy because the Poet Laureate still lives on Boar's Hill.

Here is a Laureate who is in every respect English and national, a sailor home from the sea, a hunter home from the hill. He can be trusted to interpret all our moods. *May 10*

Ruth Draper's Inspiration

London theatregoers will be delighted to learn that Miss Ruth Draper, that incomparable "diseuse," is soon to open a short season here.

Miss Draper's artistic achievements, enabling her unaided to give the impression that she is supported on the stage by a full company, are sufficiently well-known to require no comment. But I wonder how many people have heard the story, told to me the other day, of how she came first to attempt this work.

At a large dinner party one night the guest who should have sat next to Miss Draper failed to arrive, and throughout the meal she had a vacant chair on her left. Spontaneously she opened a conversation with its imaginary occupant, on whose behalf she also conducted the other half of the discussion.

So amusing did this talk become that one by one the other guests at the table stopped their own conversations in order to listen to

Miss Draper, and before the evening was over she had been urged by every person to work up this natural talent for character personation for the stage. *May 16*

Centre Court Improvements

Wimbledon, I hear, is to have a more elaborate scoring board than last year. Not only will spectators, entering the centre court, be informed of the point as well as the game score, but the name of the server will be indicated by an illuminated arrow.

These signals, for which a special corps of electricians has been engaged, will be relayed outside the court, so that all who wait may read. Perhaps one day it will be almost unnecessary to go down to Wimbledon at all—when the actual progress of a match, stroke by stroke, with every diverting incident added, will be "televisioned" to Manchester or Melbourne! *May 26*

Wimbledon

What a pity it is that the Wimbledon authorities have not yet succeeded in putting a stop to the barefaced profiteering in Centre and No. 1 Court seats, which has started again in full force.

There can, after all, be no justification for persons who find they are unable to use the seats allocated to them offering them for sale at from £15 to £20 apiece for the meeting.

Unfortunately, so long as there remain wealthy people who are prepared to buy at such prices there seems little prospect of this scandal being brought to an end. *June 23*

A Sister for Princess Elizabeth

The congratulations of a whole Empire are poured out to the Duke and Duchess of York on the birth of their daughter at Glamis.

Never, I suppose, in the world's history has a Royal marriage touched the hearts of the people so closely as that of the King's second son to one of his commoners.

In a few short years Lady Elizabeth Bowes-Lyon, a very attractive girl, seemingly very much like many other girls who were, and still remain, the friends of her youth, has won for herself a position in the heart of the Empire second only to that filled by her Majesty the Queen.

I chanced to be among those who enjoyed the Duchess's confidence in the months prior to the announcement of her engagement, and I well remember that one consideration, and one consideration only, made her hesitate to accept the high honour offered to her—nay, pressed upon her—by her Royal suitor.

That consideration was one of doubt as to her own ability adequately to occupy that central position continuously under the limelight of publicity. *August 23*

The Traffic Problem

I hear that it is more than likely that a strong protest will be made by the Property Owners' Protection Association to the Ministry of Transport concerning the increasing damage to buildings caused by the vibration of heavy traffic. The Ministry of Transport, so one official tells me, are entirely sympathetic.

It is difficult to know, however, what steps can be taken, beyond forcing all heavy vehicles to travel at a slow pace through villages and to adopt pneumatic tyres.

One striking proof of the seriousness of this aspect of the traffic problem was brought home to me yesterday. I was lunching at a club in Piccadilly which has been famous for generations for its lovely old table-glass. Noticing that the glass we were using was of very ordinary quality, I asked my host what had become of the old glass.

"We have had to pack it away," he replied: "the vibration of the traffic was so great that much of it was actually jerked off the tables and smashed."

And as he spoke motor-'buses thundered by and set the wine glasses dancing. *September 11*

A Hansom Survivor

How many hansom cabs are there in London still? I had not seen one for a long while until I hailed one as a last resort while waiting for a taxi in the dampness of Long Acre after the play.

It proved a most comfortable ride. The horse, a sturdy roan in good condition, negotiated the post-theatre traffic in Leicester

Square and Piccadilly almost as swiftly as any car could, and the cab itself was not in the least shabby. Indeed, in place of the trap in the roof through which in the old days the fare could communicate with the driver, a neat little electric light had been installed.

The driver was a genial soul. "Of course trade in the West End is not what it was," he said in reply to my inquiry, "but me and the 'oss don't look as if we're starvin', do we?"

They certainly did not. *September 19*

Lunch Hour Golf

Miniature golf has spread to the dinner and dance clubs. When I lunched at a much sought-after establishment off Bruton Street, late lunchers were politely urged to adjourn to tables at the side of the room, for in the dancing space attendants were busy laying down a miniature course, which they managed to do in a surprisingly short space of time.

Miss Tallulah Bankhead "christened" the course by driving the first ball—and doing the hole in one. Sandy Herd, who followed, took three over it. But perhaps he was being gallant.

The Portuguese and Brazilian Ambassadors, Kathleen, Lady Drogheda, and her son and daughter, Lord Moore and Lady Patricia Moore, Col. Christian Eliot, and Mr. "Willie" Boosey were among a seemingly much interested gathering of players and spectators. *September 27*

Death of Lord Birkenhead

Once more 1930, ill-starred year, has seen a brilliant life brought to an untimely close. Of all its victims none has left behind so many glittering memories of so varied a character, as Lord Birkenhead.

I am able, I am glad to say, to cherish many personal recollections of him. Some of them I have recounted in these notes on other and happier occasions. Here is one, which is a tribute to his uncanny memory.

Long before I had actually met him I was travelling down to Bristol with a friend, with whom I was disputing a passage in the trial scene from "Pickwick." Mr. F. E. Smith, K.C., as he was then, was in the far corner of the railway carriage absorbed in a newspaper.

Lowering it, with a friendly smile he remarked, "I think I can put you right." Whereupon, without faltering, he quoted the whole of the trial scene chapter from beginning to end, lit a fresh cigar, and resumed his reading. *October 1*

Paper Covers

It will be interesting to see how the scheme just announced for publishing new novels in paper covers will be received by the British reading public.

On the Continent, of course, paper covers are the rule, and they have been tried here more than once already. The experiment was each time a failure, however, chiefly because our circulating libraries account for so large a proportion of the fiction-reading public, and, naturally, library books have to be stoutly bound to withstand the inevitable wear and tear. *October 2*

A Sense of History

Professor A. E. Richardson was telling me, the other day, of a delightful sign which he saw outside a restaurant in Rouen last week.

"Jeanne d'Arc" was the name of the hostelry, displayed in flamboyant lettering, whilst immediately beneath the enterprising proprietor had added, suggestively, "English grill." *October 4*

Literary Luncheons

An ingenious attempt to bring together authors, readers, booksellers, publishers, and the man in the street who runs without reading, is being made by a famous firm of booksellers.

They have instituted a series of Literary Luncheons, the first of which is to be held at the Holborn Restaurant next Tuesday, when Lord Darling will speak on "Inelegant Literature," with Sir Gerald du Maurier in the chair.

The privilege of hearing Lord Darling pronounce judgment on literary defaulters at the luncheon table ought to prove a great draw, especially if any of the defaulters happen to be present, as is quite likely. *October 17*

Return of Ping-Pong

A notable sign of changes in taste in the minor amusements is the revival of ping-pong, which seems to be resuming something of the popularity it enjoyed twenty years ago.

One popular restaurant at the end of last week cleared out its miniature golf courses and put ping-pong tables in their place.

Ping-pong has been the rage for some time at the Royal Air Force Club. *October 20*

Psychology in Advertising

Mr. Francis E. Powell, the president of the American Chamber of Commerce in London, who has just returned after a two months' trip to the United States, told a good story the other day of a drug store proprietor in an American town, who, finding business bad owing to the slump, determined to try a little "psychology."

Accordingly he filled a large glass vessel with water and stood it in his window. Near it was a notice reading, "The Wonderful Invisible Goldfish from the Argentine."

"It needed seventeen cops to keep the side-walk clear in front of that drug store," added Mr. Powell. *November 20*

Serving the Royal Family

The announcement that the Duchess of York's housekeeper has retired after forty years spent in the service of the Royal Family leads immediately to an appreciation of the close personal interest taken by the Queen from the outset in the domestic affairs of her daughter-in-law's house.

The Queen is herself a first-rate housekeeper—a comparison of the household books at the Royal Palaces since she assumed control would give proof of that—and when her second son was married it is clear that she chose a trusted member of her own domestic staff to assist his wife in the tasks of housekeeping.

That the servants in the Royal houses and palaces stay long is generally attributed—and properly so—to the considerate treatment they receive at the hands of their masters and mistresses. But it must also be remembered that those who have the fortune so to be engaged may regard themselves as having attained the top of their own particular tree.

Etiquette Below Stairs

In the social life below stairs, perhaps even more than above, this is a consideration of real importance. For example, there are still many great houses in which the visiting servants—valets and maids—are addressed always in the housekeeper's room by the title of those whom they serve and precedence at table is taken accordingly.

Thus a Duke's valet is invariably referred to on these semi-ceremonial occasions as "His Grace," and so on down the scale, though whether this custom is carried so far as its logical conclusion in the matter of the valet to a Royal prince I am uncertain.

But, in any event, it is clear that few servants who love their profession would willingly leave the Royal Service until their time for retirement was reached. *November 25*

Preoccupied

I have just heard a charming story about Mr. Stanley Baldwin. A flag-seller, whose pitch was in St. James's, noticed among the passers-by a face which, though familiar, did not at once impress her as that of the Conservative leader.

Hurrying after him among the scurrying shoppers, she touched his arm and asked him to buy a flag. But Mr. Baldwin shrugged his shoulders and passed on.

Some few minutes later—no doubt realising that it must have been someone selling souvenirs in aid of a charity who had accosted him—he retraced his steps, and eventually discovered the table where the flag-seller was standing.

"Did you ask me to buy a flag just now?" he asked. "I'm so sorry; I didn't mean to be ungracious, but I was in the midst of composing a speech, and I was miles away." *December 18*

1931

Those who thought that 1930 had been a pretty bad year were to learn in 1931 that, however bad things may seem at the moment, there is always plenty of scope for them to get worse. Britain, however, suffered less than some.

In August the Labour Government resigned, having failed to agree on methods of balancing the budget, and was immediately succeeded by a National Government formed by Ramsay MacDonald from the rump of his own party, with Unionist and Liberal support. He was subsequently expelled from the Labour Party, along with Philip Snowden and J. H. Thomas; but at the General Election held in October the National Government was returned with a majority to which the history of the House of Commons offered no parallel. For once it appeared that the country had realized that it was living in a fool's paradise and had given the Government a free hand to put the economy in order. The Labour Party's representation fell from 288 seats to 52.

The economic storm which had begun with the Wall Street Crash in 1929 continued to blow with unabated fury throughout the year. In May Austria's largest bank, the Credit Anstalt, collapsed, precipitating a crisis which spread through the greater part of Europe and finally resulted, on September 21, in the fall of the pound from the gold standard. The suspension of gold payments, however, had an immediately stimulating effect on industry and unemployment decreased considerably during the ensuing three months. Summing up the effect of the fall from the gold standard, a journalist was able to say, "In short, the pound will purchase wholesale the same quantity of commodities as before the war, but less gold"!

In the rest of the world the year was marked as much by the wrath of nature as by financial and political turmoil. Canada, already battling with widespread rural poverty, was further afflicted by a severe drought which extended over a large part of the prairie provinces. In China disastrous floods drowned, starved or ruined millions of people; in the province of Hupeh an area as large as Scotland was turned into a lake. In New Zealand the towns of Napier and Hastings were largely destroyed by an earthquake, while Belize in British Honduras was devastated by a hurricane and more than a thousand lives were lost. Severe earthquakes also caused widespread damage and loss of life in Southern Serbia and in Managua, the capital of Nicaragua, which was virtually destroyed.

In India Gandhi was released from prison on January 26 and negotiations between him and Lord Irwin, the Viceroy, resulted in a pact under which the Congress Party discontinued the civil disobedience movement and the Indian Government released prisoners guilty of non-violent civil disobedience. In April Lord Irwin, who had gained the admiration and respect of all parties, and whose courage and vision had pointed the way to a solution of the Indian problem, gave up the Viceroyalty and was succeeded by Lord Willingdon. In September Gandhi arrived in Britain to attend the second session of the India Round Table Conference, at which, although some progress was made, Gandhi's attitude to the problem of Indian minority groups proved to be an insuperable obstacle.

There were serious disturbances in Cyprus, where the anti-British faction demanding union with Greece burnt Government House in Nicosia. Troops from India had to be sent to Burma to put down a rebellion, but in other parts of the Empire, now legally defined by the Statute of Westminster, which abolished the last traces of inequality between Governments and Parliaments of the Dominions and the Government of Great Britain, the year passed fairly quietly.

Europe, as already mentioned, was in the grip of financial chaos. The revival of aggressive nationalism in Germany became ever more apparent, and in March the Reichstag passed a budget containing grants for two of four proposed pocket battleships. The Nazis continued to gain strength but Dr Brüning managed to fight off all challenges and survived the year in office.

In Spain King Alfonso XIII abdicated and a Republic was proclaimed, of which Señor Zamora became the first president.

Other events which caught the public eye included Sir Malcolm Campbell's new land speed record of 246.575 m.p.h., the formation of a new political party by Sir Oswald Mosley, Britain's outright winning of the Schneider Trophy and a new air speed record, established by Flight-Lieutenant Stainforth, of 408 m.p.h. The year also saw the deaths of the Princess Royal, Marshal Joffre, Dame Nellie Melba and Arnold Bennett.

Peterborough, in a paragraph not included here, shows that he is as vulnerable as any other journalist to the gremlins who pull the legs of compositors. "With what ecstasy," he tells us, "did connoisseurs a generation ago listen to the venerable master [Joachim] and his three stout colleagues as they interpreted Beethoven's quarters"!

His reaction to the "new building of the B.B.C." shows how easily an "eyesore" can become a familiar and reassuring landmark, while his comments on the behaviour of the General Council of the T.U.C. lose nothing by the passage of time.

American and English Humour

As one of their audience I should have expected that the four Marx Brothers would have been well satisfied with the reception accorded them on Monday night.

Yet when I met Chico at luncheon yesterday—he is the eldest of the brothers—I found him, to my surprise, not wholly happy.

Chico was afraid that we had missed a lot of their jokes. I suggested to him that that was perhaps due to a slower sense of humour on this side of the Atlantic. But with this he refused to agree.

He thinks that the explanation is to be found in the difference between English and American dialect. He had recently been to see the Leslie Henson–Sydney Howard farce, and had laughed a lot. But he found that he was always laughing a second after the English audience.

Just in the same way he thinks the Englishman has to translate an American joke into English before he can laugh at it; which, when you come to think about it, is probably true. *January 7*

The Marx Brothers

I make no apology for returning to the subject of the four Marx Brothers, because, in addition to the success they are scoring in a London variety programme, they have been taken up by smart London and are at the moment the best "draw" any hostess can secure for a cocktail party.

Thus I found them last evening, and I am indebted to Brother Groucho for what is to me a new story at the expense of the Scotsman (incidentally, Groucho's Scottish accent is improving daily!). It all turned around a Scotsman who got some iodine on one of his fingers and then cut it in order to get the benefit. Well, if American we must be, "What do you know about that?"

I also gathered why it is that Brother Harpo gets such unusual effects when he plays on the harp. "He never had a lesson in his life," Groucho told me. "When he first took it up he didn't even know how the instrument ought to be tuned. So he tuned the way he imagined it should be, and now that is the only way he can play it. Any real harpist who tried to play on Harpo's instrument would be all at sea." *January 23*

Altering Keats's House

I hear that proposals will be placed before the Hampstead Borough Council this week for the demolition of part of Keats's old house in Hampstead.

The work of erecting a branch library and Keats museum is now in progress, and a stone-laying ceremony will take place next month. There was considerable criticism last summer of the original plans for this scheme, in consequence of which some alterations were made.

Possibly the new proposal—to pull down a drawing-room which was added to the house in the reign of George IV, and also a conservatory—with the idea of restoring the place to the exact form it had when the poet lived there, will result in further controversy.

But internally the house is not greatly changed, and on the lawn is the venerable mulberry tree beneath which Keats may have written his "Ode to a Nightingale."

Built when Hampstead was a suburban village, this is the only place in England intimately associated with the poet's memory, for his birthplace, his school, and the surgery where he lived at Edmonton have been swept away. *January 27*

That Centre Party

It may be of interest to recall, in view of the rumour that Mr. Churchill is toying with the idea of a Centre party again, that a similar report was set about when his father, Lord Randolph, resigned office and broke with Lord Salisbury.

When it reached Sir William Harcourt, he drily remarked, "I know that Centre party: it is all Centre and no Circumference"—a mot worth bearing in mind. *February 2*

The Du Maurier Tradition

Both Sir Gerald du Maurier and his second daughter, Miss Daphne du Maurier, have literary work appearing within the next ten days.

The father has written an introduction to a new edition of "Trilby," which contains some revealing glimpses of the artist-author, George du Maurier; and the daughter carries on the literary traditions of the family in a first novel of Cornish life entitled "The Loving Spirit."

Most of Miss Daphne's novel, which has a highly elaborate family tree as a frontispiece, was written at Fowey. *February 17*

Spoiling the Symmetry

The new building of the B.B.C. at the south end of Portland Place stands up very white, stark, and cliff-like, quite dwarfing All Saints at its side and the grotesque candlestick spire at which the wits have poked their fun for a whole century.

There will be no fun, I think, poked at the B.B.C. It just takes the heart out of those who used to admire Portland Place as the handsomest and broadest residential thoroughfare in the West End, especially before the builders began to pull down the Adam mansions to set up their blocks of flats, and the whole street stood for a single style and that one of singular beauty and elegance.

But now the B.B.C. rises like the vast wall of a gigantic breakwater, immensely taller than its neighbours, and the curve intensifies the clashing contrast of the styles.

The building may be perfect in isolation—I say nothing of that. But it is not in isolation, and it shatters what was left of the symmetry of Langham Place. *February 23*

Melba's Premonition of Death

Although an exceptionally strong-minded woman, and not given to any emotional nonsense, the late Dame Nellie Melba formed deep attachments both for people and for places.

Above all theatres in the world she loved Covent Garden, where she reigned as undisputed queen for nearly forty years; she was the only singer whose portrait bust adorned the corridors during her lifetime, and when she had ceased to sing there she retained her box on the grand tier, next to the proscenium—the box which for years had been that of her close friend and, in the early days, her champion, the late Lady Ripon.

On her very last visit to Covent Garden, shortly before she sailed for Australia, she was talking in quite a matter-of-fact way on business matters to Col. Blois in his private office.

Suddenly she paused. "This place is full of ghosts," she said,

"Harry Higgins, Gladys Ripon, Caruso, Neil Forsyth—they are all gone. And I shall never be here again." With that she broke down and wept inconsolably. *February 24*

Smashing Reductions

A notice which appears in a large store—"Smashing reductions in tumblers"—reminds me of the gentleman who advertised for a villa "within a stone's-throw of the Crystal Palace." *February 24*

Stage Names

By the way, should Miss Anna Neagle, who is making her first appearance as a principal in this production, ultimately attain to the dizzier heights of stardom—the measure of her immediate success is to be found in the fact that she has been "signed up" for the run of the show—some controversy may arise over the pronunciation of her name.

I remember when Elsie Janis* first came to London there developed acute dispute as to whether the first syllable should be pronounced like the Christian name, Jane, or like the first month in the year. Ultimately Miss Janis was appealed to and obligingly explained.

Now Miss Neagle tells me that her name (actually her mother's maiden name) should really be pronounced as if it were written "Nagel," with the "a" long. But as everybody pronounces it to rhyme with Eagle she has let it go at that, and, indeed, has adopted this form herself. *March 16*

Letters in Sale

The craze for literary autographs seems to be increasing, largely on account of the American demand.

Among letters, written by well-known authors, at present being sold in London is one from Thomas Hardy, priced at £16, in which he states that for years past he has not written a line of fiction or

*American actress (1889–1956). Star of *The Belle of New York*. Her real name was Bierbower!

thought of the subject. A letter by Sir James Barrie, referring to the proofs of "Tommy and Grizel," is offered for £20; and Mr. John Galsworthy's statement from Biarritz, denying that he had been interviewed by a London Sunday newspaper, is for sale at only 17s 6d.

A note of four pages from Mr. Somerset Maugham, in which he develops the lives of the hero and heroine of "A Man of Honour" after the final stage curtain, was offered at 65s. *March 19*

Conrad's Literary Style

How great was Joseph Conrad's anxiety on the subject of his style is illustrated by a letter which came up for sale at a London auction this week. It was written to his friend, Edward Thomas, thanking him for an offer to dedicate a book to him.

"I am a vagabond and a stranger in the language," he wrote. "Can't you think of someone more worthy?" He continued: "I am now passing through a phase of acute sensitiveness as to my own style. It seems the most impossible jargon, having the mere merit of being bizarre (if that's a merit), and all your, dearest fellow's, appreciation of it a most amiable, a most precious (to me) form of lunacy." *March 27*

Misunderstood

A story has come my way concerning a high dignitary of the Church—I will not mention his name—who was spending a holiday in Spain before that country plunged into revolution.

The gentleman in question had so much enjoyed a breakfast of mushrooms and coffee that he decided to ask for more. He could speak no Spanish; but at school he remembered having won a prize for drawing. So, on the back of the menu, he drew a picture of two mushrooms and a cow, the latter to represent more milk.

The waiter looked at the drawing and returned a few minutes later with two umbrellas and a ticket for a bull fight! *May 25*

Sixteen Plays at Once

Mr. Bernard Shaw, asked by a trades union amateur dramatic society for permission to produce one of his plays free of royalty, replied: "Certainly not. My fellow authors find it hard enough to compete with me as it is."

But the difficulties of Mr. Shaw's competitors are as nothing compared with the difficulties of the dramatists of Holland. There is in that country an author, Jan Fabricius, who last year had sixteen plays running simultaneously. We are to have one of his here soon.

In this country no one has beaten the record of Mr. Somerset Maugham, who had "Lady Frederick," "Jack Straw," "Mrs. Dot," and "The Explorer" all on at once in 1908. *May 26*

Sir Oswald Mosley

Little has been heard of the New party for some time past. Sir Oswald has been strangely silent. But by no means idle. He has been fishing and has caught a miraculous draught. Such speckled beauties that the political world will be thrilled by the catch.

In a word, three Sitwells, not, indeed, the three Sitwells, but, rather, three of the Sitwells, because Miss Edith Sitwell has not come over with the rest. Whether that distinguished critic and poetess is also on the road to Damascus I do not know; she may dislike politics as much as her brother Osbert says he dislikes games.

But, anyway, Mr. Osbert Sitwell and Mr. Sacheverell Sitwell—the latter accompanied by his wife, Mrs. Georgia Sitwell—have thrown in their lot with Sir Oswald Mosley, who, I suppose, has persuaded them that they were wrong in deeming "the beauty of the English language to be a more precious possession and more necessary to the country than the speeches of politicians."

Possibly they will now aspire to Sitwellise the New party programme, to give it a singing note and make things hum to a diviner air. And Sir Oswald gets not so much three recruits as an orchestra.

June 19

Two Famous Hoaxes

But for Mr. William Clarkson, whose retirement will occasion universal regret, it is probable that two of the greatest hoaxes of this century would never have been perpetrated.

The hero both of the famous visit of the Sultan of Zanzibar to Cambridge and of the Abyssinian dignitaries to the Dreadnought was Mr. H. de Vere Cole. It is doubtful, however, whether on either occasion he would have escaped exposure if it had not been for the masterly make-up of the conspirators by Willie Clarkson.

Cambridge still resents the trick played upon it shortly after the South African War, when a civic welcome was given to the pseudo-potentate while the real Sultan was being entertained in London.

The Dreadnought Hoax

Spurred by success, Mr. Cole next played a more daring trick on the Royal Navy.

This time he and his friends were painted and arrayed by Mr. Clarkson so that an Abyssinian would have accepted them as fellow-countrymen.

In due course the perpetrators of the hoax arrived, were met with great ceremony, and were conducted all over the flag-ship. Indeed, the visit passed off without a hitch.

But that the hoaxers escaped detection was almost entirely due to the consummate perfection of their disguise. *July 2*

The Baby Princess

I have just learned, on the highest authority, a small but not, I think, unimportant piece of news concerning a member of the Royal family.

Frequently, no doubt, it is those who lack personality of whom one hears but little. But although hardly anything has yet been heard of the baby Princess Margaret Rose, it is not because she has failed to evince the first signs of developing character. On the contrary, the Duke and Duchess of York's second daughter promises to be a young woman of great determination and no little charm.

Already, at the age of rather more than ten months, she is something of an authority in the ducal household. *July 10*

Expensive Boat Fares

Why is it, I wonder, that a first class ticket on the regular boat service from Folkestone to Boulogne should cost 18s 5d for a journey of some 28 miles?

A popular impression has for long existed to the effect that travel by boat is cheaper than travel by train. Can that be true where the boat fares are at the rate of 8d a mile?

By Air

This seems to me an extraordinary state of affairs, for I find that Personal Flying Services, who operate the only regular air service to this part of the French coast—in addition to ordinary air taxi work to all parts of Europe—base their charges on a rate of only 9d per passenger mile. *August 15*

Expensive Channel Fares

The reduction in passenger rates on the transatlantic route just announced by leading shipping companies gives additional point to my recent remarks on the seemingly inexplicable expense of crossing the English Channel.

The new first-class Atlantic rate would seem to work out at about 3d per mile, for which the passenger gets first-rate meals and accommodation—in fact, pension-de-luxe—plus rapid day and night travel.

This figure makes a startling contrast with the charge of about 8d per mile for the journey to France, a figure which includes bare accommodation and transport only, for should a cabin be required the cost becomes increased to something like 1s 3d per mile, or five times the rate for the American journey, to say nothing of food.

Obviously these figures do not take into account certain basic differences between the two types of journey. Nevertheless the discrepancy is sufficiently surprising. *August 17*

The T.U.C.'s Short Memory

The General Council of the T.U.C. is once more in the limelight, in their favourite role of would-be dictators. It is one in which they fancy themselves.

Yet somehow I cannot help feeling that they will have to wait a little longer for the realisation of their dream. They suffer from short memories, whereas the British public, as a whole, has a surprisingly long memory for some things.

Failure to grasp this fact brought about the dismal collapse of the General Strike in 1926. Its instigators forgot that the man in the street had so recently been put through a gruelling four-years' course of looking after himself.

Now once again the T.U.C. is blustering and threatening. Have Mr. Bevin and his friends so soon forgotten the lesson of their own impotence bought so dearly only five years ago? *August 22*

"Blue Bird's" New Nose

It is, perhaps, looking far ahead to a day when any challenger will succeed in wresting from Sir Malcolm Campbell his world's land speed record of 245 m.p.h. But should that occur, Sir Malcolm, I gather, has already made up his mind to go out for it again.

This information was vouchsafed me yesterday at the firm of coachbuilders, just off the King's Road, Chelsea, where "Blue Bird" is awaiting the fitting of a new "nose." This nose is of the utmost importance, for the streamlining experts, who have tested it on the plasticine model in a wind tunnel, have pronounced that the small change to be effected in its contours should enable the car to attain at least another ten m.p.h.

To climb into the cockpit of "Blue Bird" (as I did when unobserved for a moment yesterday) is in itself a thoroughly alarming experience. Speaking metaphorically, a large-size shoe horn is needed to assist the operation, and, once in, it becomes clear that to get out again will be even more difficult.

One's feet disappear far out of sight towards the monster engine, and, seeking some familiar pedal, find—nothing. Imagine the terror of losing the brake when travelling at 120 yards a second. But, of course, "Blue Bird" is really quite tractable. She will move off at a mere 35 m.p.h. *September 1*

Hall Caine and Trollope

Comparison has recently been made between the financial success of the late Sir Hall Caine and that of Anthony Trollope. Each of Sir Hall Caine's more popular novels usually brought the author about £10,000, whereas Trollope's total output earned him only £70,000.

As a matter of fact Trollope's highest financial score was £3,525, with "Can You Forgive Her?" published in 1864. In the same year he received £3,000 for "The Small House at Allington," and he had about as much for most of his other novels.

Hall Caine's modest £2 a week was princely compared with Trollope's first earnings with his pen. A strenuous first year of writing showed a miserable profit of £12, and "La Vendée," one of his earliest novels, brought in only £20.

A Contrast

Comparison between the two authors halts there, but we can make one interesting contrast.

When Trollope was a surveyor for the Post Office he spent much of his time travelling in trains. It was during this period that he cultivated the habit of writing in railway carriages, where the greater part of "Barchester Towers" was written.

Trollope said that his only objection to this practice was that it created an air of "literary ostentation."

When I remember Sir Hall Caine's distinctly Bohemian appearance, I do not think that such a consideration would have counted with him as an objection. *September 7*

The Granada

Mr. Sidney Bernstein's new Granada Theatre, which was opened with a cocktail party yesterday, with Mr. Raymond Massey and Mr. Godfrey Tearle as hosts, struck me as being quite the most remarkable cinema theatre in London.*

Mr. Bernstein himself insists that it is built and decorated in Italian Gothic throughout. But one could not help noticing the Russian influence of M. Komisarjevsky. Certainly I have seen nothing quite so ornate, in the best sense of the word, since I visited the Pineapple Church which is the pride of Moscow.

Amongst the scores of theatrical celebrities present were Mr. Charles Laughton, who told me that he is leaving for America in a week to play in "Payment Deferred," and Mr. Paul Robeson, who intends to sing in London, Paris and Berlin before leaving for New York in the autumn.

Mr. Robeson tells me that he is now looking not very successfully for a new play. He may one day revive "The Emperor Jones" in London. *September 8*

*The Granada Cinema, Tooting, now a bingo hall.

Sutcliffe's Triumph

Sutcliffe has outdistanced Duleepsinhji in the race for the distinction of scoring 3,000 runs during the season.

The Yorkshire professional has 161 to make, and Duleepsinhji (who is said to have backed himself to achieve the feat) 368.

Given fine weather, Sutcliffe is assured of two matches—the Champion County v the Rest of England, and the match between Mr. H. D. G. Leveson-Gower's Eleven and the New Zealanders. Duleepsinhji will also play in both, but his chances of reaching 3,000 are very slim.

One triumph Sutcliffe has practically won already. He will in all probability not only record the greatest aggregate of the year, but do so with a higher average than anybody else in the history of county cricket—with one exception.

The exception, as you may guess, is Don Bradman, who averaged 99 against Sutcliffe's present average of 96. *September 9*

Daughter for Bebe Daniels

Miss Bebe Daniels, the film star, has presented her husband, Mr. Ben Lyon, with a daughter.

The marriage was, I remember, a sensational one, not only because the bride's dress cost £2,000 and the wedding presents of diamonds had to be put under an extra police guard, so great was their value, but because eight famous film stars acted as bridesmaids. Among them were Miss Marion Davies, Miss Constance Talmadge, and Miss Betty Compson.

Not long ago Miss Daniels was seriously injured while making a film, and more than once she has been sent poisoned sweets. Such are the penalties of Hollywood fame. *September 11*

Never Heard of Mr. Priestley

Even the vogue of best sellers is limited. In the course of a conversation I had with Mr. Charles Chaplin before he left London for the week-end, he inquired blandly: "What are 'The Good Companions'?"

I had asked him if he was going to the play. But its title conveyed nothing to him. Nor did the name of Mr. Priestley.

It was not until someone pointed out that Mr. Knoblock had had a hand in its adaptation that Mr. Chaplin's interest was roused. "Oh," he said, "if Eddie Knoblock had anything to do with it,the show must be worth seeing!"

Lawn Tennis at Westerham

Mr. Chaplin was on the way to Chartwell Manor, the lovely Kentish home of Mr. Winston Churchill, where he was one of a house party.

Partnered by Mrs. Winston Churchill, he had a close lawn tennis match against Miss Diana Churchill and young Lord Birkenhead. Mr. Chaplin is quite a useful player and, as millions familiar with his early activities with custard pies will remember, is a left-hander.

September 22

Bradman's Feat

Recent news about Don Bradman is calculated to increase the eagerness of Accrington to engage him and of Australia to keep him. In his first five matches of the season the young prodigy has scored four centuries—well up to even his astonishing form.

As Bradman is a remarkably fast scorer—phenomenally fast for a man who does not lift the ball or go in for pure hitting—he would be the ideal attraction for Saturday league cricket. But I have heard nothing to weaken my conviction that he will decline the Lancashire engagement.

Bradman is, I suppose, the only batsman in the history of the game whose average throughout his career would probably exceed 100. Incidentally he is not, and never has been, known in Australia as "Boy," and would be exceedingly embarrassed by this sentimental appellation.

September 23

Misguided

Sir Oswald Mosley's "New party" is, I gather, preparing a "Defence Corps" for the protection of its own, and other, speakers from hooliganism by gangs of bravoes employed by the Socialists and Communists to break up Nationalist meetings.

If the project materialises, it will, I anticipate, draw the first official frown from Lord Trenchard in his new capacity as chief of police.

Such forces, though mobilised for purely defensive purposes, have a way of provoking the very assaults which they seek to combat and succeed only in making the work of the police more difficult. That, at least, was the view expressed to me with profound conviction by a very highly placed officer at Scotland Yard in similar circumstances at a previous General Election. *October 9*

Coward and "Cavalcade"

Several people who have been to see "Cavalcade" at Drury Lane have asked me lately what is the music of "Mirabelle," which is introduced to typify the Gaiety show of 1900.

In fact, no one could be expected to identify this music, for it is simply Mr. Coward's parody of the composers of that period.

Before he began on his score the composer went to a famous shop in the Charing Cross Road and bought £50 worth of Victorian and Edwardian music. He went home with it piled all over him in a taxi, and absorbed it thoroughly before beginning on the music of "Cavalcade." *October 20*

Conversational Privacy

It has been stated that the work-a-day vocabulary of the average man seldom exceeds 600 words, and few will deny that the vast bulk of our conversation is composed of ready-made phrases which in an age of stress and strain save much mental effort.

America has investigated this matter further, and a team of investigators have been listening in to thousands of telephone conversations. The official eavesdroppers made a complete data of thousands of calls and elicited that only 3 per cent. of the words used were not entirely ordinary.

It is hoped that no such investigation will be made in this country, for there is a disquieting side to this thirst for knowledge.

Most of us enter a telephone box happily imagining our conversation to be sacred between ourselves and the other end. I trust that this illusion will not be shattered, as it has been in America.

October 23

Exit Al Capone

Small wonder that Chicago finds it difficult to realise that Al Capone has at long last been convicted and sentenced to a term of imprisonment of unprecedented severity.

Eleven years have passed since Capone arrived in Chicago, aged 20, and, under the direction of Johnny Torrio, settled down to serious work in the beer racket.

Those were the days when Dion O'Banion, with his East Side gang, was, I think, the biggest man in the field. But the Torrio-Capone star was in the ascendant. By 1924 O'Banion had to try to put them out of the business, and for that attempt he paid with his life two months afterwards.

Two years later the Capone outfit was working on a gross basis of about seventy million dollars a year, and Capone had become politically the most powerful figure in the city.

A Strange Character

A strange character and one around whom there will always hang a certain air of inglorious romance, he has been, perhaps, the greatest personal spender in all the history of Chicago Gangland, and in pursuance of his favourite motto, "We don't want any trouble," he poured out money like water.

Moreover, in the quieter days of the racket, he would give parties for as many as 300 of his henchmen. At the outset of these affairs he would give $5,000 to the proprietor of the "ornate dive" chosen for the evening, and everybody was allowed to order what he pleased until the money ran out.

He has been a great gambler, with a liking for dice, and, up to two years ago, estimated his gambling losses at $4,000,000.

It is on record that he once won $750,000 in four days at a race meeting and left at the end of the week, having lost $250,000.

October 27

Mr. Shaw on Asparagus

Yesterday morning's post brought me a letter from an indignant "specialist in dietetics," who wants to make Mr. Bernard Shaw "eat his words, or, at least, a good helping of asparagus."

It seems that my correspondent's ire has been provoked by a passage in Mr. Mark Hambourg's recently published "From Piano to Forte," which gives a remark of Mr. Shaw at a luncheon party when a large dish of early asparagus appeared: "Take away that nasty vegetable; it's full of uric acid!"

Mr. Shaw ought to know, says my correspondent, that "uric acid in the circulation is the result of imperfect oxidation of excess nitrogenous matter. Asparagus is especially rich in sodium, calcium, iron and sulphur. The nitrogenous principle called 'asparagin,' which it contains, is not harmful."

I might add that asparagus is also free of sugar and may be eaten in unlimited quantities by diabetics, so if any of my readers share Mr. Shaw's views on diet, perhaps this new opinion may interest them. *November 6*

Prince and "The Garrick"

There is no club in London (or anywhere else for that matter) with a more interesting membership and tradition than the Garrick, whose centenary dinner on Sunday will be attended by the Prince of Wales.

Intended as a meeting-place for men in the arts and professions, it has numbered amongst its members many of the most famous artists, writers, actors, judges and barristers of the last hundred years.

The late Arnold Bennett was a regular visitor. So, going farther back, were Sir Henry Irving, Toole, Thackeray, Forster, and the great actors and novelists of the time.

The Old Tradition

To-day the tradition is still carried on, and you may see Mr. Seymour Hicks, Mr. Justice Avory, Sir Patrick Hastings, Mr. Norman Forbes (Robertson), Mr. Frederick Lonsdale and other figures representative of the professions sitting together at the long table and enjoying some of the best talk to be heard in an age when the art of conversation is not quite lost.

Business men and politicians are not eligible, and there is no club which eyes the candidate more critically.

As is only fitting, the Garrick has a unique collection of theatrical pictures, the value of which is beyond computation, amongst them a collection of Zoffanys and work by Hogarth, Sir Thomas Lawrence and Gainsborough. *November 21*

Unspoiled

It is, I believe, a fact that the potential earning power of Yehudi Menuhin is probably the greatest in the music-making world. At all events, the largest concert halls are unable to accommodate all who wish to hear him.

But however great his financial drawing power Yehudi is a simple lad. I watched him come on to the platform to play at the Queen's Hall on Monday evening.

Without a trace of nervousness or affectation he coolly surveyed the house until he found what he was looking for. Then he grinned broadly at Hephzibah and Yaltah, his two little sisters, who were sitting quite far back in the stalls, and proceeded to get on with the business of the evening.

The one thing Yehudi is rather proud about is his travelling overcoat, which was made for him by the tailors who build for the Prince of Wales. *November 25*

Wilde's Viva

One of the best Oxford stories of the Viva for "Divvers," now about to be abolished, used to be told of Oscar Wilde, when an undergraduate at Magdalen. He was asked to take a Greek Testament and translate the passage in the Acts dealing with St. Paul's shipwreck.

Wilde sailed along fluently enough, though with sufficient hesitation to create some suspicion of previous unfamiliarity with the text. After a few verses the examiner stopped him with the remark, "Thank you, Mr. Wilde; that will do."

"Pray excuse me," said Wilde, politely, "while I glance at the end of the chapter! I am so curious to know whether the good man escaped." *November 26*

1932

In 1932 all the major countries of the world, with the exception of Great Britain, Italy (by now enjoying its tenth year of Fascist rule), Russia and China, changed their governments, some several times.

In Britain the National Government, profiting from the strength of its massive majority, achieved much of the task it had been elected to carry out. It restored the solvency of the country; it balanced the budget and paid off all the foreign debts which had been incurred during the financial crisis of the previous year. Nevertheless unemployment remained a major source of anxiety and hunger marches were a feature of the year. One of the steps taken in the battle against unemployment was the abandonment of Free Trade and the passing of Neville Chamberlain's Import Duties Bill which imposed a levy of 10 per cent on all foreign imports. In September Lord Snowden, Sir Herbert Samuel, Sir Archibald Sinclair and all the junior Ministers who belonged to the Free Trade wing of the Liberal Party left office on the issue of Imperial Preference, as the exemption from this duty on goods imported from the Dominions and Colonies was known. On all other issues, however, they continued to support the Government.

In Ottawa the Canadian Government played hosts to the representatives of the nations of the Empire attending the Ottawa Conference, the aim of which was to establish closer economic co-operation between member countries. Canada's own economy, however, continued to deteriorate and it was estimated that at least 800,000 people were on public relief.

Across the border Franklin D. Roosevelt was elected thirty-second President of the United States by the largest majority ever recorded, thereby shouldering an awesome burden, for America had had another bad year. The third winter of the Depression saw the misery of unemployment greater than ever, and industrial unrest was violent and sustained. Early in the year disastrous floods caused havoc in the Mississippi valley, and, shortly after, an unprecedented feeling of universal outrage swept the country following the kidnapping and murder of the infant son of Colonel Charles Lindbergh, the first man to make a solo crossing of the Atlantic by air. America certainly had much to hope for from her new Democratic President.

In Europe governments changed with bewildering rapidity during the year. France had no less than four Prime Ministers and in May the President, Paul Doumer, was assassinated by a Russian fanatic. He was succeeded by M. Albert Lebrun who remained in office until 1940.

In Germany Field-Marshal von Hindenburg was re-elected President with 19 million votes against 13 million for Hitler. At the end of May Dr. Brüning resigned as Chancellor and the President summoned Franz von Papen who, on June 4, dissolved the Reichstag, two years before its allotted time. At the elections held in July the Nazis won 230 seats, making them the largest single party. But stalemate ensued, since neither the Nazis nor the Social Democrats would enter a coalition. Further elections in November showed that the Nazis had passed their peak and they now returned with only 196 seats. Herr von Papen resigned on November 17 and in December General Kurt von Schleicher became Chancellor.

Sweden's role in the events of the year centred round the suicide of Ivar Kreuger, the "Match King", and the discovery that his vast financial empire had been largely based on fraud. The ensuing scandal led to the resignation of the Prime Minister and seriously damaged the reputations of a number of prominent American bankers.

In Ireland Mr. Cosgrave was defeated in a General Election after ten years in office and was succeeded by Mr. Eamonn de Valera, who lost no time in making his attitude to Britain abundantly clear by abolishing the Oath of Obedience to the King and suspending payment of land annuities. It was remarked that he "showed more acquaintance with Irish history than readiness to compromise".

In India Mr. Gandhi spent the year in prison. On his return from the Round-Table Conference he decided to revive the civil disobedience movement and was arrested on January 4.

Other events which captured the headlines during the year included the opening of the Theatre Royal at Stratford-on-Avon by the Prince of Wales in April, the opening of the new Lambeth Bridge by the King in July, the secession of the Independent Labour Party from the Labour Party and the opening of cinemas on Sundays.

Much public interest was aroused by the trial of the Reverend Harold Davidson, the Rector of Stiffkey, who had been summoned by the Bishop of Norwich to appear before a consistory court to answer charges of immorality with a prostitute named Rose Ellis. Miss Ellis gave her story to the Daily Herald, *whereupon Davidson, not to be outdone, gave his account of what had happened to the* Empire News, *and was charged with contempt of court. In the end the paper was fined £100 and at the Consistory Court Davidson was found guilty of immorality, deprived of his benefice and unfrocked.*

The world of literature was impoverished by the deaths of Kenneth Grahame, Edgar Wallace, Lytton Strachey, H. H. Munro and Lady Gregory.

Even the privacy of the grave, however, was not enough to protect the late D. H. Lawrence from the censure of Peterborough, who seized upon the publication in England of a bowdlerized version of Lady Chatterley's Lover *to have another bash at his* bête noire. *The late Arnold Bennett, who is recorded as having said that, in his view, "pavement" is the most beautiful word in the English language, was let off more lightly.*

B.B.C.'s New Dance Band

Mr. Jack Payne's successor as leader of the B.B.C. Dance Orchestra, Mr. Henry Hall, is of approximately the same age, namely, in the early thirties. Like his predecessor, he has that important qualification, a pleasant speaking voice.

Mr. Hall, who in ten years rose from pianist to the control of the fourteen bands of the L.M.S. Railway Hotels, is already familiar to radio listeners as director of the Gleneagles Hotel Band, which broadcasts from the well-known Adelphi Hotel, Liverpool.

His radio orchestra, which will consist of fifteen players, has yet to be chosen. If history repeats itself, the new combination should have a swift rise to popularity. Mr. Hall, by the way, is no lover of the so-called "hot" numbers. *January 11*

Capt. Anthony Eden

To those who have watched the career of Capt. Anthony Eden, who at 35 has become Under-Secretary for Foreign Affairs, his thoroughly statesmanlike speech on disarmament will have come as no surprise.

During the nine years he has been in Parliament he has shown increasing promise. Foreign affairs have always been his metier. For three years he was Parliamentary Private Secretary to Sir Austen Chamberlain, and he did not waste his opportunities in that post of enlarging his knowledge of his subject.

At Oxford he gained First Class Honours in Oriental languages, and he has occupied all his spare time in travel. His Parliamentary career should be assured, for coupled to his admitted ability he has ease and charm of manner. *January 16*

A Birrellism

Some day, perhaps, an industrious anthologist will give us a collection of "Birrellisms." They would probably constitute one of the most enduring claims to remembrance of Mr. Augustine Birrell, who will be 82 to-morrow.

Mr. Birrell's essays, and even his legal treatises, are full of epigrammatic wit and wisdom. But the anthologist would do well, also, to hunt up the reports of law cases in which he appeared.

One of his neatest sallies was scored at the expense of Lord

Darling, before whom he was pleading in a libel suit. "If you are going to punish a man simply for having a lively imagination," he pleaded, "I don't know where we shall end."

"There wouldn't be many to punish," retorted Lord Darling. Mr. Birrell bowed. "I admit," he said blandly, "that not many judicial vacancies would be created, my lud!" *January 18*

Greta Gustafson

I am more than a little sorry that changing technique has obliged the fair Greta Garbo to talk as well as to act for the pictures. It was, I think, her very gentleness and the melting sweetness of her face that captured so many hearts.

Now, doubtless like many another, I find that there is a certain hardness in her voice that goes far to destroy the illusion—if illusion it was.

But for all that London seems to love her. The circle of the Empire was full of well-known people when I went there one night this week. *January 23*

The Vanished Catnack

The street in London famous until quite recently for the sale of Valentines was Endell Street, Long Acre. I believe one can still buy them there. But up to the beginning of the war there were many quaint little shops in whose windows were displayed not only Valentines, but "catnacks."

Catnacks, or catnaps (there are several versions of the word), were long narrow strips of paper on which were printed the words, but not the music, of popular songs. These must have completely disappeared. *February 15*

"Lady Chatterley's Lovers"

Mention of Col. Lawrence reminds me of an interesting matter in connection with a namesake, around whose personality and views controversy still rages—I refer to the late D. H. Lawrence.

Yesterday I learned that his novel, "Lady Chatterley's Lover," which has been banned in this country since the Home Office became aware of it in 1929, is to be issued in England shortly in an authorised abridged edition.

Originally printed in Florence, for subscribers only, the book related, in astounding detail, the love affair of "Lady Chatterley" and a gamekeeper in the employ of her crippled husband.

This British edition has been toned down considerably, but, all the same, I think its appearance will occasion many protests—not least from Lawrence's disciples, who have always been led to believe that had he lived he would never have tolerated any bowdlerisation of his "masterpiece." *February 19*

"Derby Day" Delights

Mr. A. P. Herbert has not exactly broken new ground with this comic opera of English life. But he has exulted in the scene with greater gusto than, say, W. S. Gilbert, who set his scenes politely on Tower Hill and Parliament Hill.

Mr. Herbert's new piece bids us

Prepare your shoulders with the rough to rub;
Most of the action centres in a pub.

In a neatly rhymed preface, he protests against the tradition which excludes England and England's poor from the comic opera stage.

All must be rich, or Royal, or Divine,
And all belong to Russia or the Rhine.
Even a peasant may be made to please
If he be Spanish, Czech, or Tyrolese.

Yet, as he asks,

. . . are the Russians really more bizarre
Than English magistrates or milkmen are?
We've colour and we've costume on the spot,
But so familiar that you see them not.

So the British people are put on the stage with tipster for hero and barmaid for heroine with all the fun of the road, the paddock and Downs on Derby Day. *February 29*

Second Best

Mr. James Agate told an excellent story against himself at a theatrical dinner the other evening; he sat beside Miss Lilian Braithwaite.

"A little while ago," said Mr. Agate, "I was fortunate enough to find myself alone with Miss Braithwaite. I hastened to avail myself of this rare opportunity.

" 'My dear lady,' I said, 'May I tell you something I have wanted to tell you for years: that you are the second most beautiful woman in the United Kingdom?'

"I naturally expected that Miss Braithwaite would ask who, in my opinion, was the woman who came before her. And I had prepared myself with a name to which it would have been interesting to see Miss Braithwaite's reaction.

"But she asked no such question. She merely looked at me with her charming smile and said, 'Thank you. I shall always cherish that, as coming from the second-best dramatic critic.' " *March 1*

Short Shrift for "Shorts"

I see that both Mrs. Moody and Miss Jacobs—the "Helens of California"—have voted decisively against "shorts" at Wimbledon.

So far there has not been a single leading player favouring the proposal. And for very good reason, I should say.

Apart from any question of taste, or even of physical comfort, women competitors would instinctively avoid a costume which might alienate the sympathy of the crowd. A friendly atmosphere is very essential in a strenuous centre court battle. *March 12*

The Altered Boat Race Course

Many rowing enthusiasts have expressed regret that the rebuilding of Putney Bridge makes it necessary to move the starting-point of the race from University Stone. This has been called "a break with tradition." But it is worth remembering that the race has been rowed over at least two other courses, and presumably there is nothing to prevent the challengers offering to row over any course they chose.

The first race, in 1829, was rowed from Hambledon Lock to Henley—and, incidentally, the start was made at 7.45 p.m.! The course for the next race, in 1836, was at Westminster. Henley was again chosen before the present course from Putney to Mortlake was selected in 1845.

This move marked the real beginning of the contest, for in the following year outriggers were used for the first time. Racing from Putney to Mortlake in keeled boats, without outriggers, must have been strenuous work!

The Boat Race Broadcast

The method of broadcasting a description of to-day's race affords a contrast with that adopted in previous years. It will be by monologue instead of dialogue, Mr. J. D. M. Snagge carrying out the task alone.

Listeners should get a more coherent account in this way, though some of the excitement that gathers in the course of a descriptive duet may be lacking. Few could face with equanimity the prospect of such a sustained extemporaneous solo effort before the microphone.

Mr. Snagge, however, has important qualifications. He is an experienced announcer at Savoy Hill, he has himself rowed in the Oxford trials, and he shared in the Boat Race narrative last year.

March 19

Mr. Wang's Rebuke

Having once spent a delightful hour with Mr. C. T. Wang, one of the Chinese delegates to the League of Nations, I enjoyed a story I heard the other day of his rebuke to a British Socialist M.P. whom he encountered at a dinner in Nanking.

It seems that the M.P., uncertain how to open up a conversation, leaned across the table as the soup came in and said, "Likee soupee?"

This opening gambit was received by Mr. Wang in silence. At the end of the dinner he was called upon to address the gathering, and delivered, in the most polished English imaginable, a speech on which he was warmly congratulated. As he bowed his acknowledgments Mr. Wang leaned across the table to the British M.P.

"Likee speechee?" he inquired blandly. *March 22*

Obscuring St. Paul's

Every lover of the beautiful must share the concern of Mr. W. G. Allen, the surveyor of St. Paul's, lest it should soon become impossible to see the cathedral from a distance owing to the rise of buildings all around.

Even now it is difficult to see St. Paul's to advantage, and quite impossible to see it as a whole. It is one of the greatest tragedies of London that steps were not taken long ago to preserve a clear space on at least the front side, so that the glorious building might be viewed in perspective as one may view many of the cathedrals of Europe from Beauvais to Rome.

Wren's Plan

Wren drew up a plan for a new and more beautiful London which would have preserved his masterpiece in splendid isolation. He wanted a large piazza all around the Cathedral, enclosed (as is the case at St. Peter's) by a colonnade.

His age was too short-sighted to adopt the plan. But we cannot blame other ages when we not merely lack the courage to clear away some of the unsightly buildings which now crowd round the Cathedral—what a view it would offer if Ludgate Hill were straightened!—but actually permit the erection of buildings which threaten, according to Mr. Allen, to obscure views of it altogether.

No wonder Canon Alexander has asked us to picture the Cathedral in twenty years' time as "practically or even literally an island—rendered even more dangerous of approach than it is now, and surrounded by a tumult of noise." *March 26*

Memorable Birthday Party

Mr. Winston Churchill has had many inspirations in the course of his career, but few of them can have been happier than the thought which led to the celebration, at once informal but memorable, of his son's 21st birthday. Its form was a dinner and its scene Claridges on Thursday.

More than seventy guests mustered at the wand of his welcome: all of them men, and many of them, like their host, distinguished fathers accompanied by promising sons. Mrs. Churchill, it is true, made a brief appearance to greet them. But from the moment the party assembled round the oval dinner table it was exclusively male.

To the right of Mr. Churchill, who sat at the centre, was the Marquis of Salisbury, and opposite him the Duke of Marlborough and Mr. Randolph Churchill, with Lord Reading at his side.

Like Father, Like Son

Many recalled a similar occasion when the late Lord Birkenhead invited the notable men of the day to celebrate his son's coming of age at Gray's Inn. It was therefore fitting that the son of "F.E." should rise and propose the health of Randolph.

He stood up, a lithe athletic figure, leaning forward with studied nonchalance like his father, and those who listened could not but believe that this adolescent master of humorous invective and adroit persiflage was not F.E. back again. No greater tribute could be paid to Lord Birkenhead than to say that his famous father could not have improved upon his speech.

In cultivated tones and language he sketched Mr. Randolph Churchill's (according to him) rather graceless career at school and indifference to discipline at Oxford. Thereafter he depicted his royal rise to fame as a public man.

Amid loud laughter, Lord Birkenhead described his inability to force a way into Mr. Churchill's office owing to the crowd of retainers and the number of income-tax collectors who came to take toll of the youngest payer of super-tax upon earned income in the Kingdom.

June 18

"Death Under Sail"

In recent years many detective stories have been written as a relaxation from hard intellectual toil, but I doubt if any of them have been produced under more dramatic conditions than a forthcoming one entitled "Death Under Sail."

The author is Dr. C. P. Snow, the Cambridge Don, who recently prepared Vitamin A—the general health vitamin—for the first time by artificial means. This 26-year-old scientist wrote his novel as a form of mental relief from experiments which may well be of importance to the human race.

He thinks that for "chasing away the cares of 'synthesis by light rays' the job of unravelling one's own mystery plots cannot be beaten."

June 21

A Great "Best Seller"

Dr. Axel Munthe is in London, from Capri, arranging with Mr. John Murray for a cheap edition of his "Story of San Michele." It has been the greatest "best seller" of recent years, and indeed no book of the kind has, I suppose, done so well since John Morley wrote his "Gladstone."

Dr. Munthe has been busy on another book—also about the notable people he has met, and his own life. When he began it he called it "Death and the Doctor," wondering whether he would ever finish it.

As yet, I gather, he has not quite done so, but we shall probably get it in the spring. *July 7*

Homes on Wheels

A friend who has just spent a few days touring in Devon, Somerset, and Dorset tells me that caravans are a feature of the landscape. These homes on wheels, often towed by quite small cars, are everywhere, and places where signs denote a camping pitch are innumerable.

While this form of touring is inexpensive and has the charm of mild adventure it makes cautious driving in the narrow, high-hedged West Country lanes doubly imperative. Some of these travelling hotels literally brush the hedges on either side of the narrower lanes.

Generally, however, the caravans were skilfully and cautiously driven. *July 26*

A Little Tactless

At dinner last night I heard an amusing story about Sir John Simon.

Candidates for Fellowships at All Souls, Oxford, in addition to doing the written examination, are also subjected to a more terrifying ordeal—dining with those who are already Fellows.

Some of the finest brains and the best conversationalists in the country attend these dinners, and great lawyers, politicians, or philosophers endeavour to "draw out" those who hope to take their places in their ranks.

One brilliant Balliol scholar—who was, however, somewhat lacking in tact—aspired to a Fellowship. He had a long family connection with India, and before long he was fully launched into the subject on which he felt himself on safe ground.

Sir John Simon's "Book"

He explained the Indian situation to his elderly and distinguished hearers with lucidity and force. One of them, however, ventured to differ from him on some particular point. The would-be Fellow turned on him and plainly showed him that his interrupter was not as well informed on the subject as he was himself.

"I am naturally extremely interested in your views on the subject," was the other's polite comment. "You see, I have just completed a book on the subject myself."

When he was asked, in a somewhat patronising tone, what the title of the book was, he replied: "Well, it is called the Simon Report." *September 9*

Origin of the Blazer

Someone asked me the other day—apropos the "Oxford Blazers"—what was the origin of the word blazer. Yesterday I heard an explanation.

According to my informant, it is derived from one of Queen Victoria's warships, the Blazer. In the days before there was an authorised uniform for the lower deck it was customary for captains to devise uniforms according to their fancies.

Thus, for example, old Admiral Dundas invariably clothed his cutter's crew in suits of Dundas tartan. In the same way the cutter's crew of the contemporary warship Tiger had striped jerseys of yellow and black.

In the case of H.M.S. Blazer, the cutter's crew had a blue jacket with brass buttons. This rig became popular on shore, and when worn by ordinary civilians was called a "blazer." *September 12*

"Sandringham Time"

In view of the mild controversy aroused as to the reason why the clocks at Sandringham are kept half an hour fast, the following explanation I heard from a friend recently may be of interest.

My friend was honoured by an invitation to Sandringham, and was warned of the change of time, first by an equerry in the train going down, then by a footman on arrival at the house, and finally by the King himself.

His Majesty's own explanation was "My father used to have big shooting parties here, and couldn't get his guests up in the morning, so he put the clocks on half an hour!"

The rule applies to the whole village and the clocks are not changed to summer time. An event was given out in church as taking place "Three o'clock, Sandringham time." *September 14*

Air Harbour for London

The model of the St. Pancras and King's Cross district being shown at the Building Exhibition at Olympia is attracting considerable attention, chiefly because of the possibilities it holds for London to have an air-port which is really accessible.

The suggestion allows for a series of runways, a couple of hundred feet wide and half a mile long, on which the aeroplanes would alight and take off. Five million pounds, the estimated cost, seems a small amount for giving the city a useful air harbour, such as must, sooner or later, be provided. *September 19*

Point Counter Point

The attempt to discredit Mr. Hoover in his struggle to retain the Presidency by a story of his being a naturalised Englishman, is reminiscent of an election canard of 130 years ago, when Jefferson and Adams were competing for White House.

Unscrupulous opponents circulated a story that Adams had married a daughter of George III, the bête noir, of course, of all patriotic Americans in those days.

In great alarm, Adam's supporters appealed to his agent to deny the story. "That would be useless," said the agent. "Once a lie like that gains currency you can never overtake it.

"No, what we must do is to declare that Jefferson has married two of King George's daughters!" *September 28*

Honouring Chopin

The French Government have just given permission for the repatriation of Chopin's remains from Paris, where they have lain —and in an honoured grave—for more than eighty years. They are to be taken back to the obscure little Polish town where he was born.

This will be a signal, and, I believe, an unprecedented, act of national homage to a musician.

Similar honour, as many Londoners will remember, was paid to the remains of the great Swedish mystical teacher, Swedenborg, in 1908.

They had lain in the Swedish Church, St. George's-in-the-East, since 1772.

Karl Marx, Too?

Spain, in 1802, when the Spanish–American War was a recent memory, brought back with great pomp from Havana to Seville the bones of Christopher Columbus—his second crossing of the Atlantic after death, for he had died at Valladolid.

Perhaps some day Germany may ask for the bones of Karl Marx, now reposing in Highgate Cemetery. But not, I think, just yet.

November 14

Sir Edward Elgar's Note

The praise of Yehudi Menuhin was in all the newspapers, but I fancy the young violinist will treasure no tribute more highly than the note which Sir Edward Elgar wrote him on Sunday night. It reads:

—I am just being hurried away, and steal one moment (I don't care if I miss the train!) to send you my warmest thanks for the complete artistry you showed us to-day. I shall write to your dear, dear father directly I get home. Again all thanks, and au revoir in Birmingham. *November 22*

Victorian Christmas Fare

According to Miss Florence White, the founder of the English Folk-Cookery Association, most people's Christmas dinners this year will be far simpler than fifty years ago.

In Victorian days Christmas dinner in a well-to-do family would begin with Palestine soup, or clear pheasant or hare soup. Then would come cod, which is in its prime at Christmas, served with plenty of cod's liver and oyster sauce.

It was a very old English custom to serve in one dish boiled meat or fish garnished, a custom which survives to-day in boiled chicken garnished with fried bacon.

The Victorian turkey, an upstart among Christmas dishes, was sometimes stuffed with oysters and served with boiled ham, tongue, or pickled pork. Sweet pickled or spiced barberries would be served separately in a glass dish.

Mince pies are, of course, much older historically than plum pudding. The shape should be traditionally oval, to represent the manger at Bethlehem. *December 24*

Beautiful Words

A New York poet and lexicographer has made a list of what he considers the ten most beautiful words in the English language.

His choice is "dawn," "hush," "lullaby," "murmuring," "tranquil," "mist," "luminous," "chimes," "golden," and "melody."

I suspect that meaning as well as euphony has influenced his judgment.

Arnold Bennett was fascinated by the same idea, but he resolutely put out of mind all that a word stood for emotionally, sentimentally. At the end of a long discussion of the subject he announced in his pontifical way that the most beautiful word in the English language was "pavement." No argument would shake his opinion.

December 24

The King's Christmas Greeting

It does not need a very vivid imagination to picture the hush that fell on a large part of the civilised world when the B.B.C. voice announced "His Majesty the King."

Untold thousands of people must have been hearing the King's voice for the first time. Every one that I spoke to had been greatly impressed by its virile vigour, but what affected them most was the note of fatherly affection which rang through every word of the historic utterance.

None who listened could help feeling that he or she was included in the King-Emperor's solicitude, and the concluding words, "God bless you," were intensely moving. Nothing could have been more simple, nothing more sincere.

Eloquent Sincerity

It is indeed the simple truth that the end of the King's broadcast was one of the great emotional moments that come seldom in a lifetime.

Each home was a microcosm of a listening world.

The loving message, spoken with such eloquent sincerity, went straight to the heart.

How many family circles acted, I wonder, as the one did of which I heard yesterday? Without a word, and with eyes here and there filling with tears, they rose and joined in the National Anthem with the B.B.C. orchestra.

A Model Broadcaster

The King is 67, but his broadcasting voice and manner were a model to many younger men. The firmness of his delivery and the intimate inflexions of tone make him pre-eminent among those whose personality is felt through the microphone.

The B.B.C. must be congratulated on a cleverly built programme; there can be little doubt that the ties of Empire are the stronger for it.

The English Tongue

The King's message came as the climax to a really thrilling broadcast. I was, I am sure, not alone in feeling there was something strangely affecting in the subtle variations of accent and intonation in which the voices of greeting came from the various Dominions overseas.

Anyone holding, as I do, that the basis of linguistic difference is to be sought in climatic conditions must have found it exceedingly suggestive to hear the English tongue undergo a series of unmistakable changes. *December 27*

1933

Without doubt the most important event of the year 1933 was the appointment in January of Adolf Hitler as Chancellor of the Third Reich and the establishment of the Nazi dictatorship. Exultant nationalism now blazed where bitter resentment had previously smouldered. The brutal persecution of the Jews, as well as of pacifists, Communists and other helpless political opponents, shocked the world but appeared to give Germany a new feeling of self-confidence and self-respect. Hitler continued to express his desire for peace but the martial parades and the bellicose speeches of some of his lieutenants did nothing to allay the fears of Germany's neighbours.

In February the Reichstag was set alight by the Nazis who then put the blame on the Communists. A young Dutchman, Van der Lubbe, who had been found in the building, was sentenced to death, but his four co-defendants were acquitted. The trial, which lasted three months, aroused worldwide interest.

In America it was the year of President Roosevelt's New Deal, as a result of which the economic situation rapidly improved, following a rigorous overhaul of the banking system, of company promoting and of Government expenditure. Prohibition, that "noble experiment", was finally laid to rest, and the Soviet Government was granted official recognition.

A World Monetary and Economic Conference was held in London in the summer and was attended by representatives from sixty-six countries, but its aims were frustrated by the policies of President Roosevelt and little was achieved.

Little, too, came of the Disarmament Conference held in Geneva, which was undermined by the sudden withdrawal of Germany in October. Germany also announced her intention of leaving the League of Nations, as Japan had done earlier in the year.

In Britain the National Government continued to steer the country along the road to recovery, although the number of unemployed still stood at well over 2 million.

France managed to clock up another three Prime Ministers during the year—MM. Daladier, Sarrault and Chautemps.

In Spain the year began and ended with revolutionary troubles, and martial law had to be proclaimed in three provinces. In suppressing a revolt at a small village in Andalusia the police shot twenty-five peasants in cold blood after the village had surrendered. This incident, which the authorities at first tried to cover up, contributed largely to the fall of Señor Azaña's Government in September.

Dr. Dolfuss, the Austrian Chancellor, spent the year wrestling with the threat of Nazism, to which end he dispensed with an unworkable Parliament and by skilful propaganda managed to keep the German wolf at bay. His visits abroad won him much sympathy and he became a popular international figure.

Sporadic fighting between Chinese and Japanese troops continued throughout the year; in May the Japanese were actually advancing on Peking which was only saved by a timely truce. The situation was made more delicate by the strengthening of Russia's "Far East Red Army" in the face of alleged Japanese designs on Soviet territory in the Far East.

For the Empire it was on the whole a satisfactory year, Canada and Australia both recording substantial progress along the road to economic recovery. In India Gandhi continued to pop in and out of prison, his release on two occasions being precipitated by fasting. The picture was not so bright in South Africa, which suffered from the worst drought in living memory; it brought ruin to hundreds of farmers and over 10,000,000 sheep died.

Other events which caught the public eye were the appearance of the Loch Ness Monster (which Lieutenant-Commander Gould, an expert on "sea-serpents", suggested was possibly "a vastly enlarged, long-necked, marine form of the common newt"), the flight of two British aeroplanes over Mount Everest, the purchase of the Codex Sinaiticus from the Soviet Government by the British Museum for £100,000, and Gordon Richards' record of 259 winning rides in one season. Scientists at I.C.I. developed polythene, Sir Malcolm Campbell raised his own land-speed record to 272 m.p.h., and the Oxford Union resolved not to fight for King and Country. Among those who died were Horatio Bottomley, Mrs. Annie Besant, Augustine Birrell, John Galsworthy and Anthony Hope.

One has had occasion earlier to remark how often a Peterborough paragraph of forty-five years ago could well have been written last week. However, in August, 1933, Peterborough says: "The

Spanish Riviera is not very familiar to English people"; and his comments on what women may or may not wear at Wimbledon, in Whitehall or on their lips and fingernails now sound like distant echoes from another century.

For Brighter Cricket

There is a monetary reward, I hear, for players in to-day's Test match who are willing to take a risk in going for hits to or over the boundary. An Australian firm offers, to the players of both sides in all five Tests:

2s for every boundary hit;
£5 for every hit over the fence;
£10 in addition for every century completed within 2½ hours; and
£1 for every catch.

Thus players who shine right through the series will be entitled, particularly if they are free hitters and good catchers—to a useful sum at the end of the rubber. I have not heard of any player who had had his amateur status imperilled by claiming the money, though similar schemes have operated in other rubbers in Australia.

January 13

France's Edgar Wallace

M. Simonon [*sic*], the French counterpart of Edgar Wallace, has arrived in London. At the age of 30 he has no fewer than 280 books to his credit.

He lives on a yacht, gets up at 5.30 each morning, and writes at the spanking pace of a chapter an hour.

I am told that his hero, "Inspector Maigret," is as famous in France as Sherlock Holmes, and is shortly to make an appearance in an English version. *January 20*

An Increase in Value

Mr. John Galsworthy, who is lying ill at Hampstead, is one of the most painstaking of modern authors. Unlike Dickens and Scott, whose work was in the printer's hands before the ink was dry, he has often rewritten novels half a dozen times before allowing them to go forth.

Even publication has not always ended his anxieties. He disliked "The Villa Roubaix" so much that he ordered all unsold copies to be destroyed, and 300 copies were torn up and a dustman given 5s to take them away.

Since then a copy has fetched £185 at auction. *January 24*

Cannibalism à la Fourchette

A missionary just returned from one of the wilder parts of Africa was asked if he had succeeded in inducing the natives to give up cannibalism.

He replied: "No, not yet, but I have got as far as teaching them to eat their victims with a knife and fork." *February 1*

Mr. Quintin Hogg

At the "English Review" luncheon I met Mr. Quintin Hogg, Lord Hailsham's son, who is one of the leaders of the movement to secure a reversal of the Oxford Union's pacifist motion.

He looks more youthful than anyone of his age that I know. These looks, however, betoken no immaturity of intellect. For his intellectual record shows him to be true son of his father. At Oxford, in addition to a double first—he is reputed to have got more "alphas" in "Greats" than any candidate since Gladstone—he was President of the Union, won many prizes, and later obtained an All Souls fellowship. *February 16*

Debating Speeches on Great Problems

The congratulations which the Prime Minister received from M.P.s in the House of Commons on Thursday night after his speech in defence of the Government's unemployment policy were a very sincere reflection of the feeling of the House.

I was talking yesterday with someone who has his finger on the pulse of the House, and he told me that many members resented the Government's being attacked continuously by methods consisting of mere debating slickness on the part of those who have no constructive contributions to offer.

He led me to understand that he was talking particularly of the vehement speeches of Mr. Lloyd George and Mr. Churchill. While members admired them as clever forensic performances, as most of the speeches of these two statesmen are, they resented the fact that the Prime Minister and the Government, grappling earnestly with tasks of paramount seriousness, should be exposed to this sort of sniping.

As he put it to me, "It reduces the House of Commons to a mere debating gymnasium." *February 18*

A Baptism of Fire

Mr. R. A. Butler, the Under-Secretary for India, had his "baptism of fire" as a Government Front Bench speaker yesterday, and acquitted himself very well. A speech to a crowded house on an historic occasion must always be an ordeal for a junior Minister.

But the son of an Indian administrator, who has been a member of one of the commissions which went to India last year, and was president of the Cambridge Union in 1924, might be expected to hold his own even in such a critical assembly—despite his mere 30 years.

Mr. Butler did so, and, moreover, made some neat retorts to the critics. He has a fresh, boyish manner, and a frank way of speaking which the House enjoyed. *March 30*

Bicycles and Shorts

The summer of 1933 seems destined to be noted as one of certain importance by those who chronicle the passing phases of women's dress reform. And once again the bicycle is to provide the medium of progress towards—who knows where?

Shorts, I observe, have this year been adopted as virtually the accepted dress for girl bicyclists. And very short shorts at that.

I wonder what would have been the reaction of Mrs. Amelia Jenks Bloomer, of New York, who nearly a hundred years ago tried to create a fashion in those most unaesthetic of female garments which remain—if they still exist—the principal monument to her memory? *May 24*

The New Sleeve

Matinee hats for some years now have been things of the past. But the present season has seen the coming of a no less irritating fashion from the viewpoint of the theatre-goer—the epaulette sleeve.

Anybody who has sat behind two fashionably dressed women in the stalls will have become aware that the matinee hat was as nothing in the matter of obstructed vision, to the epaulette sleeve.

To sit between them is hardly less embarrassing. They are so adjusted that one can neither sink into safety beneath their summits nor rise superior to their irritations. And they certainly are most unbecoming. *June 3*

Hitler versus Jazz

In Germany nowadays even dancing is subject to nationalistic criticism. Hitler disapproves of "Jazz," and has ordered its replacement wherever possible by "honest, inspiring German music"—marches for preference!

Paradoxically enough, English dance tunes—especially of the "hot" variety—are at the moment enjoying an unprecedented popularity everywhere abroad—even in Germany!

I wonder which will win in the end, Hitler or the saxophone!

June 9

Omnibus Competition

Now that all the London passenger transport services have been brought under one control I hope that we shall see an end to a particularly undesirable outcome of omnibus competition.

On a recent night an independent omnibus passed my car near Brompton Oratory, eastward bound. To keep it in sight I had to travel at 45 miles per hour, and it swerved in and out of other traffic in an awe-inspiring fashion.

But this was no record-breaking run over the whole route. For at Hyde Park Corner it waited five minutes to get a full load, and then repeated the performance down Piccadilly.

Profitable Piracy

At the top of Haymarket its stop was nearer ten minutes than five, then off it went again—not to continue its easterly journey, but to regain Piccadilly by the shortest route and carry on the profitable work of piracy, regardless of risk.

Doubtless its proprietors could show that its schedule for the total run did not exceed the legal speed limit. But a mobile police officer could have told a very different story. *July 3*

Hot-Weather Fare

There is nothing like a spell of really hot weather for putting the restaurateur on his mettle. Even the healthy appetite needs a little tempting.

I discovered at the Savoy a somewhat paradoxical dish in favour in the form of iced chicken curry. The curry is apparently prepared in the usual way, allowed to cool, and served in a bed of cracked ice.

M. Latry, the chef, has also devised a new salad which is deliciously cool—and sustaining. It consists of heart of lettuce with quarters of grape fruit and orange, and is dressed with lemon-juice and olive oil.

A falling-off in the consumption of red wine is inevitable. Peach cup provides a very attractive alternative, the basis being one of the Rhine wines. *July 26*

Jack Hobbs

Jack Hobbs, the famous Surrey and England cricketer, scored his 195th century at the Oval yesterday.

In spite of the lameness which obliged him to have a runner for nearly the whole of his five hours' innings, he batted with his usual grace—and he is in his 52nd year.

Surrey have ten more matches before them, and Hobbs therefore has quite a good chance of passing the 200 century mark this season.

He is building up a record which will probably stand for a very long time.* *July 28*

A Target for Attack

Seeing that Dr. Einstein will talk of anything but politics, I was astonished to learn that among the piles of letters which reach him daily from Germany are many which beg him to stop his "atrocity campaign against Germany."

These appeals are the result of a recent broadcast by Capt. Goering, the Prussian Prime Minister, who threatened Jewish listeners that they would have to pay dearly for everything Einstein did.

In making Einstein a target for attack, his traducers show a strange psychological lapse, for if there is one man who has the whole world behind him it is Einstein.

He is certainly a most attractive personality—his winning smile and soft brown eyes giving a radiant illumination to his features.

July 29

***Hobbs's record of 197 centuries still stands.**

Ronald Colman's Holiday

The Spanish Riviera is not very familiar to English people, and a friend who has just returned from the lovely little town of Sitges tells me that except in one of the two hotels not a word of English is spoken.

Catalan is the native speech, but a little French is understood.

Among the visitors there just now is Mr. Ronald Colman, the film actor. *August 11*

Foreign Office Fashions

Sir John Simon has returned to the Foreign Office from his holiday to find that a sartorial revolution has come about during his absence.

In the most dignified ministry in Whitehall many of the girl clerks have adopted the new fashion, and are appearing stockingless.

One of the frock-coated messengers, looking gloomily at a neat pair of bare ankles receding down the corridor, remarked to me with a bitter irony that he supposed the gents would soon be coming in shorts.

One wonders what the Foreign Secretary, one of the best and most correctly dressed ministers in the Cabinet, thinks of the new departmental fashion.

Not for the Bank

The City apparently is more particular than Whitehall in this matter. At the Bank of England a rigorous fashion censorship is in force.

Lip-stick is taboo, and anything but the discreetest shade of pink upon the finger-nails is liable to bring an official reprimand.

I cannot believe that the most daring of the Bank of England clerks has even seriously thought of entering its portals stockingless. *September 1*

Only One Classic Win

Gordon Richard's phenomenal success is due to various factors. He is light and very strong for his weight, and besides being naturally an excellent horseman has first-rate judgment.

Curiously enough, he has only one classic win to his credit, but at 29 he is still young and has therefore plenty of time to equal in this respect the record of Steve Donoghue who is twenty years his senior. *September 29*

Mr. Churchill's "Marlborough"

What, would you say, will be the most successful book of the autumn publishing season? A West End book-seller to whom I put this question yesterday backs Mr. Winston Churchill's "Marlborough," of which the first volume appears within a few days.

He said that he himself had, in advance, "subscribed" two hundred and fifty copies of it, certainly a token of confidence.

Mr. Churchill, I gather, is "well away," as they say in sporting circles, with the second volume, though we are not likely to be reading it for another year.

He can work rapidly, but he is his own constant critic, and never lets a page of manuscript or a proof go until it satisfies him.

September 30

Aquariums for the Home

In a variety of smart West End houses a new form of "decoration" is enjoying a great vogue. It takes the form of a glorified goldfish bowl or miniature aquarium.

The all-glass tank has concealed lighting in the lid and an undulating sandy ocean bed, liberally sown with growing seaweed and scattered with coloured rocks.

The water used is "matured" and seemingly need never be changed. It is kept at a constant temperature by little electric heaters and aerated slightly by the growing weed.

The fish suitable to such tanks are exclusively from tropical waters. They are very small, but rich in colour and intriguing in shape and habits.

I have seen several of these "aquariums" placed on mantelpieces or bookcase tops with fascinating effect. *December 5*

A Sage Prophecy

Some twenty-five years ago Mr. Montagu Salmon, joint founder of the great fortune of the Salmon–Gluckstein Joseph families, made a prophecy to his board.

Business in London, he told them, would move west. If his sons could find any properties falling vacant in the Park Lane belt or immediately to the west of the park they should go ahead and take them. Furthermore, they should not relinquish them unless there was an opportunity to sell at a substantial profit.

So it came about that the Salmon brothers quietly acquired the Oxford Street properties. That wise advice has been instrumental in bringing about the opening to-day of a notable addition to London's great hotels—the Cumberland. *December 12*

1934

1934

The international situation in 1934 was dominated by events in Europe, where Hitler continued to tighten his grip on Germany, and during the summer he found a solution to the problem of the rivalry between the Army and the Nazi storm-trooper movement, the S.A. The latter had served him well in the past, when they had been used for breaking up the political meetings of his opponents, but their leader, Ernst Röhm, a brutal Nazi veteran, aimed at usurping the role of the regular Army, an ambition which Hitler regarded as highly dangerous. So, on June 30, in what came to be known as the "Night of the Long Knives", S.S. murder squads shot Röhm and about 200 other people, including General von Schleicher, the former Chancellor. Later Hitler announced that Röhm had been planning a revolution. On August 2 a further obstacle to his power was removed when President von Hindenburg died at the age of 87. Hitler announced that the title "President" would not be used again and that henceforth he would be known as the "Leader" or Führer. *He reinforced his control over the army by introducing an oath of allegiance not to the State but to himself. This oath was to have important consequences, for it was later to be used by German officers as their excuse for supporting Hitler to the bitter end.*

Meanwhile, in next-door Austria, Dr. Dolfuss, the Chancellor, had been murdered in July by a group of Austrian Nazis. Hitler made little secret of his desire to bring about the union of Germany and Austria and it was only the firm attitude of Mussolini who, at this stage, distrusted Hitler and wanted to keep Austria independent, that prevented Hitler from achieving his aim.

The French spent most of the year busily tearing France apart. Vociferous public indignation followed the suicide in January of a crook called Stavisky who, it transpired, had enjoyed considerable protection in high places. It was even alleged that the Prime Minister, Chautemps, had ordered Stavisky's assassination to stop him revealing how many politicians he had bribed. In February serious rioting broke out in Paris, the police opened fire and six people were killed. Chautemps had resigned in January and his place was taken by Daladier, who in turn was succeeded by Gaston Doumergue after the February riots. Louis Barthou, then aged 72, became Foreign Minister. In order to take advantage of the breach between Hitler and Mussolini over Austria, Barthou decided to strengthen French ties with Yugoslavia and to this end invited King Alexander to visit France. Both Barthou and the King were assassinated by a Macedonian revolutionary in Marseilles on October 8. "These were the first shots of the Second World War," wrote Anthony Eden later.

The year in Russia was also marked by assassination, this time of Sergei Kirov, Stalin's man in Leningrad. It was Kirov's death which transformed Stalin into the monster of the great purges; he now decided to crush every vestige of opposition and imposed a tyranny more brutal by far than anything known in Tsarist days.

Bloodshed also stained the memory of the year in Spain, where, in September, the miners in Asturias rose in revolt. The Liberal Government sent in the Foreign Legion under General Franco who defeated the miners after fifteen days of fighting. The Legionnaires then behaved as if they were still in Morocco and hundreds of miners were tortured and shot after capture.

If in this brief survey of the year nothing has been said of events in America, in Great Britain or in the Empire, it is only because the world scene was so overshadowed by events in Europe that the relative stability and economic recovery achieved elsewhere seemed prosaic by comparison, although it must be said that President Roosevelt found 1934 a much more difficult period than the first ten months of his administration had been, and was forced to abandon some of the New Deal enterprises so valiantly begun the year before.

A few less bloodthirsty incidents managed, nevertheless, to command attention. In Canada the birth of the Dionne quins caused quite a sensation. In Britain Queen Mary launched the Queen Mary*; King George V opened the Mersey Tunnel; Kurt Hahn started Gordonstoun School and John Christie started the Glyndebourne Operatic Festival.*

The world of music suffered the loss of Elgar, Holst and Delius, that of the theatre Sir Nigel Playfair and Sir Arthur Wing Pinero, and science lost Madame Curie.

Last, but not least, in 1934 Hugo Wortham became editor of the Peterborough column.

Soccer and Baseball Finance

I wonder what our Soccer stars think when they read that Babe Ruth, at the age of 39, has signed on for another season with the New York Yankees baseball team, at a salary of £7,000.

The earnings of professional footballers in England are limited to £8 a week during the eight months' playing season and £6 a week for the remaining four months—under £400 a year.

Yet these players are drawing crowds which in three instances on Saturday carried the receipts to over £4,000. At Highbury, the Arsenal and Crystal Palace match drew £4,856.

Ruth's £20,000 a Year

Babe Ruth's contract—probably, at his age, the last player-contract he will sign—shows a drop of over £3,000 compared with his salary for last year.

Even so, it is, I gather, £3,000 higher than the salary the Yankees' president had in mind. He "figured" that he ought to be able to get Ruth for £4,000. In 1931, when Ruth was at the zenith of his career, he earned £20,000.

In one respect the negotiations seem to have been unique. They were concluded without public argument, and in a matter of minutes.

I think our Football Association system is the better. It acts as a brake on a rich club acquiring a complete team of stars.

January 29

Nizam's Vast Gold Hoard

Many investors have made small fortunes during the past few months by speculation in gold-mining shares. Names have been mentioned of men already well known in London and elsewhere whose profits have run into six figures.

I am surprised that nobody has remembered the name of the man whose increase in wealth, as a result of the rise in the price of gold, is probably in the neighbourhood of £60,000,000.

In the strong rooms of Hyderabad is safely stored an accumulation of gold bullion and coin generally estimated at not less than £100,000,000.

This gold represents part of the Nizam's personal fortune, and the computation of its value was made when the price of gold was 84s per fine ounce.

The Nizam's jewels are said to be worth another £400,000,000, but obviously his gold is a much more liquid asset, the sterling value of which has lately appreciated by a full 60 per cent.

February 5

Yesterday's Sayings

Miss Ellen Wilkinson—We are displacing labour so rapidly that soon the last man will only have to press a button to get his own funeral. *February 6*

Viscount Cecil of Ilford—It is a profound and wicked untruth that the way to avoid war is to prepare for war. *February 9*

Sir Herbert Samuel—The transfer of all industry and commerce to public control would lower the standard of living and intensify unemployment. *February 19*

Lord Desborough—Nothing separates England and America except water and ignorance. The water is very wide and the ignorance, I am sorry to say, is pretty deep on both sides. *February 22*

Dr. Dollfuss—4ft. 11in.

Perhaps it was to remove the reproach of being the smallest uniformed Fascist in Austria that Dr. Dollfuss put Rudi, his 3½-year-old son into an exact replica of his own uniform for the recent Heimwehr review in honour of Major Fey.*

I hear that university professors and school-masters have received a confidential circular ordering them to put a stop to the circulation of "jokes at the expense of members of the Government" among the students and pupils.

This apparently has not stopped the jests about the Chancellor's diminutive stature.

Here are three new stories which a friend just returned from Vienna tells me:

*Emil Fey (1888–1938) was Vice-Chancellor in Dolfuss's cabinet. The Heimwehr was an anti-socialist military force.

The dachshunds of Vienna are being "combed out" to provide Dr. Dollfuss with a suitable mount at military parades.

The Chancellor has just sprained his ankle by falling off a ladder while picking strawberries.

A dastardly plot by the defeated Socialists to assassinate him was foiled in the nick of time by his personal detective catching sight of the mouse-trap set at the door of his flat. *April 7*

Yesterday's Sayings

Mr. Justice Clauson—Even a Chancery Judge is allowed to draw to some extent on his experience of what happens after dances. *April 11*

The Chief Constable of Nottingham on the suggestion that psychologists should be attached to the juvenile courts.—The best "ist" I know is a sound spanking. *April 13*

Mr. Chamberlain, in his Budget speech—We have finished the story of "Bleak House," and we are sitting down to enjoy the first chapter of "Great Expectations." *April 18*

Lord Reading—Wives know far more of what men are thinking than men know of what women are thinking. *April 30*

A Great Conductor

When I saw Sir Thomas Beecham at Covent Garden yesterday immersed in rehearsing for the opening of the opera season next week, he radiated energy.

A good example of his readiness to turn his well-known wit even against his audience occurred in the North. At the interval of a concert he was conducting he arranged to conclude with Berlioz's "Carnaval Romain" instead of with the overture to the "Mastersingers."

No announcement was made to the audience of the change of programme, which in due course produced enormous applause.

When the audience insisted on an encore he turned, and said, "Ladies and gentlemen, the orchestra will now play the piece which you think you have just heard." *April 28*

La Goulue's Champagne

The aristocratic hunchback who was Toulouse-Lautrec is represented by two works in the "Renoir, Cézanne and Their Contemporaries" exhibition at the Lefevre Galleries, the private view of which takes place to-day.

In both "La Goulue," that vivid figure of the Montmartre of the eighties, appears, together with her inevitable companion in Toulouse-Lautrec's pictures, the saturnine man with the tall hat.

La Goulue figured in an amusing encounter with King Edward when, as Prince of Wales, he went one Grand Prix night to the Jardin de Paris.

Catching sight of him, she called out impudently: " 'Allo, Wales, vas-tu payer mon champagne?" The effrontery of her tutoiement amused the Prince, and she had her champagne. *June 1*

Versatile Journalists

There are many legends about Mr. W. R. Hearst, who is now on a visit to this country. I heard a new one yesterday.

Mr. Hearst transacts most of his business, personal and otherwise, by telegraph. On a good evening he will send out anything up to 200 messages.

These reach one of his Californian papers on a teletype. When things are quiet members of the staff amuse themselves by idling round the machines, "seeing what the boss is up to."

Recently the two giraffes on Mr. Hearst's Californian estate died. He bought another pair. These began to ail.

One night over the teletype came the message: "Get me conscientious reliable man to care for giraffes. Salary $50 a week."

By midnight 27 members of the staff had applied for the job. *July 2*

A Surprise for Hollywood

I am told that Hollywood has just heard with an incredulous gasp that perhaps the highest paid actress in the world is "an English comedienne whose name would not be recognised by 1 per cent. of American film fans."

They mean Miss Gracie Fields. Mr. J. Walter Rubin, the Hollywood director, who recently visited this country, assures

Americans that Miss Fields was paid £35,000 for her last picture, plus a share of the profits.

This may be a slight exaggeration, but Miss Fields is undoubtedly one of the world's best-paid entertainers. And her remuneration has been going up while most other stars' salaries have been falling, in many cases to but a fraction of the old fabulous amounts. *July 14*

"Soul-Searing" Tea

I remember first meeting M. Escoffier, who now lies critically ill. It was at a restaurant in the Haymarket, newly opened by one of his former subordinates. The master had come to eat and bless. He was sparing in both.

M. Escoffier, a lean figure looking much more like a French general than the world's most famous chef, talked of the gastronomic celebrities he had known in Paris during the '60's and '70's. Chief of these was King Edward, whom he praised as being both a great gourmet and something of a gourmand.

In the many years he spent in England M. Escoffier did more than anyone to shorten the Victorian menu. He failed in two things. He never succeeded in eradicating the savoury, which he considered inartistic, and our afternoon tea habit—which "seared his soul"—still remains fairly vigorous. *July 30*

A Popular Engagement

The engagement of Mr. Aneurin Bevan and Miss Jennie Lee will be popular in the House of Commons. Both have vivid personalities.

Miss Jennie Lee, when she was in the House, could always be relied upon to brighten debates. Mr. Bevan's fiery oratory makes him one of the few Labour members in the present Parliament who are capable of drawing members into the Chamber when they are up.

Mr. Bevan is particularly popular with the younger Conservatives. The older members tend to look askance at this vigorous young man with his penchant for strongly-worded outbursts.

Indeed, he had so many friends in the Conservative party that at one time there was talk of his being a convert to its creed.

But recently Mr. Bevan has swerved back violently to the Left. His marriage to Miss Jennie Lee—also a Left-Winger—is likely to stabilise his opinions. *September 12*

A Famous Oxford Figure

Three months ago I visited Mr. F. F. Urquhart, the Dean of Balliol, in whom passes a figure famous in Oxford for forty years.

"Sligger"—a nickname the origin of which neither he nor anyone else could explain—was then very ill in an Oxford nursing home. His hair could be no whiter than before, but his voice was even softer and his movements slower. The accuracy of his memory of many generations of Oxford men was more astonishing than ever.

A particular pleasure to him was the completion of Holywell Manor, the new buildings of Balliol. He had long fostered this project.

Members of his reading parties at his chalet on the slopes of Mont Blanc are not likely to forget the experience. There was the bath set athwart the mountain stream which flowed from the glacier straight through the house—the perfection of simplicity in plumbing—and the cricket ground, which solved the question of leg theory by placing the leg boundary three yards from the wicket on the edge of the mountain.

The Secret of his Charm

The secret of "Sligger's" charm is hard to define. It was compounded of a great gift of sympathy, real simplicity of manner, a deep but unaggressive culture, and, above all, a true understanding of and affection for youth and young men.

Moreover, he had those little foibles without which none of us is human and lovable. Mr. Harold Nicolson, for instance, in his book, "Some People," refers to him as "the most subtle of dons." This little compliment was much to his taste. "Some People" always seemed to be lying about his rooms. It always just happened to be open at that particular page.

He was a great civilising influence in what even Balliol men would admit was still in some respects a community of young barbarians.

September 20

Their First Meeting

Miss Madge Titheradge's first appearance last night in a play produced by Mr. Noel Coward—"Theatre Royal"—reminds me of a story I have heard her tell of their first meeting.

One evening when she was leaving the theatre after a show, a boy of 14 came up and offered her a bunch of rather faded flowers which he had clasped in a hot hand.

Amused by his offering, she asked whether his people knew he had come to speak to her. "No," he answered, very shy and frightened. "What is your name?" "Noel Coward," was the reply.

October 24

An Outsize in Louis

This letter was recently received by Charles of London, of 52, East 57th Street, New York City:

> Gentlemen—When I was in New York the other day I sent home a Louis XIV bed. I now find it is too short for my husband. Please send a Louis XV at once.
>
> Helen C.

I am unable to give the furnishing firm's reply. *October 27*

Class-War in Chess

M. M. Botvinnik, the all-Russian chess champion, has been authorised by the Soviet authorities to accept an invitation to take part in the Hastings tournament, and in Moscow hopes run high that he will beat Capablanca.

This decision is a revolution (or, should one say, counter-revolution?) in itself.

Only four years ago Nicolai Krilenko, Terrorist Chief Prosecutor and now Commissar of Justice, presiding at the "militant" congress of these games, ordered

> "Merciless Class-War both in Chess and Draughts! No quarter for the Class-Enemy! Down with Neutrality among Chess-and-Draughts-Men! Up with the Fighting Five-Year Chess and Draughts Plan!"

The abstract mind of the Russians, which makes them such good chess players, has in the past prevented their playing this and many other games with normal foreigners.

But, now that M. Litvinoff sits on the Council of the League of Nations, Botvinnik may play in the international chess tournament in Hastings.

November 20

1934

£10,000 a Year Conductor

I remember the exictement at the Royal College of Music jubilee celebrations last year when Mr. Leopold Stokowski appeared to conduct the final number of the orchestral concert.

The programme had been arranged so that each piece should be conducted by an ex-student. Luckily, no one had been chosen for the "Meistersinger" Overture, with which it concluded.

When Sir Hugh Allen found that Stokowski was in London he naturally impressed the services of the most famous conductor the College has produced.

Stokowski, however, did not learn this side of his art at the R.C.M. In his days there was no conductors' class.

His first post as organist at St. James's, Piccadilly, he once told me, was worth £100 a year.

The conductorship of the Philadelphia Orchestra, which he has just resigned, was worth a hundred times as much. *December 8*

1935

1935

In 1935 the dictators really began to flex their muscles. A plebiscite held in January resulted in an overwhelming vote for the return of the Saar to Germany, the implementation of which was successfully carried out by the League of Nations in March. Thereafter events in Germany moved with alarming rapidity. Brushing aside the idea of a general settlement of the arms question, Hitler announced that the Third Reich was to have an army of 12 corps and 36 divisions, a naval strength of 35 per cent that of Great Britain, and that conscription was to be reintroduced in October. The persecution of the Jews was intensified, and at the Nuremberg Party Congress in September it was laid down that no Jew could hold German citizenship, nor occupy any official position, nor marry an Aryan woman. At the same time the Swastika was adopted as the sole flag of the Reich. Sterilization of the unfit was also introduced and 56,000 people were so doctored during the year.

Italy's contribution to the headaches of the League of Nations in 1935 was the invasion of Abyssinia. In February troops started massing in Eritrea, then under Italian control, in alleged response to minor border incidents perpetrated by the Abyssinians. Abyssinia appealed to the League of Nations, and Great Britain and France, as negotiators, put forward proposals which, although favourable to Italy, were rejected by Mussolini. It soon became clear that he was determined to go to war, and on October 3 the advance of the Italian troops in East Africa began. The League promptly declared Italy an aggressor and proceeded to impose economic sanctions. In December proposals formulated in the name of Great Britain and France were presented to Italy and Abyssinia; but the proposals, which were the outcome of the famous Hoare/Laval Pact, were so heavily weighted in Italy's favour that public opinion forced their rejection out of hand and Sir Samuel Hoare resigned as Foreign Secretary.

In Britain the year witnessed many ministerial changes but no fundamental change of direction. In June Mr. MacDonald, who had held office since 1929 and whose health was beginning to crack under the strain, decided to resign. He was succeeded by Mr. Baldwin, who thereupon carried out a major reconstruction of the Cabinet. A General Election was held in November at which the National Government was returned with a majority of 247 over every possible combination of opponents. One unusual feature of the election was the decision of the Labour Party to oppose the Speaker, who was, nevertheless, returned with a majority of 8,000. Another surprise was the defeat of Ramsay MacDonald at Seaham by Mr. Emanuel Shinwell, who had first entered Parliament as M.P. for Linlithgow in 1922.

By far the most ambitious piece of legislation passed during the year was the Government of India Act which promised the sub-continent a measure of self-government.

In India itself the year was marred by the disastrous earthquake which totally destroyed the city of Quetta, the "Aldershot of India". 30,000 people were killed and another 20,000 left destitute. The rescue work was brilliantly organised by Sir Henry Karslake, thereafter known as "Karslake of Quetta".

In Canada it was also election year. The electorate bade farewell to Mr. R. B. Bennett and the Liberals were returned to office under Mr. Mackenzie King. In September Lord Bessborough was succeeded as Governor-General by Mr. John Buchan, who was created Lord Tweedsmuir.

France went through another difficult year, beset by financial difficulties and unnerved by the troubled European situation. In May M. Flandin resigned as Prime Minister and was succeeded by Pierre Laval whose name is forever linked with that of Sir Samuel Hoare.

In America President Roosevelt introduced a programme of "social security" considered radical by American standards. Two events which captured the headlines during the year were the murder of Senator Huey Long, the "Kingfish" of Louisiana, and the conviction of Bruno Hauptmann for the murder of the Lindbergh baby.

For the people of Britain, certainly for Londoners, the most memorable event of the year was the King's Silver Jubilee which was celebrated with suitable pageantry in May. Other notable events included the construction of the first practical radar equipment for the detection of aircraft by Robert Watson-Watt, the Normandie*'s record crossing of the Atlantic, the introduction of pedestrian crossings by Mr. Hore Belisha, and the last occasion on which a peer of the realm was tried for manslaughter by his* *peers in the House of Lords. A unanimous verdict of acquittal was returned.*

It was the year of George Gershwin's folk opera, Porgy and Bess, *the year in which the term "swing" was coined, the year in which jazz "of Negro or Jewish origin" was banned from the German wireless, and the year in which the rumba became popular.*

T. E. Lawrence, in the guise of Aircraftsman Ross, was killed in a motorcycle accident, and others who breathed their last included Lord Jellicoe, of Jutland fame, Lord Reading, former Viceroy of India, Colonel Dreyfus and Mr. George Grossmith.

Eddie Cantor's Huge Income

Eddie Cantor, who arrives in London from Paris to-morrow evening, and broadcasts the following night, has for a number of years enjoyed the reputation of being the highest-paid public entertainer in the world.

His yearly income is impossible to compute, but, including his revenue from film work, broadcasting, gramophone records, the endorsement of advertised products, and personal tours, the total is staggering.

Just before sailing for Europe recently, for instance, he had completed a 26-week broadcasting contract for a coffee company, for which he received £1,600 for one broadcast a week.

£50,000 Down for a Picture

The Metro-Goldwyn-Mayer Corporation is reputed to pay him £50,000 cash for one picture a year, plus a percentage of the gross takings.

How much extra this percentage must bring him is indicated by the fact that in the British Isles alone, four of his recent pictures are credited with earnings of over £600,000.

The personal appearance tours which he makes from time to time are particularly remunerative. A recent appearance in Brooklyn brought him nearly £2,500 in a single week. *January 1*

Out of Date

The famous "chess-board" in the Moscow Marx and Engels Institute, presented to Lenin by his devoted Bolshevik Central Committee in 1921, has, I learn, been removed "for repairs."

This board was half white and half red. The chessmen represented Lenin's Old Guard playing against the Russian Whites in the civil war period.

Each piece had a name on it. A few years ago Trotsky, who figured as a rook, if I remember rightly, had to be moved over to the White side of the board. But Zinovieff and Kameneff still retained their places among the Red chessmen.

Now, as I say, the board as been removed "for repairs."

January 10

Eton's Phonetic Speller

Dr. Alington's reference to "the distinguished Etonian," now raised to the peerage, who spelt wife without getting a single letter right, should interest the B.B.C.

I hope that Sir John Reith will lose no time in extracting his name from the former headmaster of Eton. He would form a useful addition to the Corporation's Advisory Committee on spoken English.

As one not unversed in Eton lore, I am a little doubtful, however, whether Dr. Alington has not mistaken legend for fact. I can remember the story being told by Etonians of the 1860's as current in their time. Further investigations would doubtless push it back earlier still.

A Sixteenth-Century Product

In fact, an old Etonian, learned in phonetics and archaeology, assures me that it almost certainly dates from the 16th century, when spelling allowed more scope for individual genius.

At first sight it seems rather curious that the Dean should asperse the educational standards at the school where he was headmaster for 17 years.

On second thoughts it occurs to me that he may allow himself, as an old Marlburian, a mild jest at Eton's expense.

On the other hand, the Lyttelton family—famous for their allegiance to Eton—may have something to say to him through Mrs. Alington.

She was a Miss Lyttelton before she became the Dean's yph.

January 11

Nerves

Stalin's fears for his personal safety have, I hear, redoubled since the assassination of Kirof.*

His state of nerves is indicated by a story which a diplomat in one of the Legations here tells me.

Before the Soviet Congress Stalin and his lieutenants attended a private view of an exhibition of pictures, arranged for the edification

*Sergei Kirov, Stalin's man in Leningrad, was assassinated by a young Communist revolutionary in December, 1934. Kirov's death transformed Stalin into the monster of the great purges.

of delegates in one of the Kremlin halls. One picture had won special praise from the Bolshevik hanging committee. It represented Stalin mourning beside Kirof's body.

"Tear that down at once," exclaimed the Red Dictator as soon as he saw it. "Don't you see the skeleton in my shadow on the wall?"

Then everybody did see it, of course.

My informant adds that the artist is in trouble. *February 12*

Regiment of Youth

Mr. Duncan Sandys, if elected for Norwood, will be the "baby" of the House of Commons. He is only 27. The ranks of youth are, however, unusually populous in the present House. It contains 63 National Government supporters who were born in 1900 or after.

The youngest is Lord Willoughby de Eresby, who will not be 28 until December. Next comes Mr. J. R. Robinson, the member for Widnes, who is 28 this month.

Lord Burghley, born in 1905, is among the younger "young men."

Veteran of 34

On the other hand, Mr. Robert Boothby, though among the 63, is close to what Dante put as the frontier of middle-age. That spokesman of youth is 35 this year.

He is, however, already almost a veteran in the House, of which he has been a member for 11 years.

Among Ministers, Mr. R. A. Butler is the junior. He became Under-Secretary for India when he was 29. He is now only 32.

February 23

Disputed Islands

Argentina's shadowy claim to the Falkland Islands, revived once again during the week-end, has been put forward at intervals for more than a century.

It dates from 1820, when Buenos Aires claimed the islands on the ground that Britain had not colonised them. The Falklands did not formally become a British colony until 1833.

Including Argentina, no fewer than six nations have had a hand in discovering, charting, colonising, or claiming these hundred rocky islets.

The Englishman, Davis, discovered them in 1592, and Hawkins visited them two years later. Meanwhile the Italian, Vespucci, had claimed prior discovery.

A Dutchman, Sebald de Wert, first gave the islands a name—his own—in 1598.

France in 1764 took formal possession and founded a colony, but three years later ceded the islands to Spain.

Britain had also founded a settlement, and rival claims almost led to war with Spain in 1770. In 1771, however, the Falklands were peacefully yielded to Britain.*

Non-Swimmers

There are no railways, 'buses, or trams in the Falklands, and roads do not extend beyond the capital town of Stanley, on the larger of the only two sizeable islands.

In spite of this freedom from some of the menaces of civilisation, life is scarcely delectable.

The waterproof is a national costume, for rain falls about 250 days in the year and a perpetual mist hangs over the islands.

Sir James O'Grady, when he was Governor of the Falklands, discovered that only 15 men and boys out of Stanley's 900 population could swim.

Thereupon he started a campaign for the teaching of swimming, a valuable accomplishment, considering that communication between the islands is by small boats over rough seas. *February 25*

Hamlet's "Nice Mother"

The Critics' Circle dinner to Miss Marie Tempest provided a brilliant lot of speeches. Miss Tempest herself was at the top of her form—as she always is.

Mr. John Gielgud told a good story about his Hamlet.

An old lady leaving the theatre after the performance remarked: "Of course, the young man seems to have had a very sad life, but I thought his mother seemed a nice sunny sort of a woman."

*The islands were named by one Captain Strong in 1690, in memory of Lucius Cary, 2nd Viscount Falkland, who was killed at the Battle of Newbury in 1643.

Mr. Gielgud's "Fans"

Miss Diana Wynyard—who is easily the best after-dinner speaker among our younger actresses—alluded to Mr. Gielgud's great popularity. It is impressed upon her nightly, because their respective stage-doors are opposite one another.

"It was bad enough to come out after a show and find a large circle of 'fans' waiting, all with their backs to me," she said, amidst laughter.

"The breaking-point was reached the other night," she went on, "When I was handed a batch of programmes (of 'Hamlet') to sign. I was told to be very careful of them because John Gielgud's name was on them." *March 12*

Superman

Five years ago, when things were going particularly badly, the inner ring of Bolsheviks decided to turn M. Stalin, "The Man of Steel," into a Steel God—and so satisfy Russia's strange blend of religious idealism and slavishness.

Since then, with the dictatorial machine singing his praises at full blast, this adulation has gone to amazing lengths.

Here are a few of the terms publicly applied to M. Stalin in the course of a single week:

Great
Beloved
Wise
Bold
Sage
Our darling

Great leader of the world's working-class
Genius
Inspirer
Pilot

Our own
Our guiding star
Our own dear teacher
Best friend of Soviet gymnasts

The "great leader" and "best friend" epithets may be linked with any group at the moment in favour.

M. Stalin is to be found at the head of all professions, from astronomers to film actors.

The other day I saw the Dictator—who has been a professional politician since his 'teens—described as "first and best shock-brigade collectivised farmer."

Not for Imitation

M. Stalin's is a dangerous example for lesser men to emulate.

A short time ago the "party boss" of the Mariinsk Region allowed the local newspaper to call him "Leader of the Mariinsk Bolsheviks," and to note the "stormy applause" when he was elected chairman of their district congress.

A week or two later he was degraded from his post and expelled from the party.

"The profoundly obsequious terms in which he allowed himself to be addressed," wrote "Pravda," "can arouse only feelings of disgust in everyone who remembers that the fundamental quality of a Bolshevik should be modesty." *March 14*

Mr. Sandys Between Big Guns

Very seldom does an M.P. have such a distinguished audience for his maiden speech as Mr. Duncan Sandys had yesterday.

He spoke between Sir Herbert Samuel and Mr. Winston Churchill. Although he may have been called at that stage with the idea of giving M.P.s a breather, few members left their places.

That Mr. Churchill should pay a compliment to the speech was merely observing conventional practice. It was, however, spiced by the fact that Mr. Sandy's election for Norwood was accomplished in the teeth of the opposition of Mr. Randolph Churchill.

A greater tribute was the way Mr. Churchill replied to Mr Sandy's arguments. Maiden speeches are not usually treated with this respect.* *May 3*

The P.M.G.'s Extra Millions

Until yesterday I have never known Sir Kingsley Wood mishandle figures. He is one of the best statisticians in the House.

Asked about Post Office Savings, he made the House gasp by stating that since 1931 there had been an increase in deposits of some £369 thousand million.

He repeated the figure, and when it was challenged, said: "The figure is 369,750 followed by three noughts."

It reminds one of the remark attributed to Lord Randolph Churchill when his Treasury officials confronted him with decimals: "What are these d——d little dots?" *May 28*

*Duncan Sandys was to become Mr Churchill's son-in-law on 17 September.

"Regularising" the Jews

I understand that the outbreaks of Jew-baiting in Germany—unrelated and sporadic as they appear—are the prelude to legislation regularising the "inferior" position of the Jews.

It must be realised that no outbreak of violence and no political activity can take place without the knowledge of the Gestapo—the vigilant secret police.

Jew-baiting, therefore, has official origins, however humble. Its object is to drive home to the German people the Nazi theory that the Jews have a status in Germany different from and lower than Aryans.

The new legislation to govern the position of the Jews is likely to be promulgated in the autumn. It will deal with their economic rather than their social and political status. The Jews have long since lost the right to vote.

They Once Sacked Streicher

Herr Julius Streicher, the most notorious of anti-Semites, who has had all non-Aryan guests expelled from Bad Toelz in Bavaria, was an elementary school teacher at the Scharrer School in Nuremberg.

He was one of the earliest members of the Nazi party, and owes his continued influence—as do so many other Nazi leaders—to Herr Hitler's reluctance to discard old friends.

He lost his school teacher's job because of his political views. Those who were responsible for his dismissal have long ago disappeared into concentration camps.* *August 8*

Salzburg Echo

A Toscanini story reaches me with the return of music-lovers from Salzburg.

During a rehearsal of Beethoven's "Fidelio," Toscanini was not satisfied with the way the Vienna Philharmonic Orchestra rendered a certain passage of the overture. He asked twice for a repetition.

The third time he exclaimed: "Signori, signori, I beg you to be a little more careful! Illustrissimo Maestro Beethoven—well, he was deaf. But I can hear." *September 9*

*Streicher was hanged as a war criminal in 1946.

Impressionism

A fine example of a Balfourian judgment was given by Mr. Harold Nicolson, at yesterday's American Chamber of Commerce luncheon. It was on American statesmanship.

When Mr. Nicolson was at the Peace Conference, he thought he had reason to complain of an American colleague.

He poured out his story to Mr. Balfour—"the greatest man I have ever known." Balfour was amused.

"What you don't realise, my young friend," he said, "is that you don't know anything about anything at all. All you can hope for is to have certain tendencies of impression.

"About America I have a tendency of impression which is this: We English are apt to judge America by its weather and not by its climate. The weather is very often detestable, but the climate is serene."

Mr. Nicolson said he never forgot that lesson. *September 25*

Describing Joe Louis

"Brown Bomber" seems to be the favourite title for Joe Louis, the young negro heavyweight who has, in the American phrase, "kayoed" Max Baer.

American sports writers, always inventive in the matter of nicknames for boxers, have also coined for him such lurid appellations as "Alabama Assassin," "Detroit Dangerspot," "Sepia Slugger" and "Cottonbelt Killer."

Louis's most favoured occupation is sleeping. When awake (and not punching) he reads the Bible for at least an hour every day, mainly the Old Testament.

He rarely smiles. But he laughed loudly recently when someone told him he resembled an El Greco. "Is that another Wop fighter?" he asked. "I already 'tended to Mistah Carnera."

Americans are wondering now if James Braddock, the present heavyweight champion, will draw the "colour line."

Fight is "Employment"

Even in his greatest days Dempsey did not meet Harry Wills, the then "Black Menace," and "Tiger of New Orleans." This was partly due to the force of public opinion. Wills, however, was not in the same class as Louis.

In this country, coloured boxers are ineligible for championships of Great Britain. Any other titles, such as British Empire championships, they may hold.

When a coloured boxer is prevented from fighting in England—a rare enough event—it is usually because he is an alien and has been refused a Ministry of Labour permit.

The reputable boxer and promoter do not find the Ministry obstructive.

The permit is a permit to take employment in Great Britain. The system is applied to boxers because the Ministry regards a fight as "employment"—the boxer being considered in the employ of his agent. *September 26*

Known by Their Mark

A novel method of dealing with "road hogs" in Berlin comes into force next Tuesday. The cars of drivers who persistently offend against the traffic regulations in Berlin are to be painted with a yellow cross in a conspicuous place.

This is intended to serve as a warning to the police and other road-users that the owner of the car is a dangerous driver and that they must exercise caution in his vicinity.

Cars not fit for use are to be marked with a yellow ring. They will then have to be taken to the central traffic authorities for overhaul within a fixed period.

Unnecessary use of the hooter is also to be severely punished. The aim of this measure is to train drivers eventually to dispense altogether with warning signals in the city.

Over 30 people are killed every month in the streets of Berlin. With its population of 4,000,000, this compares favourably with London, where the monthly average of fatalities from street accidents this year has been over 80. *October 11*

Another Beecham Bark

Sir Thomas Beecham's onslaught on Liverpool, which he considers "entirely uneducated" as regards opera and which he is considering "giving a miss in future," swells his fine total of places and people he has attacked in recent years.

The most recent victim was Brighton in September, where he

criticised the arrangements for his reception. This drew a severe rebuke from the Mayor, who called his behaviour "petty, childish and savouring of cheap publicity."

Last year it was Leeds which came in for censure. He declared his intention of never going to the festival again.

Worse Than His Bite

Other institutions which have come under Sir Thomas's lash are:

1934: Covent Garden Opera audience: "Savages."

1933: Covent Garden, the Albert Hall and the Queen's Hall. "The best thing for the future of music in London would be for bombs to be dropped on them."

1928: The English nation. "The laziest nation in the world already—actually becoming comatose."

Liverpool, Leeds and other cities the dust of which Sir Thomas Beecham has shaken off his feet can take heart, however.

In 1926 Sir Thomas announced his intention of going to live permanently in the United States as "England is finished not only musically, but in every other way." He is still captiously and exuberantly with us. *October 24*

Tackling the Man

Mr. Lloyd George, who has said of Mr. Chamberlain that he had "a retail mind in a wholesale business," follows the old-fashioned political method, when you have no case, of attacking your opponents rather than their policy.

In the last few days he has given some signal examples of what has always been his favourite platform method.

Of Mr. Baldwin he has said:

> He is just like some chairman of a board of directors, unrivalled when things do not go well at making comforting speeches to allay the anxiety of an uneasy shareholder at the annual meeting, but no use at pulling a business round.

Sir John Simon had been Foreign Minister for three years "and by common consent had made a bad hash of it."

Sir Samuel Hoare, of whom Mr. Lloyd George had had high hopes, "has been hopelessly outmatched and out-manoeuvred when he is put against men of the formidable calibre of Mussolini and the subtle Frenchman M. Laval." *November 6*

The Announcer's Special

Mr. Stuart Hibberd, Chief Announcer of the B.B.C., told me a story yesterday which may be a tribute to the B.B.C. or to his persuasive voice.

He and five other passengers found after midnight that they had missed the last train from Charing Cross to Chislehurst, which had left without warning from a new platform.

The marooned six went gloomily to London Bridge. There Mr. Hibberd interviewed the station authorities, and mentioned that he had just come off duty at Broadcasting House.

Presently a special train consisting of three coaches pulled into the station and carried the six passengers the 12 miles to Chislehurst.

For this purpose the whole line was kept electrified for half an hour. *November 19*

Racial Purity for Dolls

A new type of "race warfare" which, if carried through, may have far-reaching effects, is advocated in this week's issue of the "Stuermer," Herr Julius Streicher's notorious anti-Jewish publication.

It demands that the Nazi laws for the protection of "German racial purity" should be extended to waxworks and dolls.

The "Stuermer" yesterday published an attack on Jewish shopkeepers for using wax models with Aryan features in their showrooms and window displays. This, the paper states, is an insult to German womanhood.

"Wax figures used in Jewish showrooms should have Hebraic features," the "Stuermer" states. The paper also demands a law prohibiting Jews from selling dolls with Aryan features.

November 22

Mutton à la Française

At the Gastronomes' dinner some kind things were said of our English cooking. No concession, however, was made to the language of roast beef and Yorkshire pudding.

The menu kept strictly to French. Thus a saddle of Dorset mutton became La Selle d'Agneau de Dorset. Lamb in December!

Oysters from the Essex beds which won Julius Caesar's heart were merely *Les Huitres*.

All gastronomers admit the pre-eminence of France. Yet there is a limit to the extent to which the language of its cuisine should be used on this side of the Channel.

This was plainly overstepped at one of the Service clubs at which I lunched recently.

That unexhilarating friend, hashed mutton, was there excitingly presented as *Agneau Hashish Parmentière*. *December 18*

Canned Beer

A friend attempted to enliven his Christmas with the aid of a tin-opener and a sample, specially sent to him from Pennsylvania, of America's latest gift to civilisation—canned beer.

It gave him, he said, a faintly non-convivial feeling to grapple for his drink with something that looked as though it should have contained baked beans or disinfectant. The contents, however, tasted the same as ordinary American bottled beer.

Only after he had drunk it did he notice that the brand name of the beer commemorated a British disaster in the Revolutionary War.

He is rather hoping that it will not prove symbolical.

December 31

1936

DON'T LET THE KING DOWN
WE WANT OUR KING
GOD SAVE THE KING FROM BALDWIN

1936

For Englishmen by far the most memorable event of the year was the abdication of King Edward VIII; for Germans it was probably the reoccupation of the demilitarized zone of the Rhineland; for Italians it was the ending of the Abyssinian War and the formal annexation of that country; for Spaniards it was certainly the beginning of the Civil War.

Let us start with the abdication. On January 20 King George V died at Sandringham and if indeed his last words were "Bugger Bognor" The Daily Telegraph *did not record the fact. He was duly succeeded by his eldest son as King Edward VIII. For the first months of his reign Court mourning prevailed; then the date of the Coronation was announced and preparations went ahead without a hint of trouble on the horizon. By the autumn, however, ominous stories began to appear in newspapers overseas, particularly in America, about the King's friendship with a divorced American lady, Mrs. Wallis Simpson; the British Press, meanwhile, maintained a discreet silence. In October the Prime Minister warned the King that the gossip was undermining respect for the throne and in November told him flatly that he could not marry Mrs. Simpson and remain King. The climax came on December 10 when the King abdicated and was succeeded by his brother as King George VI. "The muse of the sceptred pall knows of no comparable tragedy," declaimed* The Times, *indulging in the emotion of the hour.*

On the political front the year was dominated by the belated realization that the armed services were in a deplorable state of unreadiness and that the situation must be remedied forthwith.

Mr. Chamberlain's Budget speech was followed by a curious affair which ended in the resignation of Mr. J. H. Thomas who was Secretary of State for the Colonies and had also been a close friend of the late King. It appeared that at a late hour an unusually large amount of insurance against Budget risks had been placed at Lloyd's and a leak was suspected. A Tribunal was set up which identified Mr. Thomas as the source of the disclosure.

In France the year saw the rise to power of the Socialist Party under the Jewish M. Leon Blum. The country had been virtually paralysed by industrial unrest, amounting almost to a general strike. Blum's first action was to institute paid holidays for all workers, as a result of which he received 25,000 postcards bearing the message, "Merci pour les vacances".

On March 7, disregarding the Treaty of Locarno, German troops entered the Rhineland; in the election held immediately afterwards the Nazi party gained 99 per cent of the vote—a good example of election results under a dictatorship. The country was still beset by grave economic difficulties but Dr. Goebbels declared that "Guns before butter" must be the slogan for the winter. An outstanding event of the year was the Olympic Games meeting in Berlin in August, which gave the Nazis a splendid opportunity to show off the physical fitness and organizational ability of National Socialist Germany.

In Italy the year was dominated by the waging and winning of the Abyssinian war, the official end of which was proclaimed on May 5.

The events leading up to the outbreak of the Spanish Civil War are too tangled to be unravelled here. Suffice to say that the spark which lit the bonfire was the murder of Señor Calvo Sotelo, the leader of the Monarchist Party, on July 12. On July 17 General Franco, Governor of the Canaries, raised his standard in Morocco in an effort to overthrow the Government. Franco had the support of about nine-tenths of the Army, while the Navy and the Air Force remained loyal to the Government. Franco's troops captured Badajoz in August and the insurgents appointed him Chief of State in October, while the Republican Government moved to Valencia.

The year's upheavals in Europe pushed events in most other countries of the world out of the headlines. A notable exception, however, was the re-election of President Roosevelt, who carried every state except Maine and Vermont.

In Egypt King Fuad died and was succeeded by his young son, King Farouk; and in India Lord Willingdon was succeeded as Viceroy by Lord Linlithgow. Britain witnessed the burning down of the Crystal Palace and the first television transmissions from Alexandra Palace. Max Schmeling won the World Heavyweight Boxing championship from Joe Louis, Fred Perry became Wimbledon champion for the third time, and Billy Butlin opened his first holiday camp at Skegness.

1936

Among those who went with their King to meet their Maker were Rudyard Kipling, G. K. Chesterton, A. E. Housman and Dame Clara Butt.

Peterborough saw television for the first time and, as might be expected of an ex-music critic, kept an anecdotal eye on the comings and goings of composers, conductors and singers.

An Accession Broadcast?

Eleventh King Edward

It is very likely, I understand, that the King will take an early opportunity of broadcasting a message to the Nation and the Empire.

No previous British monarch on his accession has possessed this means of reaching all his subjects. It is natural that the King should make a precedent in this matter.

His voice has not the deep timbre of his father's, which Mr. Harold Nicolson recently and aptly described as having a slight tang of the sea about it.

It is more that of the average Englishman who has been about the world.

It is marked by a meticulous care for the consonants, which foreigners always complain we clip so badly.

The king also speaks into the microphone with a deliberation even greater than that of King George.

King Edwards Before Edward I

Edward VIII is actually the eleventh Edward to be King of England.

The three pre-Conquest Edwards who were Kings of all England were Edward the Elder, Edward the Martyr, and Edward the Confessor.

It is curious that we should number our Kings from the Conquest, as William the Conqueror claimed the throne of right and not by conquest.

In France, on the other hand, though the Capetian Dynasty had no connection with the Carolingians, its Kings reckoned them in their dynastic enumeration.

Thus, Charles X counted himself as the tenth of that name, Charlemagne being the first.

Much Travelled

King Edward is the greatest Royal traveller in history, remarkable though his father's record was. It was estimated that King George had travelled 150,000 miles.

The present King, according to Sir Lionel Halsey's estimate in 1931, travelled 250,000 miles in six years. His total is probably over 300,000.

He himself once remarked that he knew every British possession in Africa but one. And he has made speeches in English, Afrikaans, Swaheli and French.

He has also spoken in Spanish to audiences in South America. So familiar has the civilised world become to him that he has been credited with a keen desire to explore the remote Arctic.

Bachelor King

In the House of Lords yesterday there was a striking evidence of the new reign.

Instead of the usual two Royal thrones for the King and Queen, with the third for the Prince of Wales, the King's throne stood by itself.

The King being a bachelor, and there being no Prince of Wales, the others had been removed. *January 22*

Knows All His Quavers

Signor Toscanini's phenomenal musical memory has once again been impressively demonstrated.

The maestro was rehearsing a transcription of "The Invitation to the Waltz" with the New York Philharmonic.

A question arose of the value of a particular note. In the score it was marked as a quaver. Toscanini insisted hotly that it should be a dotted quaver.

To settle the point the conductor's agent rang up the Library of Congress in Washington, which has the manuscript. The librarian procured it from its file and the tune was hummed over the telephone.

After Toscanini had been proved to be right he returned in an unquavering calm to his rehearsal. *February 24*

Stalin, Music Critic

The audience at the Queen's Hall performance of Shostakovich's opera, "Lady Macbeth of Mzensk," on March 18, will be able to judge Stalin's merits as a music critic.

"Pravda," the Communist party's official newspaper, has launched a surprising attack on Shostakovich, who has hitherto been regarded as the leading Soviet composer. It denounces his music as "bourgeois, unwholesome, cheap, eccentric and tuneless."

The reason for this unexpected broadside is believed in Moscow to be that Stalin heard a composition by Shostakovich for the first time a few days ago. *March 4*

German Troops Enter the Rhineland

When Herr Hitler introduced conscription on March 16 last year, I remarked that he was following precedent in timing his statement for a Saturday.

The Nazi "purge" of June 30, 1934, and Germany's withdrawal from the League (Oct. 14, 1933) also both took place on the same day of the week.

One again the Fuehrer has presented the world with a dramatic coup de théâtre which has been timed with calculated exactitude.

It is no doubt in order to leave time for consideration in the European Chancelleries that Herr Hitler makes the last day of the week his chosen time for dropping a bombshell. *March 9*

Handel in Brief

Sir Thomas Beecham has written a life of Handel. He told me the other day that he regarded it as a masterpiece of succinct musical biography.

I have now read it and can cordially agree that it possesses the quality he claims.

It is exactly 80 words long.

Here is one of Sir Thomas Beecham's portmanteau sentences:

> Afflicted with paralysis and blindness, he died wealthy and the idol of the nation.

The "life" is printed on the National Portrait Gallery postcard containing the illustration of Hudson's portrait of Handel. *March 14*

Budget Speech Refreshment

A sip or two of water is likely to be Mr. Chamberlain's only refreshment during his Budget speech to-day. This austerity, however, has not always prevailed.

Mr. Gladstone's egg-nogg—mixed by Mrs. Gladstone—was a familiar accompaniment of his Budget oration.

I remember Mr. Churchill making good Parliamentary play—during a Budget passage dealing with excise—with a coloured drink. This might have been either cold tea or Charles Lamb's favourite "cold brandy and water."

Plain water, of course, sufficed for Mr. Snowden. So it did for Mr. Lloyd George.

When he introduced the "People's Budget" Mr. Churchill's handing him a glass was one of the dramatic moments in the "longest ever" Budget speech.

Drunk With His Own Eloquence

Great Parliamentarians of earlier times were less abstemious.

Lord Brougham refreshed himself so often during one long speech in the House of Lords on Reform that he slid to his knees in passionate entreaty to the peers to pass the bill—and could not rise.

Charles Fox, on the other hand, used to suck oranges. He offered a manly and inspiriting spectacle as pips, quips and classical quotations spurted from his mouth.

Wilberforce had resort to secret and even furtive measures. To steady his nerve and arrange his ideas the anti-slavery leader took —an opium pill. *April 21*

Socialists Back Mr. Churchill

The spiritual rapprochement between Mr. Churchill and the Socialists goes on apace. Yesterday, when the Naval vote was being discussed, he interrupted Lord Stanley several times, and on each occasion the Socialists cheered.

Mr. Churchill's ardent championing of the League, his dislike of dictatorships and his critical attitude towards the Government has resulted in an enthusiasm for him on the Socialist benches not always shown towards their own leaders.

Mr. Churchill returned the compliment by encouraging members of the Opposition who also wanted to question Lord Stanley.

Once when a Government supporter cried, "Order! Order!" in an attempt to stem the tide of questions, Mr. Churchill turned sharply about and ejaculated, "Order yourself!" *May 5*

Duce's Choice of a Saturday

The Duce followed the Fuehrer's technique in choosing to make his announcement about the annexation of Abyssinia on a Saturday.

The choice, however, was prompted by very different reasons.

As I have previously pointed out, Herr Hitler, in favouring the forenoon of Saturday for a statement of policy which will bring a diplomatic crisis in its train, has done so in order to obtain a breathing space before the European chancelleries get to work.

Signor Mussolini's first object was to reach the maximum audience in his own country. For this Saturday night is the best.

He was also anxious for the news to reach as many listeners throughout Europe as possible. For this, again, the late hours of Saturday provided the best moment.

From Stockholm to Athens the cafés—except for Sundays—are fullest at about 10 o'clock on Saturday. *May 11*

Meticulous A. E. Housman

Mr. Laurence Housman has been going through the papers of his brother, A. E. Housman, which were left to him, together with his brother's fine library of books.

A. E. Housman's astonishing literary diligence and Flaubertian meticulousness in searching for perfect phrasing are revealed by the papers.

On occasion he would write 20 or 30 versions of the same line or lines.

The many variations on portions of "The Shropshire Lad" which have come to light should provide interesting controversies for Housman scholars of the future.

I believe that A. E. Housman empowered Mr. Laurence Housman to publish such portions of his unpublished works as he might think fit, and that he is likely to do so. *May 19*

Derby Result in the House

There was a dead heat yesterday in the annual race to bring the name of the Derby winner into the House of Commons. It is about 50 yards from the tape machine to the Chamber.

Capt. Margesson and Mr. Charles Edwards, Chief Whips of the Government and the Opposition, gave the result to the two sides simultaneously.

The names were passed round rather noisily. Mr. Gallacher, the Communist M.P., protested to the Speaker, asking whether it was in order for M.P.s to discuss the Derby. The Speaker merely smiled.

Had Mr. Gallacher been an older hand he would have used his point of order to give the House the result thus: "Is it in order for hon. members to interrupt proceedings by discussing the victory of Mahmoud at Epsom?"

Until about 10 years ago it was usual for some M.P. or other to announce the result in some such concealed form. The custom has died out of recent years.

Satisfied Ambition

The Aga Khan's comment on the result—

> My ambition was to win the Derby three times. I have done this in the short space of 13 years.

—is a little misleading.

Actually, all his three winners have come in seven years—Blenheim (1930), Bahrain (1935), Mahmoud (1936).

What the Aga Khan meant was that it is now 13 years—or nearly 14—since he bought his first yearling in 1922.

His first expensive yearling was Mumtaz Mahal, the fastest mare since the war. He paid 9,100 gns for her.

Mumtaz Mahal was the granddam of Mahmoud. Curiously enough, none of her offspring, including Mahmoud's dam, Mah Mahal, have been successes.

It has been left to the second generation to reassert the force of heredity. *May 28*

Soviet Babies in Gas Masks

In contrast with the laissez-faire, if not obstructionist, attitude of our own Socialists towards anti-gas measures, an anti-gas epidemic is now sweeping the Soviet Union. Here are a few examples of its ravages.

Four Leningrad students, including one "undergraduette," spent 242 hours in their gas masks, eating, sleeping, going to lectures and the opera. One of them declares, "I had never been truly happy before."

The chief surgeons of Moscow's biggest hospital perform the most difficult operations in gas-masks, and insist on their orderlies and amphitheatre sisters being similarly masked.

Women take the oath to have all their babies in masks and to mask their nurselings between feeding-times. School teachers sometimes keep whole classes of young children masked all day long.

A Moscow teacher took her entire class, suitably masked, to the pictures. When asked why, she replied, "When the Nazis drop their bombs on us my pupils will just go to the cinema."

There is an element of calculation, as well as of frenzy, in all this. Canny young men inquire, before cycling masked from Moscow to Leningrad and back, whether it has ever been done before. If it has, they do not do it. *June 17*

When Mr. Shaw Fell

Mr. Bernard Shaw tells a story against himself in his chapter on William Morris in Miss May Morris's two-volume edition of her father's works, which appears to-day.

When he dined at Kelmscott House his position as one who practises "the occidental form of Yoga"—that is, being a vegetarian and a teetotaller—was painful. "To refuse Morris's wine or Mrs. Morris's viands was like walking on the great carpet with muddy boots."

Morris did not mind about the vegetarianism, but insisted on wine—even if one ate bread and onions. Mrs. Morris regarded abstinence from meat as a suicidal fad.

With the pudding Mr. Shaw's abstinence vanished, and Mrs. Morris was at last satisfied with his healthy appetite. She pressed a second helping on him.

When he had eaten it she said, "That will do you good. There is suet in it."

Mr. Shaw adds that this was the only remark ever addressed to him by a woman whose beauty and silence were equally remarkable. *July 1*

Poet Laureate's Politeness

Mr. John Masefield spoke yesterday at the annual meeting of the London Library of the days when he was a regular student at the British Museum Library.

The room in which he used to read had various habitués. These ranged from an Anglican bishop to a syndicate who might have been working out an infallible system of gambling.

Swinburne—deaf and old—was an occasional visitor. He used to read Elizabethan folios and frequently burst out into loud laughter at what Mr. Masefield thought must be their indelicacies.

But the strangest of all the future Poet Laureate's fellow-readers was a small, slightly built man with an enigmatic and cynical smile.

One day Mr. Masefield opened the door for him—a gesture which was acknowledged by a smile of a warmer and more personal kind.

This mysterious personage was Lenin. *July 9*

Two Hundred TIMs

Over 200 people in London were trying to find out the time at half-past five yesterday afternoon.

The Post Office talking clock had come into operation a few minutes before. Two hundred subscribers can be connected with it at the same time.

I dialled TIM at exactly 5.30 p.m. I hoped to hear Miss Ethel Cain, the telephonist whose voice announces the time. Instead I heard the familiar buzzing of "number engaged."

Five minutes later I had better luck. The voice announced, "At the third stroke it will be 5.35 and 10 seconds." Three squeaks followed, and then it announced "5.35 and 20 seconds." After six such announcements the call automatically came to an end.

The signals are recorded on four glass discs resembling gramophone records. These revolve ceaselessly. One records the hours, two more carry the minutes and the fourth the seconds. *July 25*

Man of Many Tongues

The Paderewski of a generation ago would not have visited London in August. But there were no films then—and it is film work which is bringing him here to-day.

The versatility which has made M. Paderewski into a great political and social figure should serve him well on the screen.

No language difficulty confronts him. I forget how many languages he can speak. His English is perfect. As an after-dinner speaker he ranks with our leading native performers. His conversation is adorned with mots.

One of these went the rounds in New York when M. Paderewski was there some years ago.

At a party he was asserting that the differences between one man and another could always be described in a nutshell. A challenge came from Mr. Harry Payne Whitney to differentiate him from Paderewski.

"That's easy," M. Paderewski replied instantly. "You are a dear soul playing polo and I am a poor Pole playing solo." *August 4*

Mr. Attlee's Russian Harvest

On his holiday visit to Russia, Mr. Attlee can hardly fail to garner his impressions. When he brings his harvest home his trouble will begin.

Sir Walter Citrine's case shows that this deserves to be classed as a dangerous occupation.

Here are some of the various opinions given by Socialists, Labour leaders and others who have preceded Mr. Attlee on the pilgrimage to Moscow.

Lord Passfield (1932).—Russia is not a comfortable place to live in.

Mr. Joseph Toole, M.P. (1930).—Famine and misery are the chief features of the country.

Sir Walter Citrine (1935).—The standard of living is still distinctly lower than in most other countries.

Lord Lothian (1931).—The most gigantic and heroic experiment ever tried in history.

Perhaps, Mr. H. G. Wells's remark was the most caustic. He said that what was really wanted was the invention of a five-year plan to reconstruct the human brain. Our present mental apparatus, he observed, obviously lacked many things needed for a perfect social order. *August 6*

Heartburnings in Berlin

The present Olympic Games resemble in one respect some of their predecessors. They are not producing quite the friendly sporting feeling which was to be expected.

There is evidence of a certain amount of dissatisfaction on the German side and the "Angriff," the organ of Dr. Goebbels, Minister of Propaganda, is raising the Negro question.

It says:

If the American team had not brought over black auxiliaries things would look badly for it. In that case Long, the German, would have won the long jump, the Italian Lanza would have been the winner in the 800 metres, the Dutch sprinter Osendarp would have won the 100 metres, and everybody would have considered the Yankees the great disappointment of the Games.

Nazi irritation is not altogether unnatural. The German team has probably practised longer and with greater determination than any other.

It is now second on the list. But for the American Negro athletes it would be first. *August 7*

Television's Invisible Man

Yesterday I had my first experience of television. It was not entirely successful, but my impatience was as nothing to the evident embarrassment of Mr. Leslie Mitchell, the B.B.C. television announcer.

I watched not at Olympia but at a private demonstration in the West End. Something went wrong with the Alexandra Palace transmission and most of the proceedings were audible but invisible.

I saw about 35 minutes of the programme. For half this time the screen was either blank or occupied by revolving stripes of light. Every few minutes Mr. Mitchell's voice, suave but worried, would apologise fervently for the unexpected "lack of vision."

Mr. Jack Hylton was brought to the studio for an interview.

He gave an admirable imitation of Mr. Wells's Invisible Man, abruptly disappearing after his first few words, returning and then delicately dissolving into space again.

Focusing Mr. Hore-Belisha

At last Mr. Mitchell spoke with real confidence. "I know that vision is back now," he said. But he was wrong. We heard his voice, but his professionally ineradicable smile was hidden from us.

Television, from the speaker's point of view, has one drawback. When the picture is being tuned-in, extraordinary things happen to the human countenance.

Fascinated, I watched Mr. Hore-Belisha's face in a televised news-reel—swell, twist and shrink as though in a distorting mirror until correct focus was obtained. *September 5*

Ceylon's Ambition

To-day the M.C.C. cricketers will have their first game—the one-day match at Colombo. By this time they should have recovered from the staleness that caused G. O. Allen to forbid practice on board ship.

Allen has toured Australia before and knows that it takes a fit as well as a great cricketer to do himself justice in matches played to a finish beneath a grilling sun.

Besides, ship cricket is practically useless as practice.

Ceylon's request to see Hammond, which has been granted, is understandable after his brilliant English season. Since Hobbs gave up cricket Hammond alone combines his effectiveness with beauty of style.

Sutcliffe was ungainly even when most prolific. His best friend could not call Leyland elegant, fine cricketer though he is. Duleepsinhji, one of the few post-war batsmen who combined grace with dash, is still barred from first-class cricket by ill health.

Now the Ceylon public fears that Hammond, the M.C.C.'s best draw, is soon to retire. Let us hope they are wrong, for he is only 33.

October 3

Fortune From Music

The most famous living composer arrives in London on Monday. He is 72-year-old Richard Strauss, who later in the week will be conducting his "Ariadne auf Naxos" at Covent Garden.

The younger generation perhaps does not realise how great was Strauss's fame as a conductor at a time when the merits of his music were still in violent dispute.

Tall, loosely built, rather tired-looking, Dr. Strauss carries the honours of a lifetime easily. He dislikes talking shop. When I last saw him—it was in the artist's room during a rehearsal—he rolled off with immense relish the latest good stories current in Berlin.

So much did he enjoy these that when the time came for him to continue he went back to the concert room like a fourth-form schoolboy after break.

Whatever view modern critics take of his work, they cannot deny one thing. It has brought him a fortune. Of no other living composer of serious music can that be said. *October 31*

Test Match "Piece Work"

If Hammond's scoring had been in Tests he would probably have gained more than a staid paragraph in "Wisden."

Australian business men are in the habit of rewarding batting and bowling feats with cash and other prizes. Parkin, the Lancashire bowler, was once offered £1 for a hit for 6, 2s for a 4 and £1 for every run over 100. His dividend was 2s.

Another time he was luckier. Mr. Duckworth, an English M.P. touring Australia, offered him £5 for every 25 he made.

"Look here," said Parkin ingenuously to Mailey and MacDonald, "it's up to you to see I get 25." They obligingly saw to it that he got 36, and Parkin was also rewarded with 18 silk handkerchiefs for his "wonderful display."

Don Bradman's £1,000

Hobbs was once given a diamond scarf-pin by the Governor of South Australia; Parkin, who had bowled magnificently all day, had to be content with some fruit from an old lady who thought he "must be tired out."

But the gift that makes all others pale was the cheque for £1,000 given to Don Bradman when he made his record 334 at Leeds in 1930.

A telegram solemnly carried out to the wicket by a messenger is said to have been the one that broke the news. *November 3*

Mr. Coward's Impromptu

Mr. Noel Coward, who is now touring in America with his nine plays, had a great success with a gag when playing in Washington.

In "Ways and Means" Miss Gertrude Lawrence was crossing the stage to put out a light when the electrician missed his cue.

He flashed it off before she reached the lamp. Then he flashed it on again.

Mr. Noel Coward calmly took a puff at his cigarette and remarked: "The house is haunted."

An American, describing the house's reception of this impromptu, tells me that "the audience fell into the aisles." *December 3*

Herr Hitler Intervenes

I have heard very favourable comment on the restraint of the German Press with regard to the present Constitutional crisis.

Apart from a short statement by the Deutsches Nachrichtenbuero, the official agency, saying that as the causes of the dispute between the King and his Ministers are of a private character, "the German Press does not choose to take any note of them, either through news items or comment," the Press has been virtually silent.

I understand that this restraint is due not so much to Dr. Goebbels, the Propaganda Minister, who normally controls the German Press, but is in deference to the personal wishes to the Fuehrer himself.

Herr Hitler has taken the view that uninformed gossip about the head of a foreign State, and one for whom Germans have a particular regard, would consort with the dignity of neither country concerned.

December 5

How News Was Received

Mr. Baldwin's Speech

Messages from the King to the House of Commons are normally brought in, and read, by the Vice-Chamberlain of the Household. Only messages of outstanding importance are carried by the Prime Minister himself.

Mr. Baldwin's first experience of the march from the Bar of the House to the Table, with the three stately bows that have to be made on the way, was in January, when he conveyed the King's announcement of his father's death and his own accession.

Quiet as the House was then, it was even more solemn yesterday when Mr. Baldwin carried in King Edward's last message. The silence was unbroken the whole time the Speaker read the message. Thanks to the sounding-board over his chair his well-modulated voice carried to every corner of the crowded House.

Sir John Simon Prompts

There was no need for the Prime Minister to apologise, as he did in his opening sentence, for not having had time to prepare a speech. He spoke for 40 minutes, most of the time extempore. He has never spoken better.

At times he mislaid a sheet of his notes. Once or twice he turned to Sir John Simon, who has been so closely associated with him in the present crisis, to confirm a date. But those small blemishes were more than atoned for by his simplicity and sincerity.

His peroration about the House—a theatre which the whole world was watching—was admirably suited to the setting of crowded benches and galleries.

These included a full row of diplomats—Signor Grandi, who has been on terms of personal friendship with the King, among them.

Deeply Moved House

I never remember seeing the House so deeply moved. Members sat motionless throughout three-quarters of an hour that seemed much shorter. In the galleries some stood as if graven in stone.

All seemed to sense the drama and the pathos of the moment, and there was many a moist eye and husky throat as Mr. Speaker with difficulty concluded the sad duty of reading his Majesty's fateful message.

Capt. FitzRoy began in ringing tones, clearly audible in all quarters of the House. But as he reached the closing passages—"the peoples whom I have tried to serve . . . I take my leave of them"—his voice broke.

And around him many a handkerchief fluttered to restrain an urgent tear. *December 11*

Three Kings in a Year

There have before, as I have pointed out, been three kings in a year —Edward IV, Edward V and Richard III. One strange coincidence involved in 1936's three reigns was absent in 1482.

Of 1936's kings, King George V and King George VI will have reigned for almost exactly the same fraction of the year.

King George V ruled from Jan. 1 to his death at 11.55 p.m. on Jan. 20, and King George VI, will have ruled from 1.52 p.m. on Dec. 11 to Dec. 31.

There can also be few men who have had four different styles in the course of one year—Prince of Wales, King Edward VIII, Prince Edward, and Duke of Windsor.

Mr. Stephen Salter, founder of the famous firm of University boatbuilders, who was 102 yesterday, has lived in six reigns. They are those of William IV, Queen Victoria, Edward VII, George V, Edward VIII, and George VI. *December 11*

1937

1937

Throughout 1937 the international situation continued to deteriorate steadily, although many doubtless tried to persuade themselves that the two wars which captured the headlines that year—the Spanish Civil War and the Sino-Japanese War—were none of their business.

In Britain, discounting anxiety arising from troubles overseas, it can be said to have been a reasonably happy year. On May 12, amid scenes of traditional pomp and splendour, King George VI was crowned in Westminster Abbey, and his subjects, at home and overseas, were duly united and inspired by the occasion. In the same month Mr. Baldwin retired, as expected, and Mr. Neville Chamberlain became Prime Minister. The re-armament programme, under the vigorous direction of Sir Thomas Inskip, inevitably involved considerably increased Government expenditure and the standard rate of income tax was raised by 3d to 5s in the pound. Thanks to the efforts of Mr. A. P. Herbert the Matrimonial Causes Act, which enlarged the causes for divorce, was passed.

The close of the year saw no end in sight to the fighting in Spain, although the balance was tilted in favour of General Franco's Nationalists who were enjoying the assistance of upwards of 40,000 Italian troops. In April the Government-held town of Guernica was bombed by German planes, an event which horrified the outside world and inspired Picasso to paint one of the oddest creations ever to be regarded as a major work of art.

In France M. Blum, overcome by economic problems, resigned in June and his place was taken by M. Chautemps.

In Germany the main theme of 1937 was self-sufficiency, the argument being that, in the event of blockade or economic pressure from hostile countries, Germany must be able to survive on her own economic resources. The relationship between Church and State deteriorated still further and over 100 pastors were arrested in the summer for various alleged offences, among them Pastor Niemöller, who was accused of causing public unrest by his sermons.

In September Hitler received Mussolini in Berlin and the Rome/Berlin axis was officially established. In November Italy joined Germany in the anti-Comintern Pact and in December proclaimed her formal resignation from the League of Nations. In Abyssinia the Italians were finding it hard to keep the natives restful and several thousand were massacred after a bomb had been thrown at and injured General Graziani, the Viceroy.

In Russia the blood continued to flow unstaunched. The trial and execution of Zinovieff and Kameneff, long-standing party stalwarts, was followed by a purge of high Communist officials in every Republic of the Union and in every department of life. In June, Tukhachevsky, one of the five Marshals of the Soviet Union, was shot, along with seven other high-ranking generals, and scores of other senior officers disappeared without trace.

War between Japan and China broke out in August as a result of apparently trivial border incidents and the Western world was staggered and alarmed by the speed and efficiency of Japan's military success, as well as by the bare-faced effrontery of such a colossal act of brigandage. In the north 300,000 square miles of Chinese territory were under Japanese control and in December a puppet Government was proclaimed in Peking, the seat of the Chinese Government having been moved to Chunking, far up the Yangtse, in November. The entry of General Matsui, the Japanese Commander, into the capital was accompanied by wholesale massacres of Chinese.

In Palestine a Royal Commission sought in vain to settle the age-old quarrel between Jacob and Esau. The partition scheme it proposed displeased many Jews and most Arabs, and terrorism continued unabated.

Outside the world of politics and intestine strife, one of the notable events of the year was the marriage of the Duke of Windsor to the woman he loved at the hastily-borrowed château of the dubious Mr. Charles Bedaux in Tourraine. Frank Whittle produced the prototype of the jet engine, nylon stockings made their début, the Golden Gate Bridge in San Francisco was completed, Joe Louis regained the World Heavyweight Boxing Championship, and on October 1 The Morning Post *was amalgamated with* The Daily Telegraph.

On the obituary list were Ramsay MacDonald, Guglielmo Marconi, J. M. Barrie, Edith Wharton and Joan Harlow. The year also saw the passing of the Reverend Harold Davidson, the Rector of Stiffkey, who was mauled to death by a lion in a cage at Skegness Amusement Park.

1937

Peterborough, remarking upon the first television coverage of Wimbledon, says, "When television is perfected the sports commentator will become redundant." Nastase and others might well wish that his prophecy had proved more accurate.

1937

Lingua Franco

The latest Franco story comes from Berlin. It is:

"Franco can't advance any quicker on Madrid because of a shortage of interpreters to transmit his orders to his troops."

January 10

Left Wing's Take Off

The rally of 7,000 members of the Left Book Club—which was originally thought to be a club for buying up "remainders" cheap—was the nearest thing to the achievement of an intellectual Front Popular we have yet seen.

The cheers, however, went not to the sturdy Liberalism of the solitary representative of that creed, Mr. Acland, but to the forthright Communism of Mr. Harry Pollitt.

The Left Wing of the Left Book Club evidently predominated, though the audience's appearance suggested anything but labouring sons of the hammer and sickle.

Mr. Victor Gollancz, the publisher, read with some unction telegrams from France, New Zealand and, I believe, Mauritius. No telegram was forthcoming from the dictatorship countries of Germany, Italy and Soviet Russia.

We are a little embarrassed about the Soviet in our Left Wing minds just now.

February 9

M.A.D.

The department that looks after the estates of lunatics used to be called the Lunacy Department, and the colleagues of its officials nicknamed them "the Lunatics."

This was considered undignified by those in authority, who, not long ago, set to work to devise a more stately title. They thought up the imposing "Management and Advisory Department."

Unfortunately they failed to notice that the initial letters of this spell a word. The department's nickname has not noticeably changed.

February 16

Mr. Lloyd George and Hitler

Mr. Lloyd George is down to take part in the foreign affairs debate to-morrow. It will be his first speech in the House since his visit to Herr Hitler in September.

He returned from the visit proclaiming the Fuehrer "one of the greatest men I have ever met," and the Germans the happiest people he had ever seen.

When he speaks to-morrow Mr. Lloyd George can hardly help saying something about Germany. Unless he has modified his enthusiasm, his speech will bring him into conflict not only with the Socialists he sits among, but with the majority of his fellow-Liberals.

I shall also be interested to watch the reaction of his old Ministerial colleagues, Sir Austen Chamberlain and Mr. Churchill.

Pained Protests

The views Mr. Lloyd George expressed on his return from Germany drew pained protests from Liberals.

Mr. Herbert Morrison summed up the Socialist attitude by describing him as "apparently a half-baked Nazi."

In his last Commons speech on foreign affairs, a few weeks before his German trip, Mr. Lloyd George was still advancing the orthodox Liberal arguments. If France had disarmed, he said, "you would not have had Herr Hitler in power." *March 1*

Nazi Boxing Ambassador

If the world title fight between Max Schmeling, the German champion, and Braddock takes place in the Olympic Stadium at Berlin this summer Herr Hitler is almost certain to be at the ringside, flanked by Gen. Goering and Dr. Goebbels, the two other members of the Nazi triumvirate.

Max has become a great man in Nazi Germany. He is on terms of personal friendship with Dr. Goebbels. No important Nazi function is complete without him and his wife, Fraulein Anny Ondra, one of Germany's most popular film stars.

The Fuehrer takes a personal interest in Schmeling's career. After he knocked out Joe Louis in New York last summer he was received in the Chancellery by Herr Hitler, who told him how delighted he was about this triumph of Nordic over negro blood.

Herr Hitler, too, was the first to congratulate him after his victory over Steve Hamas, the American heavyweight, at Hamburg two years ago. This was the fight which signalised Max's return to championship class.

The Fuehrer personally rang up Fraulein Anny Ondra and asked her to tell her husband how pleased he was. *March 13*

Royalty on the Stage

The choice of June 21 for the première of Mr. Laurence Housman's "Victoria Regina" regularises the question of Royalty in plays.

The Lord Chamberlain has now laid it down that no Sovereign may be portrayed on the stage until a hundred years after his or her accession. Queen Victoria came to the throne on June 20, 1837.

As June 20 is a Sunday this year, the curtain will go up on "Victoria Regina" exactly 100 years and a day after her accession.

It will be interesting to see whether Miss Pamela Stanley, who originally created the part of the Queen at the Gate Theatre, and who is to play it again at Mr. Housman's special request, will be able to overcome a make-up difficulty.

Mr. Housman told me at dinner the other night that while both Miss Helen Hayes in New York and Miss Stanley in London provided remarkable likenesses to Queen Victoria in youth and old age, they found the middle years facially a difficulty.

Neither was able to achieve a satisfactory resemblance to the Queen in her forties, when she was beginning to be plump and was still not yet marked by age. On the other hand, Mlle. Gaby Morlay in Paris was more successful. *May 4*

White House Inn

While being "interviewed" before the microphone in one of her recent broadcasts, Mrs. Roosevelt was asked to describe her most amusing experience since her husband became President of the United States.

Thereupon she told how she once went into a New York department store and ordered some goods to be sent to "Mrs. F. D. Roosevelt, the White House, Washington, D.C."

The girl who was taking the order wrote this down quite calmly, and without any sign of the emotion which anyone in her position might be expected to register on realising that her customer was the First Lady.

Then, without looking up, she asked casually: "Any room number, madam?" *May 5*

The Coronation of King George VI

In Parliament Square

The weather, which promised to be the enemy, was kind after all yesterday morning.

The one disappointment for the vast crowd in Parliament Square was the long procession of foreign royalty and statesmen. All of them travelled in closed cars, many of which had only the scantiest of window space.

Even from ground level it was difficult to recognise the visitors. Spectators in the higher stands could see practically nothing. It was the same in 1911, when closed coaches were used. Every car was numbered, but the numbers bore no relation to the alphabetical list printed in the official programme.

In consequence, only a few of the notable visitors were picked out for a cheer—among them Princess Juliana and Prince Chichibu. Otherwise the cheers went to those who wore the most attractive uniforms.

Mr. Baldwin's Pleasure

Mr. Baldwin and the Dominion Premiers were also partly obscured in their closed coaches. When he neared the Abbey the Prime Minister was almost leaning out of the window to see the crowds.

He received a great ovation, and did not try to conceal his pleasure. He probably wished that he could have unsealed his roof.

Mr. Baldwin could have felt consoled, however, by the fact that two of the best seats in the Abbey were his and Mrs. Baldwin's.

May 13

Mr. Baldwin Guessed Wrong

Prime Ministerial Deputies

Mr. Baldwin's departure from active politics is hardly following the lines which ten years ago he laid down for all such valedictions.

Of public life he then said:

> Sometimes there is a certain amount of honour, but there are a great many kicks, and you always end in disaster: you are always fired out, and you are liable to be fired out without notice, and there is no pension.

Mr. Baldwin perhaps thinks that there are few in this country who remember that utterance. He is no doubt right.

It was made at Montreal during a visit to Canada, and has been recalled to me by a Coronation visitor from that Dominion.

"Might-Have-Beens"

On that occasion the Prime Minister consoled himself, however, by remarking that he had the satisfaction of feeling that he was doing a man's job. He went on:

> And if anybody doubts that, let him try my job for a week: he would never question it again.

Mr. Baldwin seems to have been particularly self-revealing during that visit to Canada. Speaking at Quebec he confessed:

> There are several things I wish I might have been rather than Prime Minister.

Canadian listeners were left to solve the riddle of his preferences for themselves, for he did not specify. Perhaps he will become more informative when released from the cares of office. *May 24*

Televising Wimbledon

On the whole the television broadcast of Wimbledon was successful. It demonstrated the differences made by the light in televising an outdoor event.

Yesterday the light was if anything too bright and made it difficult to see the ball in the general whiteness of the picture. But Miss Hardwick's back-hand strokes came out well. So did Miss Marble's service.

Another criticism one could make is that the camera does not always catch the actual stroke being played.

There is also the curious effect of slowness for those used to the ordinary Wimbledon broadcast. For some time before the commentator can record the stroke the eye has already taken it in and is ready for the next.

When television is perfected, the spoıts commentator will become redundant. *June 23*

Youth at the Oval

In one respect to-day's Test match will make history. It will, unless there are any late surprises, be the first time that both sides in a Test have played a youngster of 19. Compton is the youngest player ever to represent England. The New Zealand "baby" is Donnelly, who tops the tourists' batting averages.

Both are worth going to see, for both have a variety of strokes and usually score quickly. So impressed was Sir Pelham Warner with Compton's performances last season that he remarked that he was "the best young batsman since Walter Hammond came out as a boy."

I predicted a bright future for Compton on the first day of the season, when he made an attractive 40 against Yorkshire and hit Verity for the first six of the summer.

Neither Compton nor Donnelly need be afraid that his success will be ephemeral. Cricket prodigies have a habit of lasting. For example, Vivian, the New Zealand opening bat, first played for his country six years ago, just before he was 19.

McCabe was 19 in his first Test, and Bradman was 20. *August 14*

Bulldog Drummond's Creator

There was very little of the Bulldog Drummond in Sapper (Lt.-Col. H. C. McNeile), who has just died. He was, in fact, another illustration of the principle that most authors endow their heroes with characteristics they do not themselves possess.

Where Bulldog Drummond was enormous and bulky, "with a fist like a ham," his creator was lean and wiry, with the hands of an artist.

It is difficult to imagine Bulldog Drummond ever being ill, but Sapper looked delicate and often suffered from ill-health.

Novelist Raconteur

One thing he had in common with Bulldog Drummond, however. He was a trier.

He was a frequent visitor to Switzerland, and was an enthusiastic skater. He was always attempting figures slightly too difficult for him, and would take the most appalling tosses. Undaunted, he would try again immediately.

Sapper was an admirable companion and an excellent raconteur. Indeed, he was one of the few authors I have met who was an even better story-teller viva voce than on paper. *August 16*

The Talented King of Egypt

In spite of his youth, King Farouk of Egypt is a ruler with decided opinions of his own, as Nahas Pasha* discovered within a very short time of the death of King Fuad.

King Farouk has also got a definite and surprisingly well-developed collector's flair, particularly for the antiquities of his own country.

When he went down to Oxford during his Coronation visit to this country he surprised the authorities of the Ashmolean by a knowledge of their treasures which would have been creditable in an expert.

Like most Egyptians, he is keenly interested in anything mechanical. A friend who met him in Switzerland this year was made to go up and down in a funicular several times until the young King had thoroughly examined the working.

At Kenry House

He is also interested in photography, and shows an aptitude for chemistry and physics. He is an average all-round sportsman, excelling particularly at polo, which he has played since he was 11.

King Farouk's English leaves nothing to be desired. He perfected it during the time that he was occupying Kenry House, on Kingston Hill, which had been let to him furnished by the late F. S. Oliver, the author of "The Endless Adventure."

The young King was very fond of the large house with its big grounds, and was most reluctant to leave England when King Fuad died.

Before he left he insisted on all the English servants being brought in to be received by him. He shook hands with them all and thanked them individually for their services. *August 24*

*Egyptian statesman; chairman of the Wafd party; prime minister of Egypt 1928, 1930, 1936–7.

Prolific Mr. Priestley

By having three plays produced within the next five weeks, Mr. J. B. Priestley approaches the record which has been held by Mr. Somerset Maugham for nearly 30 years.

Two of his new plays open in London, one—"Time and the Conways"—to-night, and another on Sept. 21. A third is due some time in October, so that if Mr. Priestley is lucky with the first two, all three should be running at once.

Even then, Mr. Maugham will be ahead. In 1908 he had four plays—"Lady Frederick," "Jack Straw," "Mrs. Dot," and "The Explorer"—running simultaneously.

I should imagine that Mr. Noel Coward's industry in 1925 came nearest to disturbing this record. For a week in July that year he had three "straight" plays running—"The Vortex," "Fallen Angels," and "Hay Fever"—as well as "On with the Dance," a revue of which he was part author and composer. *August 26*

Reflected Glory

The last play in which Miss Tallulah Bankhead appeared before her marriage to Mr. John Emery, the American actor, was "Reflected Glory."

The title may have reminded her distinguished father, Mr. William Brockman Bankhead, Speaker of the United States House of Representatives, of a story which he used to tell against himself.

Arriving one night at a New York hotel, he gave his name to the reception clerk.

"Not *the* Mr. Bankhead?" exclaimed the clerk, with some excitement.

"Why, yes—Congressman Bankhead," he replied, with a modest smile.

"Oh," said the clerk, with obvious loss of interest. "I thought, maybe, you were Tallulah's father." *September 2*

Not Statesmanlike Language

Mr. Herbert Morrison is regarded as a possible Socialist Prime Minister of the future. In any case he is certain to hold high office in the next Socialist Government.

It is, perhaps, a good thing that the Foreign Office is already earmarked for Mr. Philip Noel-Baker or Dr. Hugh Dalton. International relationships would scarcely be easy with Mr. Morrison as Foreign Secretary.

Mr. Morrison's signed weekly article in "Forward" has such peace-promoting headlines as "Hitler's Slave Congress—Nuremberg's Annual Nonsense."

Mr. Morrison is also able to inform the German people that their "enemy is at home. It is the Nazi Government itself that politically and economically encircles Germany."

Whatever view is taken of the Nazi régime, when a responsible politician talks of the "nonsensical tirades" of the head of a friendly State he is scarcely using the language of statesmanship. *September 18*

Mistaking King George V

In his introduction to the correspondence between the Tsar Nicholas II and his mother, of which the first extract appears in to-day's *Daily Telegraph and Morning Post*, Sir Bernard Pares referred to the striking likeness between the Tsar and King George V.

This was so great that even the Dowager Empress Maria Fedorovna said that she had almost mistaken the one for the other.

The resemblance is illustrated by a story of which I was reminded during the week-end, and which has not, I believe, been published before.

In 1920 King George placed Frogmore Cottage at the disposal of the Grand Duchess Xenia, the Tsar's elder sister. When the Grand Duchess went to live there she took with her one or two Russian servants.

Soon after her arrival King George went over from Windsor Castle to visit his cousin. It was a cold day, and he wore a heavy overcoat.

The door was opened by one of the Russian servants, who had never seen King George before. As soon as he saw the visitor the man fell down on his knees and kissed the hem of the King's overcoat. He was convinced that it was the Tsar who stood before him. *October 4*

Quick-Fire Tchaikovsky

While the B.B.C. is anxious, as I recently pointed out, to speed up its sporting commentaries, I do not imagine it will follow the example of a leading American broadcasting conductor who is producing "quick-fire versions of semi-classical music."

He is Mr. André Kostelanetz, who was once an assistant conductor at the Imperial Opera in St. Petersburg. To make his programmes more acceptable to casual listeners, he has made drastic cuts in several well-known compositions.

In this "streamlining" process, as he calls it, Mr. Kostelanetz has reduced the playing time of Tchaikovsky's overture to "Romeo and Juliet" from 16 minutes to four minutes 45 seconds. This version, he claims, will give listeners a good idea what the composer was driving at.

The "Barber of Seville" overture has been reduced from seven minutes to one and a half, and he is now dealing similarly with works by Delibes, Rimsky-Korsakov and Mozart. *October 9*

G.B.S. and Gandhi

Mr. Bernard Shaw, as an octogenarian, has been advising India how to celebrate Mr. Gandhi's 68th birthday. In a message to the "Gandhi number" of an Indian Nationalist newspaper, he complains that 68 is too young for a celebration.

> They did not begin persecuting me in that way until I was 70, and then they nearly killed me with tender congratulations. If you want to do real service to Mr. Gandhi, ordain all over India that henceforth nobody shall remind him of his age.

But when Mr. Shaw's own "persecution" began he had a very different complaint. He was entertained on July 26, 1926—his 70th birthday—by the Parliamentary Socialist party. Mr. Ramsay MacDonald, who, incidentally, is himself 71 to-day, proposed his health.

Replying, Mr. Shaw complained bitterly that the proceedings were not being broadcast. This, a question in the House showed later, was because he had refused to avoid "argumentative political controversy" in his speech. *October 12*

Un-Teutonic Knickerbockers

By deciding that in future the Touring Club Italiano is to be known as the Consociazione Turistica Italiana, the Italians are following

Germany's lead. A fresh drive against the use of foreign words in the German language has prompted the magazine "Die Literatur" to suggest several new alternatives.

"Restaurant" would become "Gasting." "Automobile" just "Bil," while "international"—a word more detested nowadays for its significance than for its non-German origin—would be rendered by "uebermaerkisch."

Other words for which more Teutonically euphonious alternatives are proposed are "Knickerbockers," "Concordat," "Delicatessen" and "Reaction." No German substitute, however, is proposed for "Die Literatur." *October 16*

Gas Mask-minded Now

At the exhibitions of air raid precaution equipment now being held in various places, the chief excitement for visitors is the opportunity of trying on the new gas masks for civilians.

Those who care to make a practical test may enter a special chamber filled with tear gas. I found this experience rather bizarre than alarming.

In a dimly lighted chamber full of whitish fumes stood a circle of visitors wearing snout-like masks and listening solemnly to the remarks of their guide similarly equipped. The porcine suggestion was assisted by grunting noises caused by the exhalation of breath through the sides of the masks.

Breathing is perfectly normal and speech clearly audible in these masks. *October 25*

Mr. Eden—No Ornament?

Modesty may, or may not, be a virtue in a Foreign Secretary, but Mr. Eden certainly showed it in one portion of his speech in the House of Commons.

In replying to the charge of class-consciousness, brought by Mr. Dalton against the Government's foreign policy, Mr. Eden said that there was really only one difference between Mr. Dalton and himself. Whereas Mr. Dalton was an ornament both at Eton and at King's College, Cambridge, he himself was an ornament neither at Eton nor at Christ Church.

Mr. Dalton's school record may be better than Mr. Eden's, since the former was in the select for the Tomline Prize, though this would hardly make the great heart of Eton beat faster.

At their respective universities, on the other hand, Mr. Eden definitely attained higher academic distinction. He got a first in Oriental Languages. Mr. Dalton took a third in the Mathematical Tripos and a second in Economics. I have yet to meet the don who considered that the undergraduate with a first was not an ornament to his college. *November 3*

Subversive Sibelius

Sir Thomas Beecham's conducting of the Berlin Philharmonic Orchestra in Sibelius's First Symphony was given a tremendous ovation on Thursday. He was recalled five times by an audience including all the music lovers of Berlin.

Berlin's Customs authorities, however, appear to view the work of Sibelius with a much more critical eye. While in Berlin Sir Thomas had a set of test records of the same symphony sent out by post.

He was duly notified of their arrival, and a page boy was dispatched from the hotel to the Customs Office to collect them, and if necessary to pay any duty chargeable.

The boy soon returned with empty hands, and Sir Thomas was told that the matter was not so simple as that. It would take a considerable time, he was informed, before the records could be released.

Much puzzled, Sir Thomas inquired the reason. It was then explained that the records would have to be played over in the presence of an official competent to decide whether they were politically unobjectionable.

Sir Thomas Beecham Baulked

Remonstrances ensued. Sir Thomas pointed out with his usual lucidity that though the symphony consisted of several movements none of these could reasonably be regarded as a subversive movement within the meaning of the law.

He added that the mere fact that the records were addressed to him in person should be a guarantee of their innocuousness.

The Customs, however, remained obdurate. The records would have to be played through to ensure that they contained no Bolshevist or Masonic strains and no interpolated political speeches in either a major or a minor key.

At this point Sir Thomas felt obliged to call up reinforcements. It was only when diplomatic aid had been secured that the records were handed over, with assurances of regret for an excess of zeal.

Under his direction, I learn, the whole of "The Magic Flute' has been recorded in Berlin this week. *November 13*

Mozart in Ebury Street

The L.C.C. is shortly to put up a plaque on a remarkable William and Mary House—182, Ebury Street. The plaque will, I gather, read:

> Wolfgang Amadeus Mozart (1756–1791) composed his first symphony here in 1764.

In that year Mozart was brought by his father via Paris to London, where he had a great success, particularly at Court. His father called his children "prodigies of Nature" and the whole town flocked to hear them play.

Mozart's father took a chill returning from playing at Lord Thanet's and during his convalescence after the severe illness that resulted the family went to live in Chelsea.

Chelsea was then a detached village and 182, Ebury Street was the home farm to the Manor House. Not being able to play an instrument because of his father's illness, Mozart wrote his first three symphonies. He was then aged eight.

No. 182 is now the home of Lady Peek and her son, Sir Francis Peek, though it is, I believe, about to be sold. It is beautifully panelled and has a long, narrow garden which was once the site of the cow houses.

Lady Sackville's Flowers

Most of the modern part of the house was added by Victoria Lady Sackville, who was succeeded in occupation for a time by her daughter and son-in-law, Mr. and Mrs. Harold Nicolson.

In "Pepita" Vita Sackville-West describes how Lady Sackville used to plant fully-grown flowers from pots in the garden at 182 and pretend that they had grown there.

All the hawkers in the neighbourhood knew her well. Frantic tappings on the window if they passed in the morning would be followed by the appearance of Lady Sackville wearing a cheap flannel dressing gown and an historic emerald and diamond brooch, and armed with a tin police whistle.

She would buy the whole contents of the barrow and—still in the same strange garb—supervise the planting of her innocent deception, which could have deceived no one. *November 15*

The Old Churchill

Mr. Churchill surprised some M.P.s by being a silent listener to Monday's debate on the Air Raids Bill. His silence was tactical. By rising at 10.59 that evening he secured the right to speak first yesterday, and thus ensure wider attention both in and out of Parliament.

That Mr. Churchill is still the best orator in the House he made plain when he turned his guns on Mr. Herbert Morrison. The House revelled in the way he unfolded his final sentence:

"He has entered a region which baffles even the most extensive vocabulary: the facetious monstrosities of his assertions defy rejoinder, but happily do not need it because of their inherent folly."

Salvoes from Mr. Churchill's guns were fired in various directions. At the beginning it was the Socialists who cheered him most, for he was attacking the past delays at the Home Office in the matter of air-raid precautions.

Mr. Churchill silenced his Socialist supporters with the remark that his speech would be applauded by every part of the House in turn, but never by all together. His prophecy was amply justified. *November 17*

Missed a Nobel Prize?

Sir Jagadis Chandra Bose has died with one of his ambitions unfulfilled. His friends always encouraged him to believe that one of these days he would receive the Nobel Prize for Science. He would probably have presided next year over the jubilee celebrations of the Indian Science Congress in place of the late Lord Rutherford.

At the time of his death he was working on the theory of "spiritual reactions" in plant life—a belief which, in common with Mr. Gandhi, he held firmly.

The two had been friends since 1915, when Mr. Gandhi first paid a visit to Sir Jagadis Bose's laboratories in Calcutta.

The sun was going down and Mr. Gandhi expressed his wish to pray, as that was his usual time. Sir Jagadis and his pupils joined in the prayer. To his surprise the scientist saw the movements of a palm tree being recorded by the electric needle on the screen, indicating that the leaves of the palm tree were closing like hands clasped in prayer.

On Mr. Gandhi this produced a profound effect. Since then he has not allowed any of his followers to touch flowers or leaves after sunset. He believes that they either go to sleep or pray.

November 24

Bradman Out—£2,000 Less

It is natural enough that the Australian cricket authorities should be concerned at Don Bradman's enormous influence on gate receipts. But there is nothing they can do about it.

The fact that the crowd were not treated to one of his displays is held largely responsible for the loss on the New Zealanders' tour. During the last M.C.C. tour it was found that if Bradman was dismissed cheaply in the morning the expected receipts in the afternoon fell by some £2,000.

No other cricketer—not even W. G. Grace or Trumper—has ever had anything like such a box-office appeal as Bradman.

If he were a boxer or a lawn tennis player his earnings would be fabulous. Being a cricketer, and an amateur, he has to be content with the usual expense allowance.

This is £5 a day for a match in Australia and £600 for an English tour—a little under £200 a year on the average. *November 25*

To Being Polite—£8,000

Here is a Culbertson story which a lady bridge player vouches for as "perfectly true." A friend of hers, after an "inconclusive" argument whether one cut high or low for first deal, wrote to Mr. Culbertson for a ruling.

He gave it, adding, "And my fee is three guineas." Thereupon the indignant lady went to a solicitor she knew and asked him whether she must pay. "Certainly," he replied, "and my fee is half a guinea."

When I asked Mr. Culbertson about it he said, "I'm a little hurt that my fee is so low here." He explained that the same story as told in America gave his fee as $100 and that of the lawyer as $50.

Mr. Culbertson claims that it costs him $40,000 a year to be polite. In other words, he tells me that he spends this in answering bridge questions, of which he receives a thousand a day.

To all his newspaper articles an editorial note is appended saying that Mr. Culbertson answers inquiries free of charge. *December 7*

Not So High Hat Bills?

Mr. Claude Elliott, the Headmaster of Eton, has issued a notice which runs:

> Lower boys are reminded that hats are not to be kicked or knocked about. Offenders will be severely dealt with.

I see that it is said that this is due to complaints from parents about the bills for their sons' hats, and that "three or four hats a term are quite common for a lower boy."

I can scarcely believe that. The average Etonian gets one new hat a year—for the Fourth of June.

The hats, which cost just over a pound, are exactly like any other silk hat except for the slightly wider band. Most Etonians take their hats to be ironed—which is done free at the hat shops—every other day, and to be reblocked about once a term. This costs 2s 6d.

So except for those parents who have peculiarly unruly sons, hat bills are not normally very large. *December 9*

1938

1938 will always be remembered as the year of Munich and of Mr. Chamberlain's ill-fated phrase, "Peace in our time". It was also a year in which the world took several giant strides nearer to war, their size being dictated by Hitler who, in January, officially appointed himself Commander of all the armed forces of the Reich. In February, at a meeting with Dr. Schuschnigg, the Austrian Chancellor, he demanded special privileges for all his Austrian adherents. Schuschnigg asked for a plebiscite, which Hitler refused. Schuschnigg thereupon resigned, the German Army marched into Austria unopposed, and, on March 13, Austria became part of the Reich. Hitler then demanded that the Sudeten Germans living in Czechoslovakia should also be united with Germany. Lord Runciman was invited by the Czech Government to study the question and reported that the "repatriation" of the Sudetens was substantially justified. In September, in a last-ditch attempt to save what remained of his appeasement policy, Mr. Chamberlain flew to Germany no less than three times. At the Munich Conference on September 29 Chamberlain, Daladier, Mussolini and Hitler agreed to the transfer of the Sudetenland to Germany; meanwhile the remaining frontiers of Czechoslovakia were guaranteed. On his return to England Mr. Chamberlain announced that he had secured "peace in our time", although many, including M.P.s on his own side of the House, felt that Czechoslovakia had been betrayed.

Naturally such events were bound to have their repercussions. In Britain the first political shock of the year came in February when Anthony Eden resigned as Foreign Secretary in protest against Chamberlain's determination to seek an agreement with Italy. He was succeeded by Lord Halifax. In May Lord Swinton resigned as Secretary for Air in response to a general feeling that the job would be more suitably discharged by a member of the House of Commons, and in October Mr. Duff Cooper resigned as First Lord of the Admiralty, in protest at the Munich Agreement, having mobilized the Fleet the day before it was signed. Civilian training for Air Raid Precautions became a major national preoccupation and many local authorities issued gas masks.

Once again the year in France was marked by political instability and industrial unrest; Chautemps resigned in March; Blum then formed a ministry which lasted twenty-six days and was succeeded by Daladier who managed to see out the year. In July the King and Queen paid a State Visit to Paris where vast crowds turned out to welcome them, but for the French this was no more than a happy interlude in an otherwise depressing year.

Germany's occupation of Austria and the cession of the Sudetenland have already been touched upon. The third and perhaps most tragic feature of the year in Germany was the intensification of Jewish persecution to the point where they must either emigrate or die. The murder of a German diplomat in Paris by a Polish-Jewish youth was followed by a particularly horrifying outburst of Jew-baiting throughout Germany.

In Spain the Civil War continued and again Franco's Nationalists had the best of the battle, although their reputation abroad was not improved by a succession of air raids on Barcelona and the repeated bombing of British ships, both of which called forth vigorous protests from the British Government.

In Russia 1938 was yet another year of purges, trials and executions in every section of the community. Foreigners were increasingly discouraged from prying into Russian affairs, and foreign consulates had to be closed at the request of the Soviet Government, leaving, for most countries, only one in the whole Soviet Union. The Iron Curtain, though not yet christened, was already being lowered.

In the Far East the Japanese invasion of China continued throughout the year, the most significant event being the bombing of Canton which aroused worldwide protest. The city subsequently fell to the invaders with negligible resistance, having been fired by the retreating Chinese.

On a more cheerful note the year's memorable events included Len Hutton's 364 runs in a Test Match against Australia, the launching of the Queen Elizabeth *on Clydebank and of* Picture Post *on Fleet Street, and Great Britain's first victory in the Walker Cup.*

Chaliapin, Ataturk, D'Annunzio and Stanislavsky were among the distinguished dead, along with Queen Marie of Roumania and Queen Maud of Norway, both granddaughters of Queen Victoria.

Already, in 1938, Peterborough remarks on the heavy

" 'motorisation' which has long existed in England". It is perhaps as well that that incumbent died in 1959! Inevitably the dictators and their puppets find their way into his column, although, where possible, he tries to reflect the ludicrous side of their behaviour.

Piccadilly's Lure

The visit of Mr. Burgin, the Minister of Transport, to Germany to inspect her speedway system reminds me of an amusing incident which occurred when Dr. Todt, the German Inspector of Highways, was in London recently.*

Dr. Todt was so impressed by the rotary traffic at Piccadilly Circus that he could not be moved from Swan and Edgar's corner. He would stand there for hours murmuring "This is 10 years ahead of anything in Germany." Officials of the Ministry of Transport were quite unable to "move him on."

He realised for the first time that he had many years' hard work ahead before he could get Germans accustomed to the heavy "motorisation" which has long existed in England. *January 15*

Misogynist Unions

Cambridge, I see, has once again been plunged into controversy over the admission of women to membership of the Union.

The opening salvo in the latest campaign comes from the "Granta," which has published a symposium of Union officers' views. These range from the "I like women, but I don't like to hear them speak," of the president, Mr. John Simonds, to Mr. Frank Singleton's "I would welcome them."

A majority of three-fourths is required to alter the Union rules. The next step in the campaign is application to the president for a poll.

Visitors, But Not Members

This would in no case take place until towards the end of term and may be turned down, as a similar proposal was defeated less than three years ago by 81 votes. Neither Oxford nor Cambridge admits women to membership of the Union. Both houses have repeatedly rejected motions to admit them, though as visitors they are welcome.

One of their most impassioned Cambridge advocates, some nine years ago, was Lord Listowel, then, as Mr. W. F. Hare, serving his apprenticeship as a champion of lost causes.

It was during another debate at about the same time that Mr. Lionel Gamlin, later president of the Union and now a B.B.C.

*Fritz Todt was responsible for the construction of the autobahns, the Siegfried Line and, later, the Atlantic Wall.

announcer, perpetrated a mot which, unacknowledged, has cropped up again in 1938.

Referring to the proposal to admit women as full members, Mr. Gamlin declared himself unalterably opposed to "the thin end of the wench." *January 31*

Gen. Goering an Exception

To Signor Mussolini's dictum that the goose step can never be done by stout men, a subject I alluded to yesterday, there is one notable exception. Gen. Goering, despite his vast bulk, still delights to do the goose step on ceremonial occasions.

One such is the annual Nuremberg Congress. When Herr Hitler takes the salute at the Sunday march past of the S.A. and S.S. storm troopers, Gen. Goering always leaves the saluting base to lead his own detachment of the brown-shirted S.A. through the old market-place.

The sight of the enormous General throwing himself, knees perfectly straight, into the goose step, always rouses the great crowds of spectators to delighted cheers. *February 3*

Dr. Schuschnigg's Broadcast

Dr. Schuschnigg's good-bye to his people, to which I listened last night, was moving. He evidently spoke under great strain, and his voice sounded very different from what it was two days ago when he announced the plebiscite from Innsbruck.

He evidently spoke from loosely-prepared notes, and stammered at certain phrases, which he seemed to form off-hand while speaking.

He first said, for instance, that Austrian troops were ordered not to put up "particular resistance" at the entry of German soldiers. Then he corrected himself and said "No resistance," leaving out the word "particular."

His voice was overcome by emotion and he made long pauses between the words. After his last words, "Gott Schuetze Oesterreich" (May God protect Austria), he seemed to turn away from the microphone.

I could hear the crushing of paper and while the microphone was still alive the words, "Meine Herren, Ich bin fertig" (Gentlemen, I am finished), were muttered. *March 12*

Sardonic Press Chief

Yesterday's extraordinary incident at the Chancellery in Vienna, where a large number of foreign journalists were detained while Herr Hitler made his speech, marks the second event in the reign of the new Viennese Press Chief. He is Herr Lazar, who took over on Sunday night.

On his first appearance Herr Lazar, formerly the Bucharest correspondent of the "Neue Freie Presse," showed himself a martinet with a sardonic humour. Foreign correspondents were asked to go to the Chancellery at 7.30 p.m. to hear a most important announcement at 8. The Press Chief received them and announced President Miklas's resignation. Then he asked the time. Told it was 7.45, he said: "If you will wait another quarter of an hour I shall be able to give you a second extremely important announcement."

In the interval he parried questions about the German army of occupation, during which, I learn, he seemed to smile ironically. Asked what had happened to the Burgomaster of Vienna, he replied:

> I am sorry I cannot help you . . . Last night I was drinking a whisky and soda in Berlin and had no idea I should be Press Chief here to-day.

Finally, at 7.57, one of the journalists asked for his statement. But he said he must be exact. At eight p.m. he announced the incorporation of Austria in the Reich. *March 16*

The Milkman's Knock

Vienna has sufficiently recovered from recent political shocks for a new set of jokes to be going the round of the cafés. One of these tells of a German and a Dutchman who met in a railway dining car.

The German said: "We are a great nation. We have thousands of 'planes, thousands of tanks and a potential army of millions."

"True," replied the Dutchman. "We cannot compete with you. We have a very small army, only a few aeroplanes and practically no tanks. But, at any rate, when I hear someone knocking at the door in the morning I do know that it is the milkman." *April 8*

Litterateur—Not Diplomat

Sir Robert Vansittart and Mr. Bernard Shaw—playwrights both—will be the central figures in a ceremony which is to take place on the site of the National Theatre in South Kensington on April 22.*

Mr. Shaw, on behalf of the executive committee, will receive from Sir Robert the deeds of the site. As the site was purchased from the Office of Works it might have been expected that an official of that department, rather than the Chief Diplomatic Adviser, would hand the documents over.

I gather, however, that Sir Robert is participating on grounds of literary rather than of diplomatic distinction. He is coming "as one who personally believes in the great importance of the National Theatre."

Mr. Shaw is likely, I imagine, to utilise the occasion to defend the Committee's choice of the Cromwell Road site, which has come in for some criticism. In Mr. Shaw's opinion the site is not only "ideal," but "the best imaginable." *April 13*

Betting Shops Down Under

Mr. A. P. Herbert's bill to establish Government-licensed betting establishments off the course as an improvement on our betting laws is nothing new so far as the British Empire is concerned.

South Australia has its "betting shops." They were established several years ago following a Royal Commission into the ramifications of illegal betting in that State. They are now ubiquitous.

At the moment another Royal Commission is trying to sort out the tangle that has ensued.

Betting shops are licensed throughout the State, and every town of any size has at least one. They are open for mid-week betting. On Saturdays young men haunt them instead of playing cricket or football.

A Betting Control Board appointed by the Government sets out the days on which the bookmakers may operate and under what conditions. There are heavy fees for licences. Also there is a turnover tax collected by the Government.

Under the bill which established betting shops bookmakers may

*The site was opposite the Victoria and Albert Museum.

operate on the course. They were formerly forbidden to operate anywhere. The Government Tote on the course was the only medium.

May 2

Purdah for Bookmakers

In my note yesterday on Mr. A. P. Herbert's Betting Bill I referred to the situation which has resulted in South Australia from the establishment there of licensed betting shops.

Mr. Herbert tells me that his bill is designed to prevent this evil. His licensed bookmakers' offices will not be open to the public.

Cash bets must be placed in a letter-box outside. Bookmakers and their staffs will be rigorously kept in purdah. There will be no personal touch between the bookie and the non-race-going punter.

May 3

"F.E.'s" Shortest Address

A story which I have not before heard fathered on the late Lord Birkenhead was told by the Mayor of St. Pancras at the Marylebone Chamber of Commerce yesterday.

Lord Birkenhead, then Mr. F. E. Smith, had at some inconvenience gone North to address a meeting, the chairman of which promised to speak for a few minutes only in introducing him. Actually, he spoke for three-quarters of an hour.

When at last Birkenhead rose to speak, he said: "The chairman has now called upon me for my address. It is 27, Carlton House Terrace, and I'm damned well going to it!"

Thereupon Birkenhead made good his word. *May 13*

Phenomenal Mr. Luce

Arriving in London to-day is a close friend of Mr. Kennedy, the American Ambassador. This is Mr. Henry Robinson Luce, probably the most remarkable phenomenon in American journalism to-day.

Fifteen years ago, with an abandoned New York brewery for an office and two hired typewriters, he and another young man just down from Yale produced the first number of the news magazine, "Time." To-day its weekly circulation is 800,000.

Then, in the depths of America's worst depression, Mr. Luce started "Fortune." This deals with business and industry, costs a dollar a copy, and is the heaviest magazine in the world.

It proved an enormous success, and so has his latest venture, "Life," a weekly illustrated magazine. When he acquired and transformed it he hoped to start off by selling 300,000 copies.Now in the second year of his proprietorship it is selling 2,000,000 copies a week. Besides these, offshoots of "Time" include news films and, in America, broadcasting.

Not Born in a Log Cabin

At 40 Mr. Luce has an income which I have heard reliably estimated at close on £200,000. Efficient and abrupt, he lacks the flamboyance of Mr. Hearst, with whose methods he has little sympathy.

Unlike Mr. Hearst, he has kept out of politics. Whether he will continue to do so is problematical.

Although he has shown no public sign of any such ambition, Mr. Luce's name has been mentioned recently as a possible Republican candidate for the Presidency.

His past history, however, is not in accordance with the theory that the best candidates are born in log cabins. He was born in China where his parents were missionaries, and later he became an Oxford undergraduate. *May 16*

Martial Rule of the Road

British motorists visiting the Continent will be interested to hear that the fact that they have to drive on the right-hand side of the road is due to the martial habit of the early Germanic tribes. This, at least, is the explanation given by the official organ of the German police.

The German foot soldiers, it is pointed out, were armed with a spear, sword and a long shield, which was carried on the left arm. When they met another troop of armed men on the march they naturally stepped to the right in order to be covered by their shields in case of attack.

Hence the rule of the road which has been maintained ever since.

Why traffic keeps to the left in England is not explained. Presumably it is because we are a nation of shopkeepers. *June 22*

Aim Achieved Before Publication

It is not often that an author's sole object in writing a book is achieved before the book is published. This has happened to M. René Belbenoit—"Prisoner 46635"—whose "Dry Guillotine" appears to-day.

The title is the name given by the convicts to the solitary confinement cells in the penal settlement of French Guiana, which includes "Devil's Island."

Mr. William La Varre says in his introduction that Belbenoit, at 38, emaciated, toothless, and almost blind, hopes that his book will cause France to do away with the penal settlement and send no more human beings there to suffer.

The penal settlement was legally abolished by France a week ago.

July 3

Playboy with a Purpose

Mr. Howard Hughes, who has just flown the Atlantic, is known in America as the "playboy with a purpose." Fellow airmen, however, appreciate the profound technical knowledge behind his flying.

He takes immense trouble with preliminary plans. Every trip has been started only after exhaustive preparations. He has crossed the American continent in 7½ hours.

At 18 he inherited more than £3,000,000 from his father, who made a fortune from inventing oil-drilling machinery. Speed—and the machines that make it possible—has always been his hobby.

Substratosphere Speeding

Mr. Hughes has had several bad accidents with cars. He now owns his own 'plane factory and does his speeding in the substratosphere.

He broke the world's land aeroplane speed record when he was 30, and two years later he received from President Roosevelt the most coveted aviation award, the Harmon medal, for outstanding contributions to scientific aviation.

Hollywood was amused when he decided to use some of his fortune to make pictures. To the general astonishment his films were highly successful. "Hell's Angels" was one of them. It made a profit of £600,000.

He is unmarried, tall, shy, slightly deaf, extremely nervous and a careless dresser. His golf handicap is two. He does not smoke, drinks moderately and shuns publicity. *July 12*

Hollywood's Highest Brow?

For the first time for 10 years, the autumn publishing season this year will be unadorned by a new book from the pen of Aldous Huxley.

He has at last succumbed to the temptations of a Hollywood contract, and is busy on a scenario for Greta Garbo on the life of Mme. Curie. The result should be interesting. His play, "The World of Light," showed that he had mastered the trick of naturalistic dialogue of the requisite economy for film writing. His prestige value to Hollywood, as England's leading highbrow, in any case, is considerable.

Unlike his brother Julian, whose documentary films have won high praise, Aldous Huxley has hitherto regarded the film world with rather more than his normal critical detachment. His satire on the "feelies" in "Brave New World" springs to mind.

His conversion, in the Californian sunshine, has not been a sudden one. He has been living within range of the studios for the past six months. *August 12*

Nazi Place of Pilgrimage

Herr Hitler's "country retreat" in the Obersalzberg Mountains near Berchtesgaden—where Herr Henlein* has gone to confer with him —is a Nazi place of pilgrimage.

A steep and winding mountain road runs 3,000 feet up to the house. At this time of the year many thousands of Germans toil along it, hoping to see the Fuehrer or, at least, his house.

Near the house—"Berghof"—are barracks, Government offices and a large cinema. This cinema was built to entertain the hundreds of workmen who are unable to return home in the evenings.

It is like crossing a frontier to approach even the outskirts of Herr

*Konrad Henlein (1898–1945) was head of the Sudetendeutsche Partei which gained ascendancy in the Czechoslovak elections in May, 1935. He was appointed Reichskommissar for Sudeten areas after the German occupation in October, 1938.

Hitler's house. There is the usual pole across the road, with sentries armed and wearing the familiar German steel helmet.

Visitors Form Fours

All visitors are formed up on the outside of the pole in column of fours. When a crowd approximating to an army company has gathered, a sentry telephones to another sentry nearer the house for permission for the party to enter.

This given, the pole is lifted and the visitors march some half a mile along the road to the house. It stands much higher than the road, surrounded by terraces. On the terraces are soldiers and police. They scrutinise every person in the procession.

The visitors march past the house and out by another "frontier."

Sometimes Herr Hitler comes out into the garden and specially chosen visitors (many of them children) are introduced to him. They never know when this may happen, for they are never allowed to know for certain when Herr Hitler is in residence. *September 2*

Fuehrer's Prize Winners

I note that the four winners of the German national prize for scientific achievement by Germans have all made their name in applied science. The prize was established by Herr Hitler last year as a counterblast to the international Nobel prize, for which Germans are not allowed to compete.

Dr. Fritz Todt is the autobahn constructor. Dr. Ferdinand Porsche is the creator of the People's Car. The other two, Prof. Messerschmitt and Dr. Ernst Heinkel, are designers of record-breaking aircraft.

The most interesting career is that of Dr. Porsche, who is the son of a village plumber in Bohemia. He started as a mechanic in what is now Czechoslovakia. Later he set up for himself in Germany.

Like Lord Nuffield, he is self-taught. His model of the People's Car was presented to Herr Hitler on the Fuehrer's birthday this year. *September 12*

An Historic Scene Televised

Yesterday morning I drew a parallel between Mr. Chamberlain's visit to Berchtesgaden and Disraeli's to Berlin in 1878. Yesterday afternoon the same parallel, drawn more closely, was broadcast to the world.

Mr. Michael Standing, the B.B.C. commentator at Mr. Chamberlain's arrival at Heston, compared the Prime Minister's return with that of Lord Beaconsfield when he brought back "peace with honour."

I watched the scene televised—a branch of applied science in which this country leads the world. It was extraordinarily clear.

Television Triumphant

The Prime Minister's machine and the escorting 'plane did a half circuit of the aerodrome. The former landed and we had a close-up of the steps being placed to the cabin door.

After an appreciable pause, of perhaps a minute and a half, Mr. Chamberlain emerged. He was a smiling—it would not be too much to say a buoyant—figure as he acknowledged the cheers, or rather the clapping of the bystanders.

He greeted Lord Halifax and opened a letter which was handed to him. Then a woman shouted something, inaudible through the microphone, at which he smiled again and raised his hat.

A triumph indeed for television. *September 17*

Gleneagles Heart-cry

As the owner of Gleneagles, in Perthshire, where his family has lived for 800 years, Mr. Brodrick Chinnery-Haldane has for many years inveighed against the L.M.S. for giving the name of his property to a railway hotel.

The lawn tennis tournament which opens there this week has provoked a renewed onslaught from Mr. Chinnery-Haldane against all those who habitually call it "the Gleneagles tournament." In a letter which I have just received from him he claims that Gleneagles is the name of his estate at the foot of the beautiful pass through the Ochil Hills and should be used nowhere else.

> The hotel does not stand on my ground and has nothing to do with Gleneagles. All I, as the owner of Gleneagles, ask is that the name shall be respected and not mixed up with this modern railway hotel and all that it stands for.

The Haldane family has owned Gleneagles since the 12th century. It passed to Mr. Chinnery-Haldane in 1918. *September 19*

Karel Capek's Radio Appeals

An influential figure in Czechoslovakia in this crisis is Karel Capek. He has been broadcasting from Prague appeals for calm and confidence among his compatriots.

The playwright was a personal friend of the late President Masaryk and is the most prominent literary figure the Republic has produced.

I am told there is a possibility that he may be given a post in the new Czech Ministry. As the leading literary representative of the Czech ideology M. Capek's name alone would strengthen any Czech Ministry at the present juncture.

One of his latest plays, "Power and Glory," in which Oscar Homolka appeared at the Savoy a few months ago, deals with the private life of a dictator. It forecasts his downfall at the moment when war breaks out. *September 26*

Historic Television Drama

On Mr. Chamberlain's return from his first visit to Germany I said that television had been given the greatest moment in its short history. His arrival at Heston yesterday makes that remark out of date.

Television on this occasion was competing with the elements, though an expert told me that the rain effect was probably heightened by interference.

The rain was a leitmotif throughout. At the most impressive moment the wind also intervened. As Mr. Chamberlain took the "no more war" declaration from its envelope, a gust blew out the foolscap sheet, and for the moment it was the most striking object on the screen. A producer of genius could not have arranged it with greater dramatic effect. *October 1*

Capt. F. E. Guest's Prophecy

A remarkable piece of political prophecy which its author did not live to see fulfilled has just come to my notice. It consists of a letter to *The Daily Telegraph*, published on April 13, 1935, from Capt. Frederick Guest.

Capt. Guest, who was Secretary of State for Air in 1921 and 1922, wrote while the Stresa Conference was still sitting. The primary object of his letter was to urge the Government to take a determined line in foreign affairs and to cease deluding itself as to the relative strength of the British and German Air Forces.

Though three and a half years have elapsed since the letter appeared, much of it might well have been written in 1938. Referring to the many points on which a powerful Germany could make trouble, Capt. Guest listed Danzig, Memel, "the independence of Austria and the 3,500,000 German population in Czechoslovakia."

Fuehrer's Policy Foretold

Still more pertinent to-day is the paragraph in which Capt. Guest summed up.

> Any one of these situations might prove to be the necessary excuse. Germany may decide to acquire these extra blocks of population one by one. Each time she will say to Europe, "Are you going to make war for a little thing like that?"

With Capt. Guest's submission that "this is a realistic view of the situation"—his claim in 1935—there can, unfortunately, be little disagreement to-day. *October 20*

Orson Welles, Enfant Terrible

Mr. Orson Welles, the young actor who caused a panic in the United States by broadcasting a version of Mr. H. G. Wells's "The War of the Worlds" with the names of American towns substituted for those mentioned in the book, has thus set the seal on his reputation as the enfant terrible of the New York stage.

Only 23, Mr. Welles, by his energetic direction and ruthless manhandling of the classics, has made his theatre, the Mercury, the liveliest in New York.

He produced "Julius Caesar" in modern dress, stressing parallels between Caesar's Rome and Mussolini's and interpolating several passages from "Coriolanus." His next Shakespearean production is to be a hotch-potch of "Henry IV" "Henry V" and "Henry VI" entitled "Three Kings."

So freely does Mr. Welles adapt Shakespeare's lines to his own purpose that an actor at the Mercury, asked when rehearsals of one of the season's classics would begin, replied: "As soon as Orson has finished writing it."

£200 "Ha-ha!"

Mr. Welles has plenty of experience at making wireless audiences' flesh creep. At one time he broadcast every week in a radio thriller called "The Shadow."

In this he played a murderer who, after each crime, murmured in sepulchral tones, "The Shadow knows—Ha-Ha!" For several months Mr. Welles's "Ha-ha!" made him £200 a week.

At the age of 16 Mr. Welles went to Ireland. He informed the management of a Dublin repertory theatre that he was a leading New York actor.

This piece of bluff won him a series of leading parts. When he returned to New York, the experience he had gained in Ireland enabled him to become as successful an actor as he had previously claimed to be. *November 1*

Pro-British Kemal Ataturk

The death of Mustapha Kemal (Ghazi and Ataturk) is a real misfortune for this country. He was the only one among the dictators who possessed an instinctively pro-British point of view. This Anglophilism was compounded of the most diverse elements.

On the one hand there was his memory of the patronising airs which the Germans had adopted towards him during the war and which the French adopted after 1922.

We had fought him at Gallipoli and had refused to run away from him at Chanak. At the first Lausanne conference Lord Curzon managed to establish with Ismet Pasha relations of almost rollicking pomposity.

When the little Pasha returned to Angora he informed the Ghazi that whereas the French had posed as the friend in need and the Italians had wheedled surreptitiously, Lord Curzon had neither bullied nor cajoled.

He had fought the Pasha on every point, and when beaten had grinned at him with majestic geniality. The Ghazi was much impressed by these stories.

Poker a Political Asset

He discovered other affinities. Englishmen could generally play poker, whereas the French and Italians were less addicted to that pastime. Englishmen wore the right sort of riding breeches in the right sort of manner. British Ambassadors often saw the point of Ataturk's rather simple jokes.

Sir Percy Loraine, in particular, was a man after the Ghazi's heart. Few men could play poker so long or with such delighted solemnity. And then King Edward came to visit him. The old Lion of Angora was curiously touched.

Another great Albanian has been lost to Turkey. He transformed his country, and much of his magnificent edifice will survive. Yet the Turks are not by nature gifted with the ability to keep their edifices in repair. *November 11*

Chip off the Old Block

Mr. Quintin Hogg, the recently elected member for Oxford City, scored a personal triumph when he made his maiden speech last night. Rising from the Conservative benches behind the Treasury Bench, he spoke for some 20 minutes. Any member entering the Chamber without knowing the speaker might well have thought that he was listening to a man of considerable Parliamentary experience.

That the speech was on the Criminal Justice Bill, a subject with which as a barrister he is in daily touch, was, of course, in his favour. Members on all sides in a fairly full House were unanimous in endorsing Mr. Kingsley Griffith's congratulatory remark that the expectations entertained of one who bears the name he does were amply fulfilled.

Some went so far as to prophesy that they had been listening to a future Lord Chancellor. *November 30*

Novel Written in a Week-end

Edgar Wallace's extraordinary powers of work are well brought out by Miss Margaret Lane in her biography of her late father-in-law, which appears on Monday. She relates how Sir Patrick Hastings once saw him dictate a full-length novel, "The Devil Man," between Friday night and Monday morning.

Sir Patrick was staying at Chalklands, Edgar Wallace's country house. Worry over a serial had caused the host to disappear during dinner.

In the middle of the night Sir Patrick, who was sleeping badly, went to the study. There he found Edgar Wallace at his desk, holding a dictaphone mouthpiece, and beside him a cup of tea.

60 Hours' Work—£4,000

For two hours he listened to his host dictating, a servant bringing a cup of sweet tea every half-hour. With only a couple of hours' sleep, Edgar Wallace continued at the instrument till Saturday evening.

On Sunday he slept till noon. After lunch he set to work again. At nine a.m. on Monday, "pallid, unshaven and almost hysterical with fatigue," he announced that his 80,000-word novel was finished.

Then he went to bed for two days. He had earned £4,000 in serial rights alone in 60 hours. *December 3*

"The Mother of Parliaments"

In his eulogy of the late Lord Oxford Mr. Chamberlain referred to the House of Commons as "the Mother of Parliaments."

It was John Bright who coined the phrase, and few people are aware that he applied it not to the House of Commons, but to the country.

The long-familiar phrase, as Bright used it in his famous speech at Rochdale in 1865, was "England the Mother of Parliaments."

December 17

1939

1939

The Second World War began on September 1, 1939, when Germany invaded Poland, the point having been reached at which the deliberate policy of the German National Socialist Government to extend without limit the territories of the Third Reich became intolerable to Britain and France, who declared war on Germany on September 3.

The crisis of the previous September had revealed serious gaps in Britain's national defences and the intervening year was largely spent in preparation against the possibility of war. Rearmament went ahead vigorously and the strength of the Territorial Army was virtually doubled. That the threat of war was not imaginary was demonstrated in March when Hitler, in flagrant breach of the Munich agreement, occupied the rest of Czechoslovakia and, soon after, the Lithuanian port of Memel.

On April 7, which, ironically, happened to be Good Friday, Italy invaded Albania and in a few days the country was reduced to subjection. Meanwhile, in Spain the victory of General Franco's Nationalists had released the German and Italian troops serving there. The British and French Governments now extended formal guarantees of protection to Poland, Turkey, Roumania and Greece, but all diplomatic calculations were turned upside down when, on August 21, it was announced that the Nazis had signed a non-aggression pact with the Soviet Union. Then, on September 1, alleging that the Poles had rejected terms for peace, which, in fact, they had never seen, Hitler invaded Poland. The Poles offered little resistance and on September 17 the Russians crossed their Eastern frontier; on the 24th Warsaw surrendered and the country was partitioned between the two invaders.

In the west Germany made no move, although the Maginot and Siegfried lines were both manned.

On September 11 a British Expeditionary Force of eight divisions under Lord Gort crossed the Channel in complete secrecy to take its place on the French left flank.

At sea the war was waged with greater intensity. While the Germans constantly harassed Allied merchant shipping, the first major success of the war was gained by the British Navy when the Admiral Graf Spee, *a German pocket battleship, was driven into Montevideo harbour by three British cruisers where she was scuttled on the orders of the Führer, to avoid internment.*

On the outbreak of war a small War Cabinet was formed in which Winston Churchill became First Lord of the Admiralty, the post he had held at the start of the First World War. Civilian life was affected in many ways; conscription began, children were evacuated from the major cities, blackout regulations came into force, petrol rationing was introduced, and the intention to ration bacon, butter, sugar and meat was announced.

The outbreak of war found the Empire united. Australia and New Zealand declared war only three hours after Great Britain, and the Canadian Government was only delayed by its formal obligation to consult Parliament. General Herzog, in South Africa, tried to keep his country out of the war, but a revolt in his Cabinet obliged him to resign; General Smuts became Prime Minister and war was declared. In India, despite the attitude of the Congress Party, which attempted to turn the situation to its own political advantage, the population as a whole threw themselves vigorously into the task of prosecuting the war.

France, which had entered the year in a sorry state of moral and economic disarray, found in the events of March a spur to national regeneration which many did not think it too extravagant to call miraculous. As one politician put it, "By our folly we made Hitler and the new Germany possible. He in his turn has paid his debt and given us a new France." Alas, he was all too soon to take it back.

Though the war remained stagnant in Western Europe, it was being waged with bitter intensity in Finland, which Russia had invaded at the end of November. Though outnumbered by fifty to one, the Finns put up an heroic resistance and had, at the year's end, pushed the fighting line back at many points on to Russian soil.

In the Far East the war between Japan and China entered its third year. Though the Japanese continued to gain victories, General Chiang Kai-shek's guerrilla campaigns were by no means without success.

Of events which attracted public notice before the clamour of war drove all else from the headlines, brief mention should be made of the loss of the submarine Thetis *during tests; only two of her crew of seventy-nine escaped. Cardinal Pacelli was elected Pope as Pius XII; John Cobb and Sir Malcolm Campbell set up new land and water speed records, and the new Dalai Lama, aged four years and three months, entered Lhasa.*

"Earth received an honoured guest," as Auden expressed it, when William Yeats was laid to rest. It also received Sigmund Freud, another beneficiary of an Auden ode, Ethel M. Dell, Pope Pius XI, Havelock Ellis and Sir Philip Sassoon.

Peterborough duly notes the return of Churchill to office and hereafter accords him pride of place over all diplomats and musicians.

Refugee Old Masters

Mr. John Rothenstein has just completed the A.R.P. plans for the Tate Gallery's treasures. As might be expected, evacuation is the main policy. A country house has been prepared to receive the Old Master refugees in time of emergency.

The system of evacuation to be followed involves the division of the collection—like Caesar's Gaul—into three parts.

First is a list of 40 pictures—roughly 20 Old Masters and 20 moderns—including the best of the Turners and Constables. These must be saved at all costs, and will leave London immediately it becomes a danger area.

The second list for evacuation contains some 500 names of pictures the destruction of which would be considered a national calamity. The remainder of the collection will have to take a citizen's chance of survival in their own home.

Selection Secrets

The "short list" is being kept a close secret. Publication of the names of the 20 modern pictures most deserving of protection would probably start controversies beside which the more recent discords on the "overcleaned" Velasquez or the "Giorgione" panels would rank as pleasant exchanges.

The next best 500 are also secret. Every painter whose work is in the Tate can hope to have it included in one of the two lists. I believe that only Mr. Rothenstein, one or two of his assistants and the Trustees have possession of the complete plans.

Meanwhile, pictures are being grouped according to size, so that several may be packed in a single crate without loss of time if the occasion arises. For the safety of the staff a bomb-proof, gas-proof and flood-proof shelter is just being completed underneath the Gallery. *January 9*

The Umbrella

Mr. Chamberlain, before arriving in Rome, has delighted the Board of Curators of the new Umbrella Museum at Gignese, in the Italian Lakes.

They wrote asking him to present them with the historic umbrella which captured the imagination of the world when he flew with it to Germany last September.

His reply was a gentle refusal. It was based on the grounds that the umbrella was "too commonplace and worn-out" to rank as an historical relic.

The letter has delighted the museum even more than the gift of the umbrella would have done. Framed and put in a place of honour, it will be the chief exhibit when the museum is opened. *January 11*

"The Women" for London

Clare Boothe's play, "The Women," has now been licensed by the Lord Chamberlain, subject to certain minor alterations in the text. Mr. Gilbert Miller is to present it in London, probably shortly after his return from America in March.

It has a cast of 40, all women. How many of the American cast will be brought over has not yet been decided.

In New York "The Women," which might be called a textbook on the anatomy of feminine guile, had a sensational success. It is a stinging attack on rich women in New York and the trouble they cause by gossip.

They are shown playing bridge, having permanent waves and in a bathroom, gossiping all the time. The final scene shows them coming to blows in a restaurant cloakroom.

When "The Women" was first submitted to the Lord Chamberlain, I believe he refused a licence unless the title was changed to "American Women." This the author refused to do.

Two "Fortunes" in the Family

Clare Boothe, who is the wife of Mr. Henry Luce, the proprietor of the American magazines "Time," "Life" and "Fortune," must have made a fortune of her own from "The Women."

She has followed it up with another success which is now running at the Henry Miller Theatre, New York. It is called "Kiss the Boys Goodbye" and has been playing since September to over £3,000 a week.

It deals with Hollywood's difficulty in finding an actress to appear as Scarlett O'Hara, the Southern heroine of "Gone With the Wind."

January 14

Halifax Britannica

Lord Halifax perpetrated a mot during his visit to Rome which is worthy of record.

A number of Italian newspapers had gone to great lengths to prove that his family had an Italian origin, and that his name was really Halifaccio.

To journalists who asked him about this he said that his name was more Latin than Italian in origin. "You conjugate it like pax," he explained: "Halifax, Halifacem, Halifacis." *January 19*

Tender-Hearted Executioner

M. Anatole Deibler, France's public executioner, who died yesterday, suffered all his life from a weak heart and morbid shyness. The latter was induced by a fear that all Frenchmen shunned the company of "M. de Paris," as he was known.

He first realised the drawbacks to his hereditary office when doing his military service. Other recruits discovered that he was the future executioner and complained so persistently that his period of service was cut short.

In appearance he was not unlike M. Poincaré, with a spare white beard and an alert manner. His salary, until some years ago a mere £90, was only increased to £144 when Mme. Deibler appealed to the authorities.

Although her husband had executed some 400 people, he was, she said, too shy to ask for an increase and too kind-hearted to raise the rent paid by the lodgers who provided his only other income.

February 2

Infra-red Defence Problem

German military 'planes which have been making flights over the North Sea as far as the three-mile limit off the East Coast fly at very high altitudes. They also come on very clear days, which has enabled the R.A.F. to spot them the more easily.

The reason for their choice of perfect weather has not been solely one of carefree flying. The pilots, it is believed, have been testing out the new infra-red long-range cameras.

By this method of photography, which is not, of course, a German secret, photographs can be taken of objects a very long distance away.

Germans in this country can, of course, openly buy maps of London and its environs, but long-distance photography, if expertly done, can show many things not marked on the map. *February 27*

M. Bata Escapes

I see that M. Jan Bata, the biggest individual industrialist in Czechoslovakia, whose name was at one time put about as a possible President of the murdered State in October last, got away to Bucharest in time. He had his own aeroplane, which he liked to fly himself, and his own excellent aerodrome at Zlin, in Moravia, where the Bata works were situated.

A friend of mine visited him there during the Sunday of the Anschluss last year in company with other Englishmen, and they discussed the future of Central Europe.

Bata, a big, square man, whose command of English is limited and curious, listened and then delivered his remedy. "I think," he said slowly, "it would all be good if England would say 'Boo.' "

Aeroplane as Memorial

Zlin itself and the factories are somewhat reminiscent of working life in Mr. Aldous Huxley's "Brave New World." All the factory buildings are similar rectangular boxes, and the whole life of the town revolved obediently round M. Bata. He generously offered his English guests an A.R.P. rehearsal, in which he would have had a siren blown and the town would have taken to the woods.

The most curious and macabre building is the memorial to his half-brother, the late head of the firm. Like the other architecture of Zlin, it is a rectangular cube, but with a frosted glass exterior.

Inside is suspended the wreckage of the aeroplane in which the elder Bata was killed when it crashed. The letters, telegrams, and personal belongings that he had on him are all there too, preserved in a glass case. *March 18*

B.B.C.'s Fragrant Démarche

For the only touch of humour in a week-end of depressing news the B.B.C. was unintentionally responsible. In the bulletin read just before midnight on Saturday reference was made to the British Note delivered in Berlin. This, the announcer stated, was to the effect that

> The annexation of Czechoslovakia was a fragrant violation of the Munich agreement.

Puzzled by this curiously worded démarche, the announcer paused. Then, suddenly enlightened, he apologised.

I am sorry. I read that word as fragrant. It was, of course, a misprint for flagrant.

His explanation was evidently intended to convey that not he, but a B.B.C. typist, was responsible for what was indeed a fragrant moment. *March 20*

To-night's Ballerinas

Miss Margot Fonteyn and Miss June Brae, the two leading and youthful ballerinas in to-night's gala performance—Miss Brae, the elder, is just 21—are both British. Russian influences, however, surrounded their early training. Their teacher was a Russian émigrée who had a ballet school in Shanghai.

Miss Fonteyn then came to England and was followed three years later by Miss Brae. The two met again for the first time at the Vic-Wells ballet school.

June Brae adopted her dancing name by treating her surname anagrammatically. Her uncle, Mr. George Bear, is a well-known Scottish painter. Margot Fonteyn in private life is Miss Hookham. *March 22*

Unalliterative Shelters

Sir John Anderson, like Mr. Hore-Belisha, appears to be destined to have his name attached to a creation of his department. One question on the Order Paper of the House of Commons refers to "Anderson shelters."

I doubt, however, whether the name will be either universal or lasting. It lacks the alliterative attraction of "Belisha Beacon."

Few politicians succeed in leaving their names in the language. The bathing station in Hyde Park is still known as "Lansbury's Lido," and the fact that the one-time "Peeler" now answers to the name of "Bobby" ensures that Sir Robert Peel's connection with the police is still preserved in current English.

One past Commissioner of Works whose name will last as long as Parliament is Sir Benjamin Hall, after whom "Big Ben" is called. A back-bencher similarly honoured is Samuel Plimsoll. *April 10*

International Riddle

An American yesterday asked me the difference between Mr. Chamberlain and Herr Hitler. He explained it in a nutshell.

"Chamberlain," he said, "takes his week-ends in the country. Hitler takes his countries in the week-end." *April 26*

Cliveden Again

Mr. Tom Kennedy, the Socialist M.P. for Kirkcaldy, is to ask a question in the House to-day by way of protest against Lord Lothian's "pronounced pro-German sympathies and tendencies." In other words, he is trying to make that old turnip-head ghost, the Cliveden Set, walk again.

Its persistence is a remarkable example of the vitality of the false syllogism. It can be set out thus:

Lady Astor has made statements which might be interpreted as pro-German.

Lord Lothian (and other prominent men) often visit Cliveden.

Therefore Lord Lothian (accompanied by the other prominent visitors) is pro-German. Q.E.D.

Actually, as any one of the hundreds who have visited Cliveden in the past 20 years knows, social life there exists and flourishes on the basis of constant and vehement controversy.

Neither would it seem that indignant Mr. Tom Kennedy has read Lord Lothian's articles in the *Observer* or Lord Astor's speech in the House of Lords on April 14, when he said that the Axis could not be broken by soft words. *April 27*

Scriabin's Nephew

Like M. Litvinoff, his predecessor as Foreign Commissar, M. Molotoff has gone through his revolutionary career under an assumed name. Unlike M. Litvinoff, he belongs, by his real name—Scriabin—to the old Russian gentry. He is a nephew of the famous composer.

M. Molotoff is a voluminous writer and makes more and longer speeches than any other of the Soviet leaders. His public utterances entitle him to rank as their No. 1 Anti-Nazi.

His oratory suffers from a severe handicap—his tendency to stutter. This has often played him an ill turn at the wrong moment.

In his speech before the elections to the first Soviet Parliament under the new Constitution in December, 1937, everything went well till the peroration. When he came to the words, "Long live Comrade Stalin," he had to make four attempts at the name.

May 5

Dickens Descendant's Career

I shall look forward to seeing an unusual first book which is to appear shortly from the pen of a great-granddaughter of Charles Dickens.

Monica Dickens, who is in her early twenties, was found at school to be insubordinate, sullen and impertinent, and lacking in team-spirit. There seemed nothing for it but the stage. Then she discovered in the course of training that she was no actress. So she became a cook-general.

"One Pair of Hands" is an account of her various jobs. I gather from Mr. Compton Mackenzie, who writes a foreword, that Miss Dickens can not only cook but write, and that her sense of fun is no discredit to her lineage. *May 11*

Over-long Speeches

In raising the question of over-long Parliamentary speeches, and the silencing of back-benchers which they entail on important occasions, Mr. Edwards and Capt. Cazalet provided the Speaker with one of his rare chances to make a speech. Capt. FitzRoy's observations on Parliamentary brevity were witty. It is a pity that his duties normally condemn him to silence.

Possibly the Speaker's best hit was his story of Disraeli, who advised a newcomer to Westminster not to speak, on the ground that it was better for the House to wonder why he did not speak than to wonder why he did.

Capt. FitzRoy pointed out yesterday, as he has before, that he has no power to reduce the length of speeches. He could only offer advice. Yesterday he remarked that his advice had always fallen either on deaf ears or unruly tongues. *May 26*

Nazi Doctor's Dilemma

To-day's publication of the Prime Minister's book of speeches, "The Struggle for Peace," places the German Minister for National Enlightenment and Propaganda in a quandary. The German rights were sold at the beginning of March before the Nazi annexation of Czechoslovakia, and I hear that the translation is now nearly ready.

The book is being published by a firm the head of which is Professor Hoffmann, the Fuehrer's official photographer. When he signed the contract for the German edition he had obtained the official permit of the Propaganda Ministry. The question now is whether Dr. Goebbels will revoke his permission.

Since March 15 Dr. Goebbels has more or less continuously proclaimed that Mr. Chamberlain's policy is a struggle not for peace but for encirclement. He will obviously not be helping to spread that belief if he allows the publication of a book which shows clearly how far Mr. Chamberlain went to appease Germany.

German Chamberlain Cult

The danger from the Propaganda Ministry's point of view is all the greater as the spell Mr. Chamberlain cast over the German people by his visits to Herr Hitler is not forgotten.

A best-seller among picture postcards in Germany for months showed the heads of the Prime Minister and the Fuehrer together. It was made after Godesberg. It cannot now be bought.

The Chamberlain family's popularity in Germany began in fact with Sir Austen. His memoirs, to which Mr. Neville Chamberlain contributed a foreword, were translated by Dr. Pick. The volume first appeared in Germany 18 months ago, and was a book of the year. *June 1*

Lost Leader Returns

Magdalene's steadily rising academic prestige is further reinforced by the honorary fellowship which that college has bestowed on Mr. T. S. Eliot. Mr. Eliot is our leading contemporary poet. I doubt, however, whether his réclame will ever again be as great as it was in the middle twenties at Cambridge.

At that time he was the intelligentsia's pet cult. "The Wasteland," which appeared in 1922, was described by enthusiasts as equal to "The Lyrical Ballads" in its disruptive force. Later, the Clark

Lectures which Mr. Eliot delivered on the Metaphysical Poets drew record audiences from the younger members of the university.

I attended one of them and found it dull. Since then Mr. Eliot has been superseded as a leader of youthful revolt. Whatever its virtues, High Anglicanism in most people's minds has nothing to do with the overturning of traditional altars. *June 2*

D.Litt.'s Debt to Daughter

Mr. P. G. Wodehouse's doctorate will delight the English-speaking world. But I fancy that it will delight most of all his daughter Leonora.

He has often confessed that when she was a schoolgirl he tried out all his happy phrases and good situations on her before committing them to print. She was a ruthless critic, and many ideas lost their lustre when she had delivered the terse verdict, "Not funny."

The dedication of one of his earlier books ran something like this:

TO MY DAUGHTER
LEONORA
without whose constant
aid and encouragement
THIS BOOK
would have been written
in half the time

She is now Mrs. Peter Cazalet. *June 22*

St. Andrews Receives the Pros.

The last barrier between amateur and professional golfers has been removed. For the first time in its long history the Royal and Ancient club has thrown open its doors to the 200 professionals from all parts of the world who are competing in the Open Championship at St. Andrews, which begins to-day.

The decision is a belated recognition of the vast changes that have taken place in recent years in the status of professional golfers. One of them, Henry Cotton, is earning £5,000 a year. Bobby Locke, the South African youth, and Lawson Little, who is a graduate of Stanford University, California, are both making about £3,000 a year.

As there is no class distinction in America, one can imagine the surprise of Bobby Jones on the occasion when he was informed that his friend, a professional golfer, could not enter the R. and A. clubhouse. "Is that so?" said Jones, and turning on their heel they walked away arm in arm. *July 3*

Two Profitable Plays

Mr. Emlyn Williams tells me that he expects soon to sign a contract disposing of the film rights of his play, "The Corn is Green." This will add substantially to the already handsome earnings he has made from the play.

Over 250,000 people have already seen "The Corn is Green," at the Duchess Theatre. They have paid £30,000 to do so—which equals the figure reached by Mr. Williams's highly successful "Night Must Fall" in its entire run at the same theatre.

From "Night Must Fall" Mr. Williams made £25,000. From "The Corn is Green" he has so far drawn £10,000. The figures are the more remarkable since the Duchess, with a seating capacity of only 492, is one of London's smallest theatres. *July 11*

"Churchill" Discs

Curiously exaggerated stories have begun to circulate regarding the appearance of a small metal disc bearing the name "Churchill" in blue on a white background.

According to reports current yesterday, these discs have been presented to M.P.s of all parties, and 10,000,000 have been ordered.

In fact, about 10 were taken to the House on Tuesday afternoon by three Conservative M.P.s, who received them from a fellow guest at a private lunch party.

Cocktail Hour Umbrellas

They were considered an amusing commentary on a current controversy, in much the same spirit as the miniature glass umbrellas for use as cocktail sticks were regarded by M.P.s who attended the Kitchen Committee's recent cocktail parties in the House.

Only 100 of these discs exist, though 500 may be delivered to-day, and more may be ordered "if there is a demand." The author of the idea, who thinks the discs may help to determine how many people would support the inclusion of Mr. Churchill in the Cabinet, is Mr. Forbes Dennis. His wife is the well-known novelist, Phyllis Bottome. *July 13*

Hardened to Crises

The British Consul-General in Warsaw, who has circulated a note to all British subjects in Poland suggesting that they should leave within 48 hours, is Mr. Frank Savery.

Mr. Savery has been in Warsaw since the war. He knows more about Poland, Polish cooking, Polish history and Polish literature than any Briton living. Indeed, some Poles claim that on the last point he is without rival even among Poles.

He is a bachelor, has a remarkable chef and is intensely popular with all classes in Poland. He is a connoisseur of the 280 different kinds of vodka. *August 23*

The King's Broadcast

The King's broadcast last evening was perfectly attuned to the occasion. Its dignity and gravity were enhanced by the deep and level tones of its delivery.

There was no place for emotion in such a message from the King to his subjects. A personal note, however, was perhaps to be detected in the slightly greater emphasis which the King laid upon the last two words when he said, "For the second time in the lives of most of us we are at war."

The King, I hear, is showing an example of meticulousness in following A.R.P. regulations which has been commented upon by his entourage. Whenever he moves about within Buckingham Palace he carries his gas mask. Before he transacts business with his Ministers he places it on the table beside him.

Commons Overnight Change

As Mr. Greenwood pointed out in his speech yesterday, there was a remarkable change in the atmosphere of the House compared with Saturday evening. Then the Prime Minister had been heard in pained and puzzled silence when he announced delay. Yesterday morning members stood to cheer him when he took his place.

Not only was the news of war known. It had been emphasised

by an air raid warning that had sent members to the shelters before the sitting opened.

That it was a day for deeds, not words, was realised by all. Mr. Chamberlain spoke for only five minutes, and no subsequent speaker exceeded that limit. Yet nothing necessary was left unsaid. It was a model debate. Mr. Chamberlain's peroration moved the House more than any other he has delivered. It was the one part of his speech where his emotions nearly overcame him.

Mr. Churchill's Oratory

His notes for once not concealed by a Hansard, Mr. Churchill reached the highest level of oratory. His finest phrase was: "In our hearts this Sunday morning there is peace."

Restraint was shown in the cheers with which M.P.s greeted the speeches. There was no sign at all of the emotion the 1914 House displayed. Then during one early sitting that August the House burst into singing the National Anthem.

Even more remarkable was the restraint with which members listened to the unpopular view of the microscopic minority voiced by Mr. McGovern. It was not until he declared that the national unity would be broken in six months that he evoked any interruptions.

Only one speaker made direct allusions to 1914. Appropriately that was Mr. Lloyd George, who was given a loud cheer on rising, and when he offered his services to the Government in any humble capacity.

Back to No. 10

Mr. Churchill's inclusion in the Cabinet has long been expected and there was no surprise mingled with the relief with which the news was heard last night.

Comments, rather, ran on the remarkable career of a great public figure who twice has been at the Admiralty at the beginning of a titanic national struggle. *September 4*

Our Resourceful Recruits

A nervous young recruit to one of the women's home defence services was being examined by her grimly efficient commandant.

"Where is your indelible pencil?" she was asked.

"I didn't know I needed one. What is it for?"

"To write the names and addresses of the casualties upon their foreheads, of course," the Commandant replied briskly.

The recruit pondered this. Then an idea struck her.

"But what do I do if the casualty is a negro?" *October 4*

High-speed U.S. Press Methods

I heard a remarkable example yesterday of the tempo at which American journalism will be operating throughout the war. The weekly magazine "Time" decided at short notice to publish an article on Stalin. No one, the editor considered, was better qualified to provide an intimate study of the Russian ruler than Trotsky.

A long-distance telephone call was put in on a Thursday from New York to Mexico City, where Trotsky lives. Next day the foreign editor of the magazine flew the 1,300 miles to Mexico and went through the article with Trotsky, correcting his English here and there.

By Saturday he was back in New York with the article. Trotsky's remuneration for it was, I believe, in the neighbourhood of £200.

October 7

World War II?

Americans are puzzled over how to describe the war. "Time," the American magazine with the three-quarters of a million circulation, calls it World War II.

In the latest number to reach England it prints letters from its readers objecting to this, as it implies that America will be drawn in. "Time's" answer runs: "Nobody ever kept out of a riot by calling it an altercation." *October 13*

Fifth Form at St. Stella's

The Dowager Lady Reading, chairman of the Women's Voluntary Services for Civil Defence, is "Stella" to her friends. I hear that the staff at her headquarters in Tothill Street now call themselves "the girls at St. Stella's."

Certainly the W.V.S. uniform has an academic and indeed youthful air. It consists of a green hat with W.V.S. on the ribbon and a grey dress. A green overall with the badge is also worn in office hours.

As the new name of the W.V.S. organisation is likely to spread throughout the country, the London headquarters staff, I gather, has already taken for itself the designation of "the Fifth Form at St. Stella's."

November 4

Statesmen's Lien on Fame

Mr. Churchill's vitality, again exemplified last night in his broadcast, no less strikingly than it has been in Parliament, is the more remarkable since his lien on fame is of greater span than that of any other living statesman.

Turning over a "Who's Who" for 1902, I found that he had 33 lines. They began with "M.P. (C.) Oldham since 1900; late Lieut. the 4th Queen's Own Hussars." Mr. Lloyd George had only six lines.

Neither Lord Baldwin nor Mr. Ramsay MacDonald appeared at all. Mr. Chamberlain also is not included, but his more precocious brother, the late Sir Austen, has a place. Lord Halifax appears simply as heir to his father as "the Hon. F. Lindley Wood, b. 1881."

A Sir John Simon is included. He was a surgeon, born in 1816, who was officer of health to the City of London as far back as 1848.

November 13

Search the Cupboards

The late Tom Hodge, of Sotheby's, could have written a wonderful book of recollections of historic sales of literary relics and rarities. I know that he counted his greatest adventure to be the discovery of a Mazarin Bible in a disused medicine cupboard.

He had travelled to Queensferry to make an inventory of the Hopetoun Library, 50 years ago. After he had done this he had a few minutes to spare before catching the train to London. The trap was waiting at the door. But Hodge espied a corner cupboard and insisted on the butler opening it.

Behind some musty old bottles he found the two dusty volumes of Gutenberg's first issue of the Bible. At the Hopetoun sale this brought £2,000—a great sum in 1889. When the Soviet Government sold their Mazarin Bible in 1931 the price paid was over £30,000.

The Mazarin Bible is so-called because the first Gutenberg Bible to be identified was found in the Cardinal's library. *December 7*

Gunners' Patron Saint

St. Barbara, whose festival the French gunners celebrated by salvoes against the German lines, is a third-century Saint. She is supposed to have lived in Egypt and to have suffered martyrdom at the hands of her own father. The legend runs that on his way home, after cutting off her head, this strict pagan parent was struck by lightning.

It is owing to this occurrence that she became the patron saint of artillerymen when cannon began to come into use 11 centuries later.

Makers of fireworks also venerate this Egyptian virgin martyr. So do architects. This is because before her death she was imprisoned in a tower with two windows. St. Barbara changed them into three in honour of the Trinity. *December 8*

Symbolic Regimental Tie

When I mentioned that the French artillery had celebrated the feast of St. Barbara with salvoes against the German lines, I omitted to say that the saint is also remembered by our own Royal Regiment of Artillery.

The lightning which killed the pagan father after he had martyred his daughter caused St. Barbara to become the patron saint of artillerymen. The R.A. regimental tie consists of red zig-zag lines on a dark-blue background.

These represent the lightning of the legend. Very few of those entitled to wear the tie realise its symbolism. *December 13*

Speakers' Chairs

My note on presents to the Speaker, and the way in which time has modified them, brings a letter from a correspondent who reminds me that the phrase, "The Speaker took the chair," had for many years a double meaning.

Until the time of the fire of the Houses of Parliament a century ago it was the recognised practice for the Speaker on retirement to take away his chair.

These elaborate canopied thrones are still to be found in some old country houses. But Capt. FitzRoy will have no regrets at the passing of the old custom. He lives in a small house near Henley-on-Thames.

The Speaker has also lost the right to retain for his personal use the whole of the plate from the official residence. *December 27*

A Bas la B.B.C.

I charge the B.B.C.'s announcers with corrupting the King's English. Recently one of them informed me that "Ravel's imagination peoples the wood with goblins and satires." One might think that accents mean very little to the announcers. Ally, for instance, whether noun or verb, has its stress on the second syllable. The B.B.C. almost invariably accentuates the first. Here are some other surprising errors which I have noticed or which have been pointed out to me:

"Decrease" and "increase," alike as substantive or verb—also "détail" and "rétail" in like manner.

"Longtitude" or "longditude" for "longitude."

"Says"—pronounced with genteel phonetic accuracy.

What infuriates many people, though I cannot say that it sets my teeth on edge, is margarine with a hard "g."

Monte Video and the Pedants

Mr. Winston Churchill, by the way, is an admirable exponent of pronouncing foreign words in the classical English way. For him Nazis are Nazis, not Natsis—just as Mozart used to be Mozart and "Moat-sart" was looked on as an affectation.

In his last broadcast he spoke of Monte Video (with the accent on "vid"), as every English schoolboy used to call the capital of Uruguay—not Urugwy. The B.B.C. pronunciation is Monte Ve-dao.

Admittedly that is how the inhabitants call it. But if we are to pronounce the names of all foreign towns and countries with phonetic accuracy there is no end to our difficulties. Paris, for instance, should become Paree. And there are Brussels and Rome, where we have modified the names to suit ourselves.

So hurrah for Monte VIDeo, I say, and down with the pedants.

December 27

"Marjerine"?

As the result of my paragraphs on B.B.C. English, I have to record activity along the whole pronunciation front.

This is specially marked round the word "margarine." Mr. Frans Jurgens, managing director of Van den Berghs and Jurgens, is definite on the subject. The correct pronunciation, he says, is with the "g" hard and there is no justification for any other.

Many other correspondents, one of whom quotes Greek, support him. "Margarine" has the same derivation as "Margaret," both coming from a Greek word meaning pearl.

Mr. Jurgens tells me that the reason for this is that in one of the processes used in margarine manufacture, when it was invented 70 years ago, an emulsion of thousands of tiny globules was formed. These looked like a mass of pearls.

So no more "marjerine" from the B.B.C. *December 29*

1940

From the Allied point of view 1940 was a year of almost unrelieved anxiety, although it was a year on which the British could look back not without some feeling of pride. The "phoney war", as the stalemate in Western Europe had become known, was broken on April 9 when Hitler invaded Denmark and Norway. Britain and France sent troops to Norway but they were ill-equipped and numerically quite inadequate to withstand the German onslaught, and within six weeks Germany had overrun both countries. The Allied defeat in Norway, however, had one immediate result of incalculable value to their cause. Dissatisfaction with the Government's conduct of affairs led in May to the resignation of Mr. Chamberlain as Prime Minister and the assumption of office by Mr. Winston Churchill at the head of a Coalition Government. Ironically Churchill himself bore no small share of the responsibility for the Norwegian fiasco. As he later wrote, "It was a wonder I survived."

On May 10, the very day of Mr. Chamberlain's resignation, the Germans launched another lightning attack, this time on Holland and Belgium. Holland fell in five days; the Belgians fared little better and on May 28 King Leopold capitulated. Two days earlier the British evacuation from Dunkirk had started and by June 3 it was complete. To the south and west many British troops who had been employed on the lines of communications were left behind, but most of these managed to get away. All heavy equipment was, however, abandoned.

On June 14 the Germans entered Paris and on the 17th the French sued for an armistice which was concluded on the 22nd. The Allies were obliged to face the fact that they had been no more effective, when faced with the might of the German blitzkrieg, *than Poland had been nine months earlier.*

Mussolini, reckoning that the Allies were now facing inevitable defeat, jumped aboard the German bandwagon on June 10.

Hitler now began to make plans for the invasion of Britain, an undertaking which clearly demanded a formidable degree of air and naval superiority. In the middle of August the Battle of Britain began in earnest. It was to last until the middle of September and cost the Germans 1,389 aircraft and the British 792. Far from achieving air superiority the Germans were actually falling behind; more important, they were losing pilots faster than they could train them. So it was decided to concentrate all their efforts on bombing London in one final attempt to crack the morale of the British. It was to have exactly the opposite effect and Hitler was forced to the conclusion that he would have to postpone the invasion of England until the spring of the following year. But as the year closed fires were still smouldering all over the City of London, which had been the target of a great incendiary raid on December 29.

The war in North Africa began on September 13 when the Italians advanced into Egypt. It should be remembered that, at the time, Egypt and Libya respectively formed part of the British and Italian overseas territories and troops were garrisoned there in peacetime as a matter of course. There were about 20,000 British troops in Egypt under General Wavell. The Italian forces under Marshal Graziani numbered 200,000. The Italian advance was halted after five days, the Italians having lost 3,000 men, the British 150. In December the campaign began in earnest. On the 9th the British surrounded the Italian position at Sidi Barrani and took 38,000 prisoners. At the end of the year the Western Desert Force, commanded by General O'Connor, was still on the advance.

In October Italian troops based in Albania invaded Greece, but the Greeks resisted stubbonly and once again the Italians sustained very heavy casualties.

In America President Roosevelt was elected for an unprecedented third term and at the end of the year he announced the introduction of "lend-lease", whereby America would lend Britain not money but actual munitions to the full extent of British needs and American productive capacity.

In such a fleeting survey of so turbulent a year space forbids much mention of events not connected with the war. Exception should be made, however, for the assassination of Leon Trotsky in Mexico City on August 21. Among others who gave up the struggle were Mr. Chamberlain, Lord Tweedsmuir, better known as John Buchan, George Lansbury and Sir Abe Bailey.

Although they are not included here, it is interesting to note that Peterborough, in his frequent references to William Joyce, always refers to him as "Lord Hee-Haw." His addiction to the Eton College Chronicle *as a source of material is particularly noticeable in the year which marked the 500th anniversary of the school's foundation.*

A Mitford Nuisance

Miss Unity Mitford's return would better have been marked by silence. But she has only herself to blame if she finds herself starred in the sensational Press.

In normal times the vagaries of a young woman who uses her social position to try and play a rôle in international politics may be dismissed with a smile. This is a free country, as cranks of every political colour know well enough.

Unfortunately for Miss Mitford, however, the times are not normal, and her vagaries became rather a nuisance. Her wearing of a Swastika badge at election time in Prague in the summer of 1938 infringed the law and caused diplomatic complications. *January 4*

"Ready, Aye Ready"

I spent a few hours in Edinburgh this week-end and admired its preparedness for air raids.

On each table, for instance, in the lounge of one of the principal hotels was a typed sheet of A.R.P. instructions. The last paragraph ran:

"Dining room customers who wish to go to the shelter should tell their waiter, who will present their bill immediately."

January 8

Mr. Churchill's Peaked Cap

What was Mr. Churchill wearing when he went to France last week? According to messages received here, hc was seen on different days in a soft hat with a "white brim" (whatever that may have been), and in a peaked cap.

Although it has been suggested that the latter was a yachting cap, it is more likely to have been the plain peaked cap which, in conjunction with a blue suit, constitutes the correct attire for the First Lord and other civil members of the Board of Admiralty when paying official visits. It was devised by Lord Monsell shortly after be became First Lord.

When Mr. Churchill paid a previous visit to France as First Lord, over a quarter of a century ago, he wore the uniform of an Elder Brother of Trinity House. A story, probably apocryphal, credits him with having replied to an inquiry from his host on the subject. "Je suis un frère ainé de la Trinité," to which the duly impressed Frenchman responded "Mon Dieu!" *January 10*

Sub-Machine Gun v. Rifle

Gen. Sir Hubert Gough is interested to read that the Finnish infantryman is armed with a light machine gun. He advocated this in some articles which he wrote for *The Daily Telegraph* as long ago as March, 1934.

It has also not escaped his notice that "an army much nearer home"—as he put it to me—is also discarding the rifle and bayonet for the sub-machine gun.

In regretting that our General Staff seems to be slow in assimilating new ideas, Sir Hubert thinks that they may be too busy dealing with the vital question of officers wearing woollen scarves.

This side of soldiering has never appealed to him. He tells me he is glad to say that his confidential report of 1895, when he was a young captain in the 16th Lancers, contained this severe stricture: "He takes no interest in dress." *February 16*

Van Eyck—1872 and 1940

I am enabled to state that Van Eyck's great picture, "The Three Marys at the Sepulchre," is to remain in this country.

In making his great purchase of a portion of the Cook Collection at Doughty House Mr. Nathan Katz, the Dutch art dealer, assures me that notwithstanding his offer of over £100,000 for this very famous picture, no bid could be entertained by the Cook trustees. I gather than it is ear-marked for the nation whenever public funds are again available for art.

The late Sir Herbert Cook's grandfather, Sir Francis Cook, acting on the advice of Sir Charles Robinson, Queen Victoria's Surveyor of Pictures, was able to buy it for only 315 guineas at Christie's in 1872. Collectors were then falling over each other to acquire the story-telling pictures of living Royal Academicians.

A few weeks after the Van Eyck had fetched this paltry sum a work by Thomas Webster, R.A., illustrating Charles Lamb's "Essay on Roast Pig," was bought by a Middlesbrough ironmaster for 2,500 guineas. *March 21*

"Peace with Honour"

Lord Wakefield told a City audience yesterday that it was at Guildhall that Lord Beaconsfield used the phrase "Peace with honour," to describe the result of the Berlin Congress of 1878.

I always understood that the occasion was when he was speaking from a window of 10, Downing Street, though it is quite likely that he repeated the words at a Guildhall banquet. He certainly did not coin the phrase, which had been used by Burke in a speech on conciliation with America a century before.

But he realised its value as a slogan, as is shown by the fact that he employed it on another occasion many years before he went to Berlin. *April 26*

The Pope and the Duce

The difference of opinion between the Fascist régime and the Holy See is, I learn, going much deeper than is generally believed. Relations between the Vatican City and Mussolini are seriously strained.

Pius XII is opposed to the entry of Italy into a conflict, especially on Germany's side. There is evidence that he personally warned Signor Mussolini against the risks of a war fought by Italy in alliance with the Nazis.

The Pope, I understand, has gone so far as to threaten openly that in the event of Italy joining Germany he will be compelled to leave the Vatican City and go to Portugal.

A point stressed by the Vatican is that the Pope cannot be cut off from contact with the great Roman Catholic community. Were Italy to become a belligerent this would inevitably happen to him. *May 3*

Anti-Communist Drive

The Socialist party purge continues. An Indian, Mr. V. K. Krishna Menon, Socialist candidate for Dundee, is the latest to fall under the disciplinary axe. Action has been taken against him, not by headquarters, but by the local organisation.

His candidature has been withdrawn by the Dundee Trades and Labour Council because, it is stated, he spoke at a meeting of a body associated with the Communists.

Transport House had originally endorsed his fitness as a candidate. But in view of their strong line against heterodoxy I forecast that no objection will be taken to the action of the local Socialists. *May 5*

Churchill's Oratory

Mr. Churchill's survey of the war situation yesterday was the best speech that has been made in the House since the war began. Apart from his brief request for a vote of confidence when he formed his Government—when he spoke for only eight minutes—it was his first real speech in the Commons since he became Prime Minister.

He used all his powers of oratory to the full, and held the House spellbound as he unfolded the story of the withdrawal of the B.E.F. and their French comrades.

True B.E.F. Insularity

More than ever he was resolutely insular in his pronunciation of foreign place-names, a trait which has the full approval of the men of the B.E.F. Amiens was pronounced like aliens with an "m" substituted for the "l." Abbeville was two distinct words, Abbey Ville.

His Narzi has already succeeded in introducing the right touch of scorn into one's abhorrence of the National Socialist party. Even Napoleon's Grande Armée became the Grand Army. *June 5*

The "L.D.V.s"

A number of ex-Service men, including majors and captains, have joined the Local Defence Volunteers. They are known as the "Long Dentured Veterans." *June 10*

R.A.F. Problem

A friend who has just passed into the R.A.F. as a pilot tells me he failed hopelessly in one question in the intelligence test. He was set this problem:

You are in a completely dark room and can see nothing. In front of you is a tray with 10 white socks and 10 black socks. What is the smallest number of socks you must pick up and take away in order to be sure you have a pair—either a pair of black or a pair of white?

His answer was 11, but he realised when he came away that this was wrong. *June 18*

The Other Winston Churchill

The Prime Minister's American namesake, Mr. Winston Churchill, the author, is, I hear, about to publish his first book for more than 20 years. This is "The Uncharted Way," a psychological analysis of Christianity.

In their younger days the two Mr. Churchills were constantly confused, especially in the U.S., where the American's novel, "The Inside of the Cup," was a best seller before the last war.

It is due to this that the Prime Minister's name always appears as Winston S. Churchill on the title-page of any book he has written. Some 40 years ago he wrote to the American Mr. Churchill suggesting that, if both were to continue writing, one or other had better change his name. The American replied that, as he was three years the senior, it was not for him to do so. Our Mr. Churchill agreed and thereafter inserted the "S." *June 24*

Short Cut to Economy

A journalist working at the Ministry of Information submitted some "copy" for censorship. He was summoned by the censor, who said he could not accept the material because it consisted of two different stories on the same sheet of paper.

The writer could not persuade the censor to join him in his paper-saving campaign; there was a regulation about it. Finally he cut the paper across and handed in the two separate sheets.

The censor was full of admiration. "I had not thought of that," was his comment. *June 25*

Black and White

The question in the R.A.F. intelligence test which I mentioned recently has brought me many solutions. The correct ones are surprisingly few. Here is the problem:

You are in a completely dark room and can see nothing. In front of you is a tray with 10 white socks and 10 black socks. What is the smallest number of socks you must pick up and take away in order to be sure you have a pair—either a pair of black or a pair of white?

If you reason as follows its presents no difficulties: From the table you take a sock which may be either black or white. You take another. Either this makes a pair of white or black, or you have one white and one black sock. You therefore lift another, which may make three white or three black socks, but must make two of one colour or the other.

The answer, therefore, is three. *July 1*

Orders Is Orders

A Local Defence Volunteer in a lonely spot cried "Halt!" to a man in a car, who promptly halted.

"Halt!" said the L.D.V. again.

"I have halted," said the motorist. "What do you want me to do next?"

"I don't know," said the L.D.V. "My orders are to say 'Halt!' three times and then shoot." *July 15*

L.D.V.s' New Name

The Prime Minister, speaking in his broadcast of the Local Defence Volunteers, added "or, as they are much better called, the Home Guard." To the public the name will be a new one though Mr. Churchill's phrase suggests that it is current in Whitehall.

I shall be interested to see whether as the result of the Premier's imprimatur it becomes generally current.

Sir Herbert Morgan, in a letter to *The Daily Telegraph* on May 28, said that "parashot" was a confusing sobriquet for the anti-parachutist forces and suggested calling them Ironsides.

Sir Edmund Ironside adopted this title for his mobile Regular troops, though I am unaware how far it is popularly used in the Army. Certainly "parashots" is now dead, and to-day "L.D.V.s" holds the field.

Nothing is more difficult than inducing the public, once it has chosen a name of this kind, to change it for another, even an obviously better one. *July 16*

Canadian Kipling

Yesterday at lunch I met the Canadian Rudyard Kipling. He is Mr. Robert Service, whose ballads on Canadian life are known in every Dominion household.

Mr. Service is in his sixties, has a fair complexion, almost white hair and talks with a soft Scots accent. He left his villa near St. Malo in the middle of June and hopes to fly to his home in Vancouver.

He began writing poems for pleasure and found by accident that they were profitable. When a bank clerk in Klondyke he sent a collection of them to a firm of publishers, with a cheque to defray their cost of publication.

Some time later he received a letter saying that their salesmen had advance orders for 17,000 copies. They suggested a contract on a normal percentage basis.

The book was "Songs of a Sourdough." Its sale is now nearly 2,000,000 copies. *July 17*

Young England's Response

The private schoolboy has found a way of bringing his weekly letter home to a graceful conclusion.

This is how one ended an unusually short Sunday letter: "I am afraid I must close now as the rest is of military importance."

July 20

Refugee Makes Good

Artur Schnabel, formerly a German national, was at one time the biggest draw for London audiences of any pianist. He has now settled in New York.

His actor son, Stefan, is also in America. A publicity agent called on him recently. After drawing Mr. Schnabel out about himself, she said, "Are your parents in America?" "Yes." "And your father—what does he do?"

Mr. Schnabel said his father was Artur Schnabel. "I see. But what does he do?" "He's a pianist," Stefan said. "He played at Carnegie Hall several times this season."

"That's nice," the lady beamed. "I'm always so glad to hear of a refugee getting on well." *July 29*

Those Tough Maiden Aunts

An evacuated preparatory school boy has two maiden aunts who live at X.Y.

In a letter home, after evincing anxiety about the safety of his father and mother, he asks: "Have any bombs dropped on X.Y. yet? If so, don't let them worry you, as it does not worry me in the slightest." *July 30*

R.A.F. Latin

A certain fighter-bomber squadron has been thinking up a motto.

They wanted something classical on the lines of "Per ardua . . ." Many suggestions were made. At last a pilot noted for his sang-froid suggested "No Bono Panico"—No good getting the wind up.

August 3

H.G. First Cavalry

A signal honour has just been paid the mounted Home Guard recruited from the Devon and Somerset Staghounds. This is an inspection by Field-Marshal Lord Cavan. It was held in a field adjoining the Hunt kennels and the unit mustered in force.

When the story of the Home Guard comes to be written, the Devon and Somerset Staghounds means to establish its claim to rank as the senior mounted unit. It held its first mounted parade on May 21, and ever since has regularly patrolled the moors.

N.W. Frontier to Exmoor

The unit has had three C.O.s. The first was the Master, Mr. S. L. Hancock, who soon afterwards was called up. One of the joint secretaries, Mr. Bernard Waley Cohen, succeeded him.

Now Mr. Waley Cohen is required for Government work, and Col. R. Alexander, former Master of the Exmoor Foxhounds, takes his place.

Col. Alexander, in his service on the North-West Frontier of India, has realised the advantages of mechanisation. But I have not heard that so far he entertains any project to mechanise the Home Guard of the Devon and Somerset Staghounds. *August 9*

"Scram"

"The enemy is over there—scram," was a platoon commander's order. His men understood it and "scrammed" most effectively.

"Scram" is one of the new words to find their way into the military vocabulary. Many military commands have been shortened. Some of them have not been officially sanctioned.

To-day officers have considerable licence in coining short, snappy words to convey the meaning of the enterprise to be carried out with speed, spirit and resolution.

None of them is snappier than the classical American effort: "Into fours—git." *August 22*

B.N.C.'s Reputation

In "Memory Hold-the-Door," the late Lord Tweedsmuir's just-published book of memoirs, there is a story about Lord Haig that is new to me.

It goes back to the Boer War, when the young officer who was then John Buchan had to carry dispatches to Haig, then Chief of Staff to Gen. French. He had been, as they both knew, at the same college at Oxford. Buchan overslept in the train and had only just time to leap out of the carriage at Colesberg in his pyjamas and a British-warm. So arrayed, he took his dispatches to the general's quarters.

Haig glanced at him as he took the papers. All he said was, "Brasenose never was a dressy college." *August 27*

Judge's Obiter Dictum

The words of Mr. Justice Humphreys, in dismissing the appeal of the Leeds murderer, Wright, are likely to be remembered with grim amusement in the Inns of Court. I have never heard the popular idea, that motive must be proved in a prosecution for murder, more drily and devastatingly treated. The judge said:

> No motive was suggested why the murder should have been committed by the appellant. On the other hand, provable motive was equally absent on the part of the rest of the inhabitants of this country.

In other words, if all the evidence clearly points one way, discussion about motive is moonshine. As Lord Chief Justice Coleridge said long ago, most murders are common assaults that have had an unfortunate termination. *August 28*

There's No Fun Like Work

A request for hospitality in Scotland was made for Australian soldiers on leave. One of the replies it produced was as follows:

> Hospitality in Scotland for Australians. Many farmers in Scotland are willing to take Australian soldiers into their homes while on leave. These men will be charged £1 per week, and will only be required to work should they themselves desire.

It is now posted on the orderly room board of an Australian unit somewhere in England. *September 13*

Likes Fast Bowling

The political future of Lord Dunglass* has been discussed with some interest. His experience as Mr. Chamberlain's Parliamentary Private Secretary would certainly qualify him for promotion to a Government post now that his chief has resigned.

I am told that he may shortly take up a military appointment. For some years he has been a major in the Lanarkshire Yeomanry.

There is some doubt, however, whether he is medically fit. His indifferent health has been keeping him away lately from the House of Commons.

Lord Dunglass served Mr. Chamberlain as P.P.S. for more than four years. The association began when Mr. Chamberlain was Chancellor of the Exchequer.

Parliamentary cricketers regretted that secretarial duties often kept Lord Dunglass away from the cricket field. Like the late Peter Eckersley he was one of the few bats in the side who could face really fast bowling. *October 12*

*Now Lord Home of the Hirsel.

A Kennedy as Author

Mr. John Kennedy, son of the American Ambassador, has just produced his first book. The young Harvard man has done this at an age when undergraduates at Cambridge, England, are concentrating on their triposes.

His book, almost needless to say, deals with the things uppermost in his mind during the last two years, when he was watching British affairs through his own and his father's eyes. He calls it "Why England Slept."

Mr. Henry R. Luce, proprietor of Time, Life, and Fortune, in a foreword describes it as the most dispassionate account of British pre-war policy yet written. That, I think, is a not undeserved tribute.

Mr. Luce on Roosevelt

Mr. Luce also makes one or two remarks of his own. Talking of the Presidential election, he wonders whether Mr. Roosevelt believes America is ever going to fight—or alternatively whether he is "just playing politics."

As regards Mr. Wendell Willkie Mr. Luce says:

"All his genius of personality and industrial management will be bitter ashes in our mouths if Mr. Willkie goes forth to prepare for a war which he leads us to believe isn't really ever going to happen."

The author, by the way, dedicates the book to his father and mother. *October 17*

Cecil Rhodes—

Lt-Col. Frank Johnson, in his book of reminiscences, "Great Days," which appears to-day, tells the story of the origin of Rhodesia. In December, 1889, at breakfast at the Kimberley Club, he met Cecil Rhodes, then faced with the problem of occupying Mashonaland.

He had been told that a force of 2,500 would be the minimum. When he repeated this to the author, then a young man of 23, he replied, "Two thousand five hundred men is absurd," adding that 250 would be enough.

After breakfast Rhodes asked him to work out the cost. He did so between breakfast and lunch and found it would be £87,500.

Rhodes was enthusiastic and offered him the leadership of the expedition. Johnson refused and left for Cape Town that evening.

—and Rhodesia

Six days later he received a wire from Rhodes asking him to meet him at Cape Town station at 7.30 the next morning. Rhodes then repeated his offer, which was again refused. They walked up and down outside the station for two hours. "We must have that country for the Empire," Rhodes said.

Finally Johnson said:

> All right, you win. I'll go. But only under one condition. You give me a cheque for £87,500, supply me with field and machine-guns, rifles and ammunition, and I will undertake to hand Mashonaland over to you fit for civil government within nine months. But I want you to remember that I am not your servant but your contractor.

Rhodes walked on in silence for over 100 yards. Then he stopped suddenly and said, "I will give you the cheque. Now let us go to Poole's and get some breakfast."

That was the beginning of Rhodesia. *November 7*

Inventor of Syllabics

The centenary of a remarkable achievement by a forgotten genius occurs this month. He was James Evans, a Methodist missionary whom the Hudson's Bay Company sent out to the Cree Indians in 1840.

Finding he could not express the language in ordinary characters, he invented the method known as Cree Syllabics. This is now used for many languages in Polynesia and Asia, as well as for those of the American Indians.

Evans also cut and cast type, the metal being lead from bullets. Ink he made with chimney soot mixed with fish-fat. His paper was birch bark.

The printing press was one of the company's fur presses. He only obtained permission to use this grudgingly and on condition it was to be employed for printing only the Bible and hymns. Some of his books exist in Canadian museums.

Admired by Savants

There is no more honoured name among the few savants who are interested in semantics. The late Sir Denison Ross used to marvel at James Evans's invention of syllabics.

I remember him saying that since history began there had been only two mental concepts by which language could be written down —the pictorial (ideographic) and the alphabetical. "Then this fellow comes along and produces an entirely fresh notion."

Evans has found no place in our literary Pantheon—the Dictionary of National Biography. *November 8*

Maugham on Eliot

"Perhaps you don't all of you know that the most famous poet living in England to-day is an American bank clerk from Boston. If we have a great poet in England to-day, it is T. S. Eliot." I quote Mr. Somerset Maugham speaking in New York.

Mr. Maugham went on to talk of T. S. Eliot's thrilling and original poetry, and added that the most stimulating and significant verse now being written in England by our young poets bears Eliot's mark.

These observations provoked another speaker, Carl Sandburg, poet and historian of Abraham Lincoln, to express violent disagreement. "T. S. Eliot," declared Mr. Sandburg, "is anti-democratic . . . he is mediaevalist . . . he is royalist . . . and he's so close to Fascist that I'm off him, to use a truck-driver's phrase."

So there it is. *November 16*

Retort Feminine

An Oslo girl sitting in the lounge of an hotel was approached by a German officer asking her to dance. She refused, and shortly afterwards he returned and spoke in rather a threatening tone.

'Is it because I am a German?' he inquired.

"Oh, no," she said, smiling sweetly, "not at all. It is merely because I am a Norwegian." *November 25*

Churchillian Oratory

The men of a section of our coast defences are delighted with a visit paid to them recently by Mr. Churchill and with the speech he made at the end of it. The weather was bitter, and the men were lined up growing visibly colder as he completed his inspection.

He advanced to the microphone and the troops were wondering whether any oratory, even Mr. Churchill's, could make them forget the cold.

Mr. Churchill spoke. "If the clods come," he said, "push them back into the sea. Good-day to you." *December 2*

When Bonar Law Resigned

Sir Ronald Waterhouse when he served three Prime Ministers as Principal Private Secretary was known as the Oyster. Lady Waterhouse in "Private and Official," which is to appear at the end of the week, makes amends. One of the stories she tells is how Lord Baldwin became Prime Minister in 1923.

Owing to the state of his health Mr. Bonar Law was unable to offer his resignation personally. In his letter to the King he had offered no guidance as to his successor. This was taken to the Royal Pavilion by his son-in-law, Sir Frederick Sykes. Sir Ronald Waterhouse accompanied him.

King George's first thought was to send for Lord Curzon. The difficulty of his being in the House of Lords was considered and overruled. So, too, with the question whether Lord Curzon could continue as Foreign Secretary if he became Prime Minister.

Finding a Premier

King George seemed to have made up his mind when Sir Ronald suggested another obstacle. He pointed out that many M.P.s thought Lord Curzon would be unsuitable. He represented that section of privileged conservatism which in these changing days could not be too assiduously exploited.

The King paced backwards and forwards between Queen Mary, who was standing by the fireplace, and Sir Ronald in the centre of the room. He suggested calling a meeting of the Privy Council.

Sir Ronald proposed consulting two ex-Presidents of the Council, Mr. Balfour and Lord Salisbury, and the Conservative leaders of the two Houses—Lord Curzon and Mr. Baldwin.

This Queen Mary supported, but King George still considered Lord Curzon's claim to the Premiership as outstanding.

"Baldwin—I'm Afraid"

Sir Ronald Waterhouse, however, that morning had had a talk with Mr. Bonar Law which he had been pledged not to reveal. He now decided that this must be divulged and asked the King's permission to repeat it textually.

He had pressed his chief to name a successor. The Prime Minister had refused. "You must tell me," said Sir Ronald, "what your answer would be if you should have to give it."

B.L.: "But I would not and I will not."

Ronald: "If I give you my word of honour to preserve your confidence?"

B.L.: "In that case . . . I am afraid . . . I should have to say—Baldwin."

It was thus that King George, though he consulted the various personalities mentioned in the conversation, decided to ask Mr. Baldwin to form a Government. *December 2*

Far-sighted General

Sir Archibald Wavell has successfully solved a problem which he visualised as the result of the trend towards Army mechanisation when he wrote his book, "The Palestine Campaigns," published in 1928.

Discussing the power of mobility and drawing comparisons between cavalry of the traditional type and mechanised cavalry, he put this question:

> How would a small mechanised force, though greatly superior in fighting power to a mass of cavalry, have dealt with a multitude of prisoners?

"It is a problem," he added, "that may puzzle a mechanised force some day."

His Own Query Answered

That day has come and Sir Archibald happens to be the man to discover a solution. He held the view that a mechanised force would often require the co-operation of a force capable of fighting on foot.

Such a force would be able to secure tactical features which denied freedom of movement to mechanical vehicles. He pointed out that this co-operation would also assist in solving the problem of handling large numbers of prisoners. *December 16*

Collecting Made Easy

The impending sale of another assortment of the vast collections of Mr. W. R. Hearst, the American newspaper millionaire, will be a major event in the New York art dealers' world.

He has always had, however, a lavish manner in purchasing. When he heard of a good thing going anywhere he would cable to his agents to buy it, and that was that.

He bought his famous castle in Wales, St. Donat's, without having seen it. "Buy St. Donat's" was the order. His agent, also without having seen it, bought it. Now it is leased to the Government for the duration.

Once Mr. Hearst took a fancy to collect ancient church tapestries from Europe. When the first consignment arrived at New York it was found that the rooms of the Hearst palatial flat were not lofty enough to display the treasures.

The remedy was simple. Mr. Hearst took the flat above and had the intervening floor and ceiling removed. The result, if odd, was undeniably impressive.

When one is worth £40,000,000 one can afford to gratify a little whim from time to time. *December 31*

1941

The two major events of this year were the German invasion of Russia and Japan's attack on Pearl Harbour, with the result that, whereas at the beginning of the year the British Empire had faced the enemy alone, by its close Russia and the United States had joined in the struggle. Since the major countries of the world are all now involved in the war it is easier to follow the course of events theatre by theatre rather than looking at them country by country.

In North Africa General Wavell's troops continued their rapid advance which finally halted at El Agheila, 150 miles south-west of Benghazi. 130,000 Italians were taken prisoner, though at no time throughout the campaign did the strength of the entire British force exceed 31,000 men. But in January Hitler decided to go to the aid of his less martial ally and in April Rommel launched a counter-offensive which in a few weeks took back practically all the territory that had been gained during the winter.

Troops had been withdrawn from North Africa to go to Greece where once again Germany had come to the assistance of her ally. The German army entered Yugoslavia on April 6 and had reached Athens by the 27th. The last Imperial troops left Greece on May 2, prepared to make a further stand on the island of Crete. This intention was frustrated, however, by the first invasion in history based solely on the use of airborne infantry. The attack was ultimately successful but the German casualties were so high that they never again attempted an airborne invasion.

In November General Auchinleck, lately Commander-in-Chief in India, who had exchanged commands with General Wavell, launched a massive tank offensive and by the end of the year the Germans had been driven back out of Cyrenaica.

The German invasion of Russia began on June 22 and the impetus of the attack was such that vast areas of Russian territory were soon in German hands. By November they had reached Rostov in the south and were approaching Moscow, while in the north Leningrad was already entering the fourth month of its epic siege. At the end of November, however, the Russians staged a remarkable recovery and the entire German army from the Baltic to the Black Sea fell back, on the lame excuse that they were straightening their line. The appalling suffering inflicted on the invaders by the Russian winter could not be concealed from the

German people at home and the situation became so critical that Hitler assumed personal command of his armies, which, he said, would henceforward be guided by his intuition. By the year's end the campaign had already cost each side a million men. British reaction to the invasion of Russia was that enemies of the Nazis were allies of Great Britain, notwithstanding differences of creed, and Churchill at once promised Russia the fullest aid.

In the Far East Japan had for some time been baring her fangs for war. In September, 1940, she had signed a pact with Germany and Italy whereby she would come to Germany's aid if America entered the war on Britain's side. In the west, however, it was felt that Japan was too fully committed in her struggle with China to embark on any further military adventures, a belief which was fostered by a Japanese mission to Washington to discuss American/Japanese relations. But the talks were mere pretence and on December 7, 1941, a large Japanese force under Admiral Nagumo attacked the U.S. Fleet in Pearl Harbour, inflicting enormous damage. The following day Great Britain and the United States declared war on Japan, and Japanese troops landed in north-east Malaya. Two days later the Japanese sank the British battleships Repulse *and* Prince of Wales, *the only two British capital ships in the Far East, and by Christmas Day Hong Kong had fallen.*

At sea British policy was based on the blockade of Germany, whose aim was to prevent American lease-lend supplies from reaching Great Britain. Happily, by the beginning of the year the Americans had come to see that their future and that of Great Britain were indivisible. Co-operation steadily increased and on August 14 Roosevelt and Churchill signed the Atlantic Charter.

The most notable single event of the war at sea was the sinking of the veteran HMS Hood *on May 24 by the German battleship* Bismarck *and the swift retribution meted out by British naval and air forces when the* Bismarck *herself was sunk three days later.*

One event not connected with any particular theatre of war which deserves a mention was the arrival in Scotland by parachute of Rudolf Hess, Hitler's Deputy and greatest friend. He was made a prisoner-of-war, as indeed, to all intents and purposes, he remains to this day.

At home neither bombing, rationing, the Home Guard nor Civil

Defence could prevent people's brave endeavours to carry on as normal. The Derby, run at Newmarket, was won by Owen Tudor at 25–1. The Eton and Harrow match, played at Eton, was won by the home team by 136 runs; and the M.C.C. took a team to Rugby to celebrate the anniversary of the match described in Tom Brown's Schooldays.

The world of literature was impoverished by the loss of Mrs Virginia Woolf, who drowned herself, and by the deaths of James Joyce and Sir Hugh Walpole. Kaiser Wilhelm II also died, after twenty-two years in exile.

Peterborough repeatedly makes it clear that he had no love for the Scots and could not resist telling jokes at their expense, one of which is included here. He also endeavoured to keep his readers cheerful, in spite of all, with a barrage of perfectly appalling puns. Here is a sample: "Hitler is reported to have fallen foul of some of his generals. Surely a case of the pot calling the Keitel black."

Greater Than The Chief

Mr. Duff Cooper is telling this story against himself. He was challenged recently by a Home Guard sentry at the Ministry of Information who demanded to see his pass.

He replied that he was the Minister, but the sentry persisted. "I do not think you understood," said Mr. Duff Cooper. "I am the Minister of Information." The sentry was firm. "I am sorry, sir," he said, "but I should still have to see your pass, even if you were Sir Walter Monckton himself." *January 6*

41 Years for a Sequel?

Mr. James Joyce, who has died at Zurich after an intestinal operation, had constantly visited that town to consult doctors. He used to go there for his eyes, and he underwent a dozen major eye operations in the past 10 years.

Some time ago Dr. Alfred Vogt, of Zurich, who numbers Mr. de Valera and Dr. Axel Munthe among his patients, succeeded in making an artificial pupil for Mr. Joyce's left eye, set below the position of the normal pupil.

It is two years since Mr. Joyce's last book, "Finnegans Wake," appeared. It took him 17 years to write. Its predecessor, "Ulysses," occupied him for seven years.

At this rate of progression a sequel to "Finnegans Wake" would, I calculate, have taken him 41 years to complete.

Reading and Understanding

Personally I have always thought that Lewis Carroll, in "The Jabberwock," turned gibberish to better account than Joyce.

Most people who have ploughed through "Ulysses" are, I fancy, in the position of Mr. Bernard Miles's rustic in "Diversion No. 2" at Wyndham's. He proudly says, "I could read when I was a boy—but not so as to understand it."

One reason for Mr. Joyce's strange desire to enrich or to destroy the English language—I have never been sure which was his aim—may have been his own remarkable powers as a linguist.

He was teaching in a Berlitz school while he wrote "Ulysses." He spoke perfect Italian and French, fluent German, and had a good knowledge of Erse and half a dozen other tongues, including Lapp. *January 14*

Monopoly of Scarlet

The 1941 Vatican year book, the "Annuario Pontificio," shows 15 vacancies in the Sacred College of Cardinals, 55 instead of the full complement of 70. Pius XII has reigned for 22 months, and has not yet bestowed a single Red Hat. In fact, no Cardinal has been created for three years.

It is unlikely that the Pope will make any new creations while the war lasts. Should there be an appointment the new Cardinal might have some trouble in obtaining his robes. I am told there is only one manufacturer in the world who has the correct scarlet dye for cardinalitial dress, and he is a Herr Burtscheid of Aachen.

It is a jealously guarded secret and has been a monopoly of the Burtscheid family for three centuries. *January 28*

Those Bullish Cows

At a recent meeting of local millers and corn chandlers in Exeter an official form was produced giving details of the rationing of cattle foods.

Among the various classes of livestock were included "Bulls, two years, and Bulls, under one year—Male and Female." *February 14*

Our Inventive Premier

Mr. Churchill, always the Nazis' bête noire, is now said by them to have invented the incendiary leaves "which British airmen drop on German territory, particularly on farms."

I take this information from the Deutsche Allgemeine Zeitung, the German paper making the discovery. It reveals that Mr. Churchill learned such methods "when he fought for Spain 40 years ago in the Cuban War of Independence."

To add verisimilitude to an otherwise bald and unconvincing narrative it quotes a picturesque passage purporting to have come from a report made at the time by Mr. Churchill to the British Government:

Cuban native rebels are setting sugar-cane crops on fire by attaching phosphorous plaques to the tails of reptiles. The wax is set on fire by the rays of the sun, causing the phosphorus to burn. The fields catch fire rapidly without it being possible to discover who did it.

The Deutsche Allgemeine Zeitung comes to the crashing conclusion: "There is no doubt that the British Premier is the guilty party to this sort of crime committed by British pilots."

February 15

Napoleon and Hitler

Sir Charles Petrie, now working on a book about the Napoleonic wars, tells me that he has come on something very topical. This was a report from Napoleon to the Directory. It was dated Feb. 23, 1798.

Napoleon had been on an inspection of the "invasion ports" between Etaples and Ostend. His conclusions were:

(1) France could not gain supremacy at sea for some years.
(2) Without that no operation could be more hazardous than an invasion of England.
(3) A surprise was only possible in the long winter nights.
(4) Their preparations were too backward for such an attempt that year.

Napoleon, at the time a General under the Directory, then obtained permission to strike at Great Britain in the Eastern Mediterranean. His abortive Egyptian campaign was the result.

February 24

Menzies—Mingies

The Australian Premier's pronunciation of his name as it is written has caused a Scottish Menzies to send me a Limerick:

There was a young lady named Menzies
Who said, "Do you know what this thenzies?"
Her aunt with a gasp
Said, "My dear, it's a wasp,
And you're holding the end where the stenzies."

After that I need not emphasise that Menzies north of the Tweed is pronounced Mingies. *March 1*

Evasive Action

A Flight Lieutenant who had been given command of a squadron rang up the Directorate of Postings at the Air Ministry.

"I want Pilot Off. Jones posted to my squadron," he said, "And I want him posted now. I don't want any of the inefficiency your department is known for."

"Do you know whom you are speaking to?" said the voice at the other end.

"No."

"I am Air Marshal Brown."

"And do you know whom you are speaking to?"

"No."

"Thank God for that," said the young officer, and rang off.

March 20

Capital of Bloomsbury

Mrs. Virginia Woolf, whose death is presumed, did not long survive the tall house which she had made the capital of literary Bloomsbury.

A German bomb tore it rudely in half some time ago, leaving exposed to the public eye the mural paintings by Duncan Grant and Vanessa Bell, Mrs. Virginia Woolf's sister, with which the living rooms were decorated.

The house, round which for 20 years so many writers revolved, was the home of the Hogarth Press as well as of Leonard and Virginia Woolf. She wrote either there, in a large, half-subterranean room, surrounded by unbound books, parcels and MSS, or at her cottage in Sussex.

Classic Spoof

To many of those who revered Mrs. Woolf as the austere, uncrowned Queen of Bloomsbury it may come as a surprise to know that, as Virginia Stephen, she took part in the most elaborate prank ever perpetrated by that famous practical joker Horace Cole, brother of Mrs. Neville Chamberlain.

Wearing a false beard and Oriental robes, she was one of the retinue of the fake African potentate. This "Sultan" was solemnly received by a British admiral and the entire ship's company of the warship to which, with Cole as cicerone, a "state" visit was paid.

April 4

Florence Nightingale II

The death of Sister Agnes removes the most dynamic figure in the history of contemporary nursing. Miss Agnes Keyser, who has often been compared with Florence Nightingale, founded King Edward VII's Hospital for Officers in 1899.

From being a social figure, interested in racing and sport, she became the matron of a hospital which henceforth was her life's work.

King Edward had known her when he was Prince of Wales. Owing to him she was able to continue with her hospital after the South African War was over.

Throughout his reign he watched the progress of her work and often dropped in for a chat at the hospital in Grosvenor Crescent which had formerly been her private house.

Succeeding generations of the Royal family kept up the friendship. At Balmoral she was frequently the only visitor outside the Royal circle.

Four Cigarettes a Day

Small, with searching blue eyes and a quick manner, she ruled benignly yet firmly both patients and doctors. In the last war the number of her nursing homes grew to five or six.

Everywhere she insisted on her rules being strictly kept. One of these, a maximum of four cigarettes a day, her patients sometimes tried to evade.

They were rarely successful. *May 14*

Stage and Church

Miss Jenny Dolly, one of the Dolly Sisters, who has died in the United States, at one time enjoyed a special fame in Oxford, thanks to a bearded and venerable-looking ecclesiastic.

He was Dr. Darwell Stone, for 35 years Principal of Pusey House, who died last February. He possessed a caustic humour altogether belied by his patriarchal appearance, his long sermons, and his patristic learning.

A freshman anxious to draw him out asked Dr. Darwell Stone what he thought of the Dolly Sisters. "Let me see now," he answered gravely, "are they a Roman Catholic or an Anglican Order?"

The retort flourished in the university for years. *June 4*

End of Eton Jackets?

An Old Etonian has, as I imagine, settled the question whether Eton boys are to continue to wear the black tail coats and Eton jackets which I believe they first adopted as mourning for George III. Mr. Oliver Lyttelton's rationing scheme looks like making some sort of change inevitable.

It is obvious that schoolboys will have to wear the same clothes in the holidays as they do at school. So I suppose that Eton boys in a few months will begin to appear in grey or blue suits.

As the Eton dress has already been under fire for some time I doubt whether there will be any reversion to the old order after the war.

At the same time the conservatives might still fight a battle for the most distinctive part of the school dress. Top hats do not come under the rationing scheme. *June 4*

Historical Form

On June 16, 1487, the army of Henry VII, grandson of Owen Tudor, defeated the army of Lambert Simnel at Stoke-on-Trent. On June 18 the Pretender was languishing as Henry's prisoner, and was contemptuously made a scullion.

To-day, June 18, 1941, Lambert Simnel is favoured to beat Owen Tudor in the Derby at Newmarket. Let those who back horses from omens rather than a study of the form book make what they can of it.*

As the history professor said to his wife at breakfast yesterday: "I have been advised to back a horse in the Derby, dear, but I cannot think of the name. Ah, now I remember—Perkin Warbeck!"

June 18

M.O.I. Experts

Mr. Hamish Hamilton, the publisher, has joined the American Division of the Ministry of Information. Hitherto he has been serving in the Military Intelligence.

In his new job he will be very much at home. Mr. Hamilton knows the journalists and writers of New York almost as well as he does those of London. Two Americans on his more recent publishing lists have been Clare Boothe and Virginia Cowles.

*Owen Tudor won at 25–1.

Mr. Douglas Williams, the head of the American Division of the Ministry of Information, believes in having experts for dealing with Press and publicity work. He has already recruited four Fleet Street journalists who learnt their America on the spot.

To them he now adds a publisher. *June 24*

Admiral into Ham

In the recent Common Entrance Examination the candidates were asked to translate into French the phrase "Admiral Cunningham." A boy of 12 entered for Oundle obviously liked the question. His version was "Amiral Rusé-Jambon."

I feel sure the Admiral himself will enjoy the answer. *June 26*

Should He Pay?

After two years of married life the wife of an Aberdonian was suddenly taken ill, and was successfully operated on for acute appendicitis. The surgeon said to the husband, "Your wife is lucky to be alive. She should have been operated on three years ago."

The Aberdonian sent the bill to his father-in-law. *June 28*

What H.M.S. Means

Lord Halifax is telling his friends in Washington a story about a British sailor. He belonged to a British warship being repaired in an American yard, and was sight-seeing in Boston when a woman stopped him. She proceeded to ask him what the letters H.M.S. on his hat stood for.

He replied, "High mustn't say." *July 15*

Sands of the Desert

I have already referred to the written conundrums and the picture puzzles which the psychologists are using to discover the "mental age" of Army recruits. I am now told that as a last resort a form of oral examination imported from America and known as the "Kent" test is being tried.

Men who appear backward are gently asked a series of questions such as "What are houses made of?" and "Why does the moon look bigger than the stars?" Marks are awarded in accordance with the degree of appropriateness of the answers.

Thus, if when asked "What is sand used for?" a recruit replies, "To make glass," he is given four marks, but only two if his answer is "For industrial purposes." Only a single mark is given if he says for scrubbing or for play.

The examiner himself was puzzled, however, what marks to award to the young soldier who told him: "Sand is mainly used for camels to walk on." *August 18*

Diplomats in Iran

The diplomatic quarter of Teheran, where many eager discussions are now taking place, is a sight worth seeing. It stands a little apart from the colourful city which centres on the Shah's official palace, and is near the foot of the Demavend, a beautiful snow-capped mountain which rises precipitously to a height of about 18,000 feet.

No diplomatic quarter in the world, I believe, covers so large an area. Each legation is in itself a large compound which, Indian fashion, contains several separate bungalows.

The compound of the British Legation is particularly spacious. A semi-tropical sun shines through the handsome trees which line its drive and paths.

The Minister and the senior members of the Legation staff occupy separate residences of their own. In the grounds there is the Legation church. The whole place is exactly like a British cantonment in India.

Teheran—Listening Post

Teheran has been a magnificent listening post ever since the end of the last war, and the talk of the European diplomats who meet each other in the Teheran Club is always stimulating.

The British Legation, incidentally, is the birthplace of Mr. Harold Nicolson, who about 16 years ago returned to the city where his father, the first Lord Carnock, distinguished himself when he was the British Minister. *August 20*

"The Water Poet"

Lord Halifax, at the naming by Lady Halifax of a Halifax bomber yesterday, referred to the "simple prayer" used, as he said, from time immemorial in Yorkshire:

From Hull, Hell and Halifax,
Good Lord, deliver us.

The "prayer," in fact, occurs in one of the innumerable doggerel effusions of John Taylor, self-styled "the water poet," who flourished, or at any rate scratched up some sort of a living, in Elizabethan and Stuart days.

Taylor was a Thames waterman by trade, and afterwards "served Eliza Queen" as a pressed man in the Navy. Later he made a livelihood by describing, in uncouth verse, his various eccentric journeys on foot. One of his walks was across Europe to Bohemia, where he was entertained by the Court at Prague.

Finally he settled down as a publican in Long Acre, where he died in 1653. He left behind him an enormous mass of bad verses, which are nevertheless of no small value as a mirror of his time.

September 13

Bob's Your Uncle

A story is going round the Service clubs about one of our best-known generals. As the yarn goes, he was discussing the war with a Free French officer. He explained his views in pidgin French, and ended with the remark: "Si vous faites ça, alors Robert sera votre oncle."

September 23

"Per Ardua ad Astra"

I have been asked who suggested the R.A.F. motto. The answer is Mr. Harold Baker, now Warden of Winchester, and sometimes known as "Bluey" Baker.

He was an Oxford contemporary of Raymond Asquith and together they swept the academic board. Mr. Baker then went into Parliament. It was while he was Financial Secretary of the War Office before the last war that he was asked to provide a motto for the Royal Flying Corps.

"Per Ardua ad Astra" was the result.

Someone recently asked him to translate it. "It can't be done," he said. "That is its merit." *September 26*

Publisher's First Decade

Mr. Hamish Hamilton is celebrating his first 10 years as a publisher—the anniversary was this week—by a commemorative anthology, "Decade," a long and fascinating volume of extracts from some of his publications.

The collection calls attention to the important books he has issued, many of them the work of well-known American correspondents. Among the authors are John Gunther, Walter Duranty, Vincent Sheean, Virginia Cowles, Dorothy Thompson and Clare Boothe.

Mr. Hamilton has secured William L. Shirer's "Berlin Diary" for this country. He is bringing out this remarkable book, the American edition of which was reviewed at length in *The Daily Telegraph* on Sept. 16, on Friday.

After two years in the Army Mr. Hamish Hamilton has recently joined the American Division of the Ministry of Information. Last night at a party at Grosvenor House he was greeted by some of his authors and other friends. *September 27*

Scoring Off Teacher

In a certain Alsatian village a German school teacher has replaced the nuns who used to run the village school. This Nazi tried to teach the children to make the Hitler salute, but without success.

One day in exasperation he said to a small boy of 11: "All right. Then say 'Vive la France.' " He cried, with tremendous enthusiasm "Vive la France," upon which the teacher said, "Now say 'Heil Hitler.' " The child declared he could not. Asked why, he replied, "La langue ne tourne pas."

That was the end of trying to teach the children to make the Hitler salute. However, some days later the teacher, being, as I say, a thorough-going Nazi, talked to them about Hitler and compared him with the great national hero, Napoleon.

Whereupon one of the children with an innocent air enquired, "Sur quelle ile le mettra-t-on?" *October 13*

M.P.'s Plain Duty

A pair of Bristol cups and saucers, painted with the election colours of Edmund Burke, fetched 50 guineas last week. It was at this 1774 election that Burke expounded the plain duty of a member of Parliament.

He said to his constituents: "I owe you not only my industry, but my judgment, and I should betray you instead of serving you if I sacrificed my judgment to your opinion." *October 20*

Haitian's Challenge—

Diplomats at Vichy are chuckling at M. Abel Leger's adroitness in securing from the Germans marks of respect for his national flag which Adml. Darlan may well envy him.

Early last year M. Leger, who is Haitian Minister to France, removed the Legation to his residence at Beauvais. When the Germans arrived there they requisitioned the house and broke down the mast from which the Haitian flag floated.

M. Leger, who is a lawyer of note, at once wrote to the German headquarters demanding that a general having the rank equivalent to his in the Diplomatic Service should meet him in a duel. In reply he was asked to call at the commandant's office.

—and the Nazi General

There he was told that his request would be granted and was offered the choice of weapons. M. Leger admitted to no great skill in the handling of any weapons, but stated he was quite willing to be killed for the honour of his country.

This embarrassed the German G.O.C., who saw possible international complications looming. He therefore asked whether M. Leger would care to accept reparation.

The Minister agreed on condition that it included the solemn rendering of honours to the flag by a detachment of 200 German soldiers.

After some demur the terms were accepted, the Germans re-erected the flag-mast, evacuated the house and rendered the ceremonial honours. Large notices in German were also posted all around the estate forbidding any German to enter under penalty of severe punishment. *October 27*

Pass Before Meat

Having hired a taxicab to take him in the black-out to a restaurant which he had not visited before, a hungry man walked into the building outside which he was set down.

In a dimly lit corridor he was asked for his pass. "I will show you my pass, certainly, but why should I have to show a pass when all I want is a meal?"

"Meal, sir?" said his challenger. "You won't get a meal here. This is the Ministry of Food." *November 12*

Super-Sheikh

After Hitler has become "Lord of Europe" he plans to become Overlord of the Moslem world, my intelligence service tell me, under his old title of the Sheikh-el-Grueber. *November 14*

Wavy Navy Dinner

The Connaught Rooms, as someone put it to me, was awash with Ocean Swells for the R.N.V.R. dinner. Among them was Adml. Ghormley, U.S.N., who accompanied Mr. Winant.

Adml. Sir Dudley Pound got the laugh of the evening for his story which had a sly dig at his hosts.

While waiting his turn to bat at a cricket match at Dartmouth, he got into conversation with a sub-lieutenant of the R.N.V.R. The young officer told him that he was in the Tiger, at that time Adml. Pound's flagship.

"Then we are shipmates," he replied. "I do not think so," said the sub-lieutenant, "because I have never seen you before in my life." *November 17*

Eire's Sure Shield

An old lady on a Dublin tram exultantly remarked at the time of Dunkirk: "Thanks be to God, the English now are properly bate."

"Yes," said a fellow passenger. "I suppose now the Germans will soon be coming here."

"Faith," she replied indignantly, "the English Navy would never allow such a thing, surely." *November 18*

A Private's Tastes

A Sergeant-Major stopped a recruit who was walking out in battle dress and brown shoes.
S.M.: "Where did you get them shoes?"
R.: "I had them in private life, sergeant-major."
S.M.: "What were you in private life?"
R.: "On the Stock Exchange."
S.M.: "Did you have a silk hat as well?"
R.: "Yes, sergeant-major."
S.M.: "Then why don't you wear that?"
R.: "I don't care for a silk hat with brown shoes." *November 27*

Excursion into French

French-Canadians had their wish when Mr. Churchill suddenly broke into French in his speech last night. So many of them who listened-in speak no language but their own, and his French was such as every one of them could follow.

As I heard him, it struck me that he had made considerable strides since earlier days. I had just been turning up a passage in the late Lord Oxford's Memories, where he describes a war-time (1915) lunch at which Delcassé and Cambon were present.

"Winston," wrote the then Prime Minister, "was very eloquent in the worst French anyone ever heard. 'S'ils savent que nous sommes gens qu'ils peuvent conter sur,' was one of his flowers of speech." *December 31*

1942

Events now crowd in so closely upon each other that this brief summary must perforce become even sketchier. At the beginning of the year, although Britain had now been joined by Russia and America, the outlook was hardly encouraging. By its close, however, there was a glimmer of light on the horizon, and with hindsight it can certainly be said that 1942 was the turning point of the war.

Let us look first at the Far East, where the year opened upon a scene of unrelieved gloom for the Allies. Hong Kong had fallen on Christmas Day of 1941; Malaya was to prove no more of a problem and Singapore fell on February 15. Sixty thousand men were taken prisoner in what Churchill called "The worst disaster and largest capitulation in British history". Only in the Philippines did the Japanese encounter any serious opposition, where the Americans put up a gallant fight on the Bataan peninsula and later on the island fortress of Corregidor. But gallantry was not enough and on May 6 the Americans surrendered. Meanwhile the Japanese had advanced into Burma, reaching Moulmein by January 31. On March 8 the British evacuated Rangoon and by May 14 the whole of Burma was in Japanese hands. Although this marks the nadir of Allied fortunes in the Far East, the tide was already on the turn, for in the Battle of the Coral Sea between May 4 and 8 the Americans had administered the first severe check to Japanese aggression. Then, in June, Rear-Admiral Spruance scored a brilliant tactical victory over Admiral Nagumo at the Battle of Midway. Although the end was still three years away, from now on the Japanese were on the defensive.

Now to North Africa where, apart from a brief offensive in January, Rommel remained relatively inactive until May, when, in a series of engagements as complex and as hard-fought as any in the war, he soundly defeated the troops under General Auchinleck. On June 21 Tobruk fell and by July 5 Rommel had advanced as far into Egypt as El Alamein. But here too the tide was soon to turn. In August Mr. Churchill paid a visit to Cairo and in the ensuing reshuffle General Alexander took over from General Auchinleck and General Montgomery assumed command of the Eighth Army. The first test came on August 30 when Rommel launched the Afrika Corps in an all-out bid to open the road to Suez. After three days' fighting he was in full retreat, leaving behind him a trail of burnt-out tanks. This engagement was known as the Battle of Alam Halfa. Then followed at the end of October the Battle of El Alamein, the real turning-point of the war in North Africa. Soon after Alamein, on November 8, an Anglo-American force under the command of Lieut.-General Dwight Eisenhower landed in Algiers and started advancing eastward. By the year's end the Eighth Army had taken Benghazi and was advancing on Tripoli.

On the Russian front German morale was at its lowest ebb. The soldiers were poorly clad and their lines of communication were stretched to, often beyond, their limits. The Russians, however, were soon to learn the truth of the popular German song:

Nach jedem Dezember
Gibts wieder ein Mai,

for on May 8 General von Manstein launched his offensive in the Crimea and, after heavy fighting, the Russians were overwhelmed. Further to the north three Soviet armies were surrounded when trying to liberate Kharkov, Stalin having forbidden the troops to withdraw. In order to safeguard the left flank of their advance into the Caucasus the Germans recognized the necessity of taking Stalingrad, thereby gaining control of the River Volga, but it was at Stalingrad that their plans were doomed to failure. The German Sixth Army, under General von Paulus, reached the outskirts of the city on August 23, expecting it to fall the following day. But the Russians fought back with all the fanaticism and doggedness of those who have nothing left to lose but their lives and as summer turned to autumn the deadlock seemed no nearer to resolution. Then on November 19 the Russians sprung the trap and completely encircled the city. To look ahead for a moment, all resistance in the city ceased on February 2, 1943, and 90,000 German troops were taken prisoner. They were all that remainded of twenty-two divisions.

Even this briefest of summaries of the three main theatres of the war in 1942 leaves little room for mention of other events. At sea the German U-boats continued to play havoc with Allied shipping. After America's entry into the war Hitler switched the spearhead of the offensive to American coastal waters and the result was nothing short of a massacre. In the month of February alone 71 ships, totalling 384,000 tons, were sunk off the Eastern seaboard, and for many months to come the production of U-boats was to exceed by far the number sunk in action.

To relieve the gloom for a moment one might recall that this was the year of Noel Coward's In Which We Serve, *of Greer Garson's* Mrs. Miniver *and of Walt Disney's* Bambi.

On December 1 the report of Sir William Beveridge was issued to the public, fulfilling at last the Fabian plans laid down by the Webbs before the First World War. As A. J. P. Taylor said, "It came forty years too late and provided, as might be expected, against past evils."

Peterborough derived much amusement from a splendidly awful fellow called Billy Brown, who crops up frequently throughout the year. In his name London Transport urged travellers to follow the rules with such couplets as:

Face the driver; raise your hand.
You'll find that he will understand.

Severe paronomasia is still evident, breaking out in one instance with the following: "An actor tells me that a recent outbreak of colds among the members of the theatrical profession is not to be attributed to influEnsa."

Royal Dukedoms

Lord MacDuff, by becoming Duke of Connaught, creates what I believe to be a precedent in English history. He will be the first holder of a dukedom created for a son of the Sovereign not to be a Royal Highness.

During the past three centuries other Royal ducal titles have either died out through lack of male heirs or have been merged in the Crown through their holders ascending the Throne.

This latter event happened in the present and the last generation. Both the King and his father were Dukes of York.

Forfeited Titles

The Duke of Saxe-Coburg-Gotha, a son of Queen Victoria's youngest son, Prince Leopold, would still be Duke of Albany had he not been deprived of his title during the last war.

The German descendant of another Royal duke, according to the Almanach de Gotha, still keeps his British title. He is the Duke of Brunswick, the present head of the former Royal family of Hanover. He is descended from George III's son Ernest, who became King of Hanover on Queen Victoria's accession to the Throne.

In fact he forfeited his British dukedom of Cumberland at the same time as his somewhat remote cousin of Saxe-Coburg. *January 20*

Cricket Brotherhoods

Yesterday at lunch I met the oldest IZ. Naturally he talked about the late Dr. Edward Lyttelton, former Headmaster of Eton, and one of the great cricketers in the great time of English cricket.

Canon Lyttelton was captain of the famous Cambridge eleven of 1878, the greatest side ever put in the field by either University. They celebrated their victory over the Australians by a dinner in the academic surroundings of King's, that Etonian *pur sang*, Oscar Browning, being host.

Thanks to the Lytteltons Eton holds the palm for family cricketers. Seven of the eight Lyttelton brothers got their colours.

Their rivals were the Fosters and the Fords. Seven of the Fosters played for Malvern and seven Fords for Repton.

In county cricket the Fosters rank first. Four of them played for Worcestershire. R. E. Foster's 287, at Sydney in 1904, set up a record for England v. Australia matches that stood till Bradman's 334 at Leeds in 1930. *January 30*

Skeleton at the Feast

Many London Welsh people must have secretly echoed Petty Officer A. P. Herbert's naive question, "Why am I here?" when the Chiswick bard found himself among them at their St. David's Day lunch at Grosvenor House on Saturday.

So far as can be ascertained, Mr. Herbert has no Welsh ancestors. His father, it is true, always wore a signet ring with the crest of the Earls of Pembroke, whose name happens to be Herbert. This, however, Mr. Herbert ceased to wear when he reached the age of discretion and learnt something about the significance of armorial bearings.

As he admitted, about the only reason for his presence at the lunch was the fact that he was the only one present who had written a Welsh hymn.

Cry from the Heart

This lyric ecstasy arose out of a holiday he once spent in North Wales. It rained every day, but his friends kept on insisting that he would find the hills really beautiful once they emerged from the mists.

They never did emerge. In the train on his way home he was inspired to the following effect:

Wales! Wales!
Land of the leeks and the snails.
In buckets and pails
The rain falls in Wales
And when it's not raining it hails.

March 2

Pleasant Weakness

Mr. Somerset Maugham's new book, "Strictly Personal," an absorbing and sometimes harrowing account of "the small things that happened to me during the first 15 months of the war," is dedicated to Sir Edward Marsh, K.C.V.O., most famous of private secretaries. Thereby an unsuspected chapter of our literary history leaps to light.

Not only has Sir Edward corrected, and very stringently corrected, the proofs of all Mr. Maugham's books for years past—excepting this one, written in America—it is also revealed that "many of the best writers of our generation are indebted to you for such proficiency as they have acquired in the practice of writing our difficult language."

I have always thought of Mr. Maugham as one of the most studiously careful writers of English. In fact, despite this evidence, I propose to go on thinking so.

Still, if ever I come across a colon in my re-reading of him, I shall attribute it to Sir Edward: he has, it seems, "a pleasant weakness" for this detail of punctuation. *March 2*

The Prime Minister's Name

Someone yesterday put it to me that the Court Circular's hyphenation of the Prime Minister's name (the Right Hon. Winston Spencer-Churchill) was a misprint. In fact it was perfectly correct.

Owing to the title descending through the female line the family name of the Dukes of Marlborough in the 18th century was Spencer. The fifth Duke in 1807 assumed by Royal licence the additional surname of his distinguished predecessor. John Churchill, the first Duke.

Though the family surname has since remained Spencer-Churchill, the Prime Minister is merely following the example of his father in abbreviating it for daily use. The Victorians, who were more particular than ourselves on such matters, only knew him as Lord Randolph Churchill.

Mr. Churchill is not, however, described in the Court Circular by his full name. This is Winston Leonard Spencer-Churchill.

March 12

Auden and Brother Poet

Mr. Hugh Auden, the British poet, now Associate Professor of English at the University of Michigan, finds himself in juxtaposition with a New Jersey taxicab driver, Mr. George Zabriskie, as one of the recipients of two poetry fellowships awarded by the John Simon Guggenheim Memorial Foundation.

Eighty-two fellowships, which usually carry a stipend of £625 apiece, have been granted this year to research workers, scholars, artists and others judged "most capable of adding to the scholarly and artistic power" of the United States.

There were more than 1,500 applicants.

Mind—Not Muscle

Mr. Zabriskie, like Mr. Auden, is a strong individualist. He failed to graduate at Duke University because he refused to participate in the physical education part of the curriculum. He did so on the ground that his object was study and not the development of his muscles.

Although he is only 23, he worked as a mop salesman, a farm labourer and a journalist before becoming a taxi driver. His first volume of poetry, published last September, is entitled "The Mind's Geography." *April 10*

Racehorse's £500 Dugout

The famous racehorse Nearco, unbeaten during his racing career and winner of the Grand Prix de Paris four years ago, lives in a £500 air-conditioned dugout on a Newmarket stud farm. Nearco was bred in Italy, but has some of the finest English thoroughbred blood in his veins.

His sire was Pharos, one of the best of Lord Derby's stud horses. After his Grand Prix triumph Nearco was bought by Mr. Martin Benson, of Newmarket, for £65,000—the highest price ever paid by an individual owner for a racehorse.

The horse is in great demand by breeders and earns £15,000 a year in fees. His first crop of two-year-olds will be seen on the racecourse in the new season which opens at Newmarket on Tuesday. *April 11*

Budget Clerihew

The imminence of the Budget has inspired Mr. E. Clerihew Bentley, inventor of the Clerihew, to this forecast:

I am sure Sir Kingsley Wood
Tax us less if he could.
But considering the size of the bill,
I doubt if Sir Kingsley Will. *April 13*

Composer's Hat

Mr. Arthur Bliss, the recently appointed B.B.C. Director of Music, looks like—in fact is—an ex-Guards officer. The other day he decided that his hat was really too shabby for a man in his new position.

He went to a hatter's not far from Broadcasting House and said he wanted a new hat. "I think a black one with a fairly large brim," he added.

The assistant put his head on one side. "No, sir, I think not."

"What do you mean?" Mr. Bliss asked.

"Not for you, sir," the salesman replied. "That is the kind of hat musicians wear." *April 15*

Mandalay

Kipling undoubtedly was responsible for creating the impression in English minds that Mandalay is a city hoary with history. Actually it was founded in 1857, the year of the Indian Mutiny, and was the Burmese capital for only 28 years.

It was the last of the capitals of the Burmese kings, who were in the habit of giving expression to the saying, "A new king, a new capital." Only two kings reigned in Mandalay—Mindon, who founded the city, and his son Thibaw, the last of the Burmese monarchs.

The foundation was attended with the customary human sacrifices. A woman was offered up to be the guardian spirit of the new city, and four of the people were buried alive at the four corners of the city walls.

Mindon died in 1878. Thibaw fell in 1885, when Kipling's old flotilla went chunking from Rangoon up the road to Mandalay, carrying Gen. Prendergast's expeditionary force. *May 5*

Real Dutch Courage

Queen Wilhelmina's broadcasts to her Dutch subjects throughout the world have played a great part in sustaining the spirit of a people who have a name in history for dogged resistance to foreign tyranny.

Yesterday's address to those in "the home country" is the Queen's reply to the increased brutality of the German terror since Himmler arrived in Holland this week, and 460 more civilian hostages were arrested.

In speaking of the German "hangmen" she used a word which

carries, in both Dutch and German, much more force of denunciation than it does in our own language. The Queen employed it a fortnight ago in her broadcast on the murder of 72 hostages in one day.

Her people know that Queen Wilhelmina and her Ministers might have had peace with dishonour when Holland was invaded two years ago. They are proud of her refusal to accept slavery on their behalf, although the German answer was the ghastliest crime in even Hitler's record—the bombing of Rotterdam, with 30,000 victims.

May 23

A New Word?

Ossian Goulding, *The Daily Telegraph* Stockholm correspondent, knows better than most people the effect on the German mind of such raids as that on Cologne. He is in Britain on leave at the moment, and we discussed it last night.

He recalled some of the stories that circulated in the Swedish capital after the raids on Rostock on April 23 and afterwards. For days the rumours spread and multiplied, as the refugees, evacuated to Berlin and Magdeburg, began to talk. The effect in Stockholm, which was considerable, must have been far short of the total influence of these first-hand stories.

The word which became common currency to describe the new British bombs was "Bezirk." It means "district" indicating their vast range of destruction.

It may be that the word "Bezirk" will join "blitz" and "panzer" as future enrichments of the English language, this time with a victory connotation.

June 1

Brontë Pupil

Probate, I read, has been granted to the copy of a will which had been destroyed in an air raid and which bequeathed a number of Brontë relics to Mr. Patrick Brontë Branwell, a descendant of the Miss Branwell who sent the Brontë sisters to Brussels.

These are almost the last relics to be privately owned. The others are at Haworth, the desolate Yorkshire village in which the Brontës lived with their father.

The Parsonage was bought for the nation by the late Sir James Roberts. A farmer's son, he went to the Haworth Sunday School, where his teacher and special friend was Charlotte Brontë.

Later he worked in a local mill, made good and became the millionaire owner of the Saltaire Mills, near Bradford.

Sir James had two passions—Brontë literature and Russia. He firmly believed that events would bring about a deep understanding between Great Britain and Russia, and during the last war he founded the Russian chair at Leeds University.

Even the Lenin revolution did not disturb his belief that the two countries would come together in a time of real emergency. When he died, six years ago, the last personal link with Charlotte Brontë was broken.

His son-in-law is Sir Frederick Aykroyd, who recently concluded an arduous year as High Sheriff of Yorkshire. *June 3*

Unknown Celebrity

No successful writer has ever so successfully avoided publicity as Ernest Bramah, who has died at 74. For half his lifetime his "Kai Lung" and his "Max Carrados" stories have been among the recognised treasures of humour and of detective fiction respectively. Also he wrote admirable prose.

Yet no one has ever known anything about him except the fact, which leaked out somehow, that his full name was Ernest Bramah Smith. His age was never disclosed while he lived.

His publishers and literary agents were sworn to secrecy about everything connected with his personal life. He never appeared in public.

A year or so ago I had the rare distinction of receiving a letter from him, commenting politely on some comment of my own. I should have replied—but there was no address on his letter.

His Chinese story-teller and his blind detective were above all original creations. His way of accepting his fame was original, too. *June 29*

Sir Roger Keyes and the Premier

Yesterday's was one of the most crowded Houses I have seen even for an important Commons debate on the war. The atmosphere was charged with electricity, and it was not long before there was a discharge.

Sir John Wardlaw-Milne, a tall, commanding figure with a crimson carnation in his button-hole, made a good start. He threw the House into bewilderment, however, by his suggestion—which he admitted had no relevance to the debate—that the Duke of Gloucester should be appointed Commander-in-Chief of the British Army.

The hubbub which this created held up his speech for some moments, and he never fully recovered the command of the House.

During Sir John's speech Mr. Churchill called up Mr. Lyttelton from his seat lower down the front bench. Mr. Lyttelton displaced Sir James Grigg, and from then on the Prime Minister sat between him and Sir Stafford Cripps. Mr. Churchill was in frequent consultation with the Minister of Production.

Mr. Churchill Beamed

The Prime Minister was obviously much touched by the support accorded to him personally by his old friend Adml. of the Fleet Sir Roger Keyes, the seconder of the motion.

He positively beamed when in answer to an interruption the Admiral exclaimed: "It would be a deplorable disaster if the Prime Minister was forced to go." This provided an irresistible opportunity for pointing to a difference of aim between Sir John Wardlaw-Milne and the Admiral. Mr. Lyttelton seized it.

He, too, after a good start, was thrown off his balance. He came into conflict with that very expert Parliamentarian Mr. Maxton over his refusal to allow a question, and was a good deal worried by other questioners. *July 2*

New Angle on Eton

An American passing through Eton was astonished to see the boys in top-hats. "What is this?" he exclaimed. "Is it an Octu for undertakers?" *July 14*

No Precedent for Churchill Visit

Mr. Churchill's historic business journey to the United States last winter had precedents in Mr. Ramsay MacDonald's decidedly less fruitful pilgrimages to Washington in 1929 and 1933; but no British Prime Minister has ever until now visited Russia while in office.

There was, however, a projected war-time visit which might have had even more tragic consequences than, in fact, it did. Mr. Lloyd George, six months before he became Prime Minister in 1916, planned to go to Russia.

He was then Minister of Munitions, and his intention was to accompany Lord Kitchener to discuss problems of supply with the Russian Government.

A few days before the Hampshire sailed Mr. Asquith wrote to Mr. Lloyd George asking him to meet the Irish leaders in an effort to negotiate a settlement. He accepted, and Lord Kitchener left for Russia alone.

"But for Mr. Asquith's letter I should have been with him and shared his fate," writes Mr. Lloyd George in his "Memoirs." "This escape, at least, I owe to Ireland." *August 18*

New College Julep

When Mr. Barry Bingham, son of the former American Ambassador in London, was here early this year Mr. Willard Connely took him to his Oxford alma mater, New College. There Mr. Connely showed Mr. Bingham, who had been his pupil at Harvard, all over the college.

Mr. Bingham has now written an article in one of his papers, the Louisville Courier-Journal, on an American tradition in that old and famous foundation. This is the New College julep.

It appears that in 1845 William Heyward Trapier, from South Carolina, visited New College and was asked to stay and dine in hall. The day being hot, his host asked him what he would like to drink. Mr. Trapier asked for a mint julep.

As no one knew how to mix it, this Southern gentleman prepared it himself. It was such a success that Mr. Trapier declared that henceforth New College must always have its mint julep.

Secret Recipe

Accordingly, he presented the college with his family julep recipe, a Georgian silver cup and a sum of money for an annual college julep festival.

Trapier never fulfilled his promise of returning. But every year his memory is celebrated on June 1, the anniversary of his visit.

Mr. Bingham says that New College scholars have sought details of Trapier's career with little success. So also little success attended Mr. Bingham's questions to the steward about the recipe.

He apologised for not being able to disclose it. "I learned it from the dying lips of my predecessor," he announced, solemnly, "and I swore I would never pass it on except to the man who will some day succeed me."

Mr. Bingham, whose last visit to London was to study A.R.P., has just returned as a lieutenant, U.S.N. *September 4*

Eureka!

How strangely some phrases find their way into history! The name, "The United Nations," to describe the greatest alliance the world has known, will live in the record of our time. How did it arise?

The answer is given by Mr. Forrest Davis and Mr. Ernest K. Lindley, two veteran Washington journalists who have just published in America a study of recent United States policy and action as observed at close quarters in the capital.

They disclose that the phrase was shouted to Mr. Churchill through a White House bath-room door last December by Mr. Roosevelt, who had just thought of it in bed.

A few days later the "Declaration by the United Nations" was signed by the 26 plenipotentiaries in Washington. *September 21*

The Misses Shelley

Freshwater, Isle of Wight, is celebrating to-day the 50th anniversary of the death of its most distinguished inhabitant—Tennyson.

I once heard the story of a tea-party discussion in Freshwater in the 70's, when it was excusably poetry-minded. In this two old ladies by the name of Shelley took part.

One of them who had a sharp tongue remarked: "I once had a brother who wrote immoral poetry, but I am thankful to say I never read a line of it."

No one had realised before that the Misses Shelley were the sisters of Percy Bysshe Shelley, who had died some half-century previously. *October 6*

Ship That Did Come Home

When Major-Gen. F. A. M. Browning, chief of our airborne troops, was on his recent holiday in Florida, he saw a man whom he had long wanted to meet. This was Mr. Frank Huckins, the noted Florida boat-builder.

Some years ago the General wrote to Mr. Huckins saying that he had long admired his boats, and hoped to buy one—if a book Mrs. Browning was writing was successful.

Mr. Huckins replied that he had never heard of Mrs. Browning. He added that since he had left Harvard, 30 years before, he had read no books whatsoever—and was practically illiterate.

When Gen. Browning arrived in the United States on a fortnight's leave his one request was to visit Mr. Huckins. Gen. Marshall at once put a 'plane at his disposal.

Mr. Huckins has since been saying that he "may be building" a boat for Gen. Browning after the war. Mrs. Browning is Daphne du Maurier. The book referred to was "Rebecca." *October 6*

Oldest Profession

A doctor, an architect and a Civil Servant were arguing which of them belonged to the oldest profession.

The doctor's claim that a member of his profession must have been present at Adam's major operation was countered by the architect. He pointed out that the world was created out of chaos, and where there is creation there must also be an architect.

"Ah," said the Civil Servant, "but where there is chaos there must always be a Civil Servant." *October 13*

Omarian Jubilee

A jubilee occurs to-day of the literary dining club formed to honour the master poet—and his English translator—who wrote

> Here with a Loaf of Bread beneath the Bough,
> A Flask of Wine, a Book of Verse . . .

The quotation, however, hardly does justice to the Omar Khayyam Club, which has counted many literary sybarites among its members. Their oratory matched in mellowness the wines and viands in which they celebrated the memory of the master.

The Omar Khayyam Club held its first dinner at Pagani's on Oct. 13, 1892. It has since remained faithful to that restaurant.

This 50th anniversary is being kept in cold storage till after the war. *October 13*

With Hardly a Rag

An English lawyer was entertaining at his club a member of the New York Bar, now in the United States Army. The Englishman showed his guest a picture of Gandhi in an illustrated paper and said: "You'd hardly believe it, but Gandhi used to be a lawyer."

"Is that so?" said the American. "He looks to me more as if he had been a lawyer's client." *October 26*

Refugee's Pious Vow

A book written in fulfilment of a vow is to be published on Monday. The author is Franz Werfel, the German-Jewish playwright and novelist, an active opponent of Nazism who had taken refuge in France.

When Paris fell he was in great danger as one of the men proscribed by the armistice. He escaped to unoccupied France and found sanctuary for some weeks in Lourdes. There he came to know the facts about St. Bernadette and the healings that followed her visions.

He made a vow that if he succeeded in getting out of Europe he would write the Song of Bernadette. The novel with that title has for many months been a best-seller in America. It is a work of compelling beauty and understanding. *October 28*

Mr. Gielgud Puns

In Mr. James Agate's latest "Ego," just published, there is a letter of last April from Mr. John Gielgud quoting a misprint in a Liverpool notice of "Macbeth." This referred to Mr. George Woodbridge (who played the Porter) as an "engaging Portia."

"I could not forbear," wrote Mr. Gielgud, "to murmur that the quality of Mersey is not strained." *November 14*

Dean Farrar's Daughter

Lady Montgomery, widow of Bishop Montgomery, and mother of the Eighth Army's Commander, who has cabled her congratulations to her son on his 55th birthday to-day, had a distinguished father as well as a distinguished husband. She was one of the five daughters of that eminent Victorian cleric, Dean Farrar.

During her girlhood her father was Canon of Westminster and Rector of St. Margaret's. She thus passed some of the most formative years of her life in the shadow of the Abbey.

At that time Canon Farrar had an immense reputation both as preacher and writer. His versatile talents, keen sympathies and handsome presence made him an outstanding figure in the London of that day.

As a teetotaller his grandson follows in his footsteps. Canon Farrar took the pledge and became a temperance advocate as the result of the drunkenness he saw around him in the streets of Westminster. *November 17*

U.S. Song of Freedom

Here is the song that has swept the United States:

Down went the gunner,
Then the gunner's mate.
Up jumped the Sky Pilot,
Gave the boys a look
And manned the gun himself
As he laid aside the Book,
Shouting,
"Praise the Lord and pass the ammunition.
Praise the Lord and pass the ammunition.
Praise the Lord and pass the ammunition.
And we'll all stay free."

So popular is it that the American Office of War Information has had to restrict the number of times it can be broadcast daily. Over 250,000 gramophone records of it have already been sold and over 125,000 copies in sheet music.

It was written by Frank Loesser, now a private in the United States Army. He is the Hollywood composer who also wrote "I want spurs that jingle, jangle, jingle," and "I don't want to walk without you baby." Each has brought him in a moderate fortune. *November 21*

"To Meet Gen. Hertzog"

Sir Ian Hamilton recalled to me yesterday how he had once been invited by Mr. Churchill to dinner to meet Gen. Hertzog.

He was just making his bow to Mrs. Churchill—who received her guests but did not dine with them—when Gen. Hertzog advanced upon him with outstretched hands.

They plunged at once into an exciting talk about Cape Colony, Kimberley and the Jameson Raid. Nothing, however, was said about Zilikats Nek, where, in Sir Ian's phrase, "each had done his best to do the other in."

Then, as dinner was announced and they were on their way to the dining-room, Hertzog turned and said: "By the way, there used to be an old fighting general, Ian Hamilton. He's dead, isn't he?"

November 24

1943

1943

In 1943 the Allies dominated and dictated the whole course of the war, a situation which both demanded and grew out of ever closer and more elaborate inter-Allied planning. In the middle of January President and Prime Minister met again, this time at Casablanca, from whence it was announced that the war would be waged until the "unconditional surrender of all the Axis powers" had been achieved; and at the end of November Roosevelt, Churchill and Stalin met for the first time at the Teheran Conference.

Let us start this time with the Eastern Front, where the surrender of the German Sixth Army marked the turning-point of that campaign. The shattering cost in terms of men and equipment was as catastrophic to the German cause as was the loss of prestige and the weakening of morale. Henceforward a German soldier sent to the Eastern Front went with the resignation of a martyr. Moreover, the balance of manpower was now beginning to weigh heavily in favour of the Russians. In November, 1942, the opposing forces had faced each other on terms of numerical equality; seven months later, at the Battle of Kursk, the Russians outnumbered the Germans by two to one. The three titanic tank battles of Kursk, Orel and Kharkov resulted in enormous casualties on both sides, but the Russians were better able to absorb them.

*The war in North Africa ended on May 13 and the invasion of Sicily, the largest amphibious operation ever attempted, was launched on July 10. Although the Germans fought back bitterly, it soon became clear that the spirit of the Italians was broken and that the invaders were indeed looked upon as deliverers. Organized resistance on the island had ceased by August 17 and on September 3 two divisions of the Eighth Army crossed the Straits of Messina. On September 8 the Italian Government surrendered and an armistice was granted, a situation which gave rise to acute political complications. The U.S. Fifth Army, under General Mark Clark, landed near Naples on September 9 and ran into severe trouble at Salerno. Meanwhile the Eighth Army, under Montgomery, was advancing up the Adriatic coast. They occupied Termoli on October 8 and then pushed west to join up with the Fifth Army. However, at this stage, on the line of the Rivers Sangro and Garigliano, the "*winterstellung*", as it became known, the Germans turned and bared their teeth. So began the long and* *painful battle for the waist of Italy. A year later the Allies had only advanced a further 250 miles.*

In Burma the Arakan offensive early in the year came to nothing, though Brigadier Wingate's controversial Chindits did considerable damage to Japanese lines of communication and managed to hold the attention of large numbers of the enemy. In the Pacific the Americans continued to maintain the offensive. A two-pronged attack was planned, one under General MacArthur to advance on Japan through New Guinea, the Philippines and Formosa, the other under Admiral Nimitz, to approach Japan across the Central Pacific, island-hopping via the Gilbert, Marshall, Caroline, Mariana and Bonin Islands.

Nothing has been said of the war in the air since the Battle of Britain. To recap briefly, Bomber Command, which for the first two years of the war had been a small and relatively ill-equipped force, came under the control of Sir Arthur (Bomber) Harris in February, 1942, and thereafter its fortunes began to look up. The introduction of Radar, the formation of the Pathfinder Force and the Lancaster Bomber all played their part in this change of fortune. On February 25, 1943, a raid on Nuremberg by the R.A.F. opened the campaign of round-the-clock attacks which was carried on throughout the year, the Americans bombing by day and the British by night. Two successive mass bombing assaults on Hamburg in July produced what Goebbels described as "a catastrophe the extent of which simply staggers the imagination". 800,000 people were made homeless.

At sea the situation was also looking up, although the Germans still managed to sink 597 Allied ships during the year. However, by June more German submarines were being sunk than Allied merchant ships. The Royal Navy ended the year on a high note by sinking the enemy's last active capital ship, the Scharnhorst, *on December 26.*

Back home it was a bad year for literary ladies, Elinor Glyn, Radclyffe Hall, E. M. Delafield, Beatrice Webb and Beatrix Potter all penning their last lines. In July General Sikorski, head of the Polish Government in exile, was killed in an aeroplane crash at Gibraltar and was accorded a fulsome tribute by Peterborough, in whose column the puns continued to rain down. Here is a selection of wince-makers: "German farmers believe that visits of the R.A.F. to Essen have completely upset the rotation of Krupps"; "If the raids on Essen get any heavier, it has been suggested that the directors and shareholders will be 'Bang Krupps' "; "Is the January income-tax demand a shed Yule?," and, under the heading "Darn Likely", "I understand that girls are hoping the new fully-fashioned stockings will give them a good run for their money."

The Beast of Revelation

It has been pointed out to me that the Book of Revelation has a reference to Hitler. This is contained in Chapter 13, Verse 18.

"Here is wisdom. Let him that hath understanding count the number of the beast; for it is the number of a man, and his number is Six hundred threescore and six."

The clue is an easy one. Numbering the letters of the alphabet and starting with 100 one gets the following figures:

H 107
I 108
T 119
L 111
E 104
R 117

Their addition makes 666. *January 7*

Too Much—or Too Little

Soldiers who have felt a little aggrieved at the freedom with which American troops are able to spend money will enjoy the story I have just heard from India.

An American, having hired a tonga for a distance, the ordinary fare for which would be half a rupee, magnanimously handed the driver a 50-rupee note.

The man shook his head violently and demanded 60. "No," said the American, "that's enough. I shan't pay any more."

The Indian thereupon accepted the money and walked away leaving the tonga and pony with the purchaser. *February 24*

Passed for Comment

Sir Charles Harris, formerly Permanent Head of the Finance Department, War Office, entered his 80th year yesterday. His mordant wit still remains a tradition in the Civil Service. A characteristic example of it goes back to over 40 years ago when he was a mere Principal Clerk in the W.O.

The question of giving military rank to Army doctors was being discussed, and the papers were being duly circulated for comments. Harris's note was the following:

> I suggest that the relative rank of these doctors should follow established custom. What is wrong therefore with this grading—Mr. Practitioner, Lieutenant Practitioner, Captain Practitioner, Major Practitioner, Colonel Practitioner, and, finally, General Practitioner?

As they say in unofficial circles, this nearly queered the pitch.

March 3

Affectionate Peer

Socialist Lord Faringdon frequently treats his fellow peers to vigorous expositions of his views. These are always forcible, as one might expect from one who in the Upper House a year or two ago described himself as a pacifist.

At yesterday's sitting he showed the love for his fellow-men implicit in his political philosophy by addressing the Lords as "My Dears." Smiles lit up the grave faces on the benches.

To do him justice, Lord Faringdon also joined in the amusement caused by this unusual indication of affection. *April 7*

Von Arnim in 1913

Von Arnim who is reported to have replaced Rommel in Tunisia, was described to me yesterday by an Englishman who identifies the Nazi general as a man he met in Potsdam 30 years ago. He remembers him as stockily built, fair-haired, of medium height, keen on tennis and talking perfect English.

When my informant congratulated him on his English he replied that he ought to be able to speak it as his mother was an Englishwoman. It appeared that she was the Countess von Arnim who wrote "Elizabeth and Her German Garden," a best-seller of the late '90s.

Her husband died in 1910, and she afterwards returned to England. In 1916 she married the late Earl Russell. Her death took place in February, 1941. *April 26*

63 Years a Great Nobleman

The Duke of Portland, who died yesterday, was a great nobleman in the style that was so dear to the heart of Disraeli, whom he knew well.

The by no means opulent young Guardsman who woke up one day 63 years ago to find himself one of the greatest landowners and wealthiest men in England might well have figured in "Lothair" or "Coningsby."

Welbeck Abbey may serve as a symbol of the change that has come over the scene since those days.

The house, which is one of the stateliest private residences in the world, where he had been host to Kings and Ambassadors under the old order, was kept up by the Duke despite all difficulty; but some years ago he remarked that there could be "little doubt that those who come after me will not be able to do so." *April 27*

"Father Could Do It"

Disraeli's friendship for the late Duke of Portland and his family, to which I referred the other day, had a very solid basis—that of gratitude. Looking through the Duke's memoirs I find the story which he himself did not know until long after he came into the title.

One day in the '40's Lord George Bentinck, the late Duke's cousin, was asked by his brother Henry, "What's the matter, George? You seem out of sorts." Lord George explained that he had found "an ideal leader" for the Protectionists in Benjamin Disraeli, but the other party chiefs would not hear of a man who was "not a landed proprietor." "Let us make him one," suggested Lord Henry: "father (the fourth Duke of Portland) could do it, and he seems in a very good humour this morning."

No sooner said than done. The Duke advanced to Disraeli, on easy terms, the money to buy Hughenden, in Bucks, and Disraeli became the Tory leader.

It remains to add that the Duke's successor, who was a Free Trader, called in the remainder of the loan soon after he came into the title, and Disraeli paid up "at great inconvenience to himself." *April 29*

Lord Randolph's Schooldays

I have just seen the list of serving old boys from one of the oldest and most famous preparatory schools in the country. This is Cheam School, once usually known as "Tabor's," to which the Prime

Minister's father went to be taught by the first of the Tabor family who were connected with the school.

The names include two who have recently distinguished themselves—Lieut. Lord Milford Haven, R.N., who won the D.S.O. this year, and Sqdn.-Ldr. Clyde-Smith, who has both the D.S.O. and the D.F.C.

Other old boys now with the Forces are Vice-Admiral Sir Robert Hornell, Major Lord Tennyson, who is attached to a Fleet Air Arm station, and Col. Sir Lionel Fletcher, now of the Royal Marines.

When Cheam School was forced to leave its old home owing to the growth of Greater London it moved to Headley, near Newbury, where it now flourishes under the Rev. Harold Taylor. Mr. Churchill has often said that Lord Randolph's religious streak came from his passion, at Cheam, for declaiming the Bible to enthralled listeners.

May 3

Captain to Viceroy

The choice of Field-Marshal Sir Archibald Wavell, C.-in-C., India, as Lord Linlithgow's successor is in curious contrast to the last wartime appointment to the Viceroyalty, that of Lord Chelmsford in 1916. When the announcement was made he was serving in India as a captain of the 4th Battalion of the Dorsetshire Regiment.

The secret that he was being groomed for Viceroy was not suspected by an old major, veteran of many wars, who two days before the appointment was announced assured him in an expansive moment that "a man in your position ought to be able to get a job."

Even less was it suspected by a lady whom Lord Chelmsford met at an official dinner in a provincial capital. She complained very bitterly because the wife of a man in her husband's official position —not, in fact, a very exalted one—was taken in to dinner by a captain in the Territorials. Seven days later the Territorial captain was the Viceroy-elect.

June 21

Popular M.P. Returns

Those M.P.s who have come into the House of Commons since the war began were a little puzzled yesterday to hear a back-bencher being cheered when he rose to put a private notice question.

They did not know that the older hands were welcoming back to

Parliament Lord Dunglass, M.P. for Lanark, who was P.P.S. to Mr. Chamberlain both at the Treasury and at No. 10, Downing Street.

Lord Dunglass is recovering from a very serious illness that has kept him out of the House for more than two years.

His recovery and appearance were also welcomed by the staff of the House of Commons, who remember vividly the half-centuries he used to compile in the Lords and M.P.s v. Staff cricket matches at the Oval. *June 23*

Oldest Air Transport Line

Air Commodore A. C. Critchley has been having numberless talks with civil aviation experts since he became Director-General of the British Overseas Airways Corporation five weeks ago. One of the most important people he has seen in this respect is Mr. Wilmot Hudson Fysh.

Mr. Fysh, a Squadron Leader and D.F.C. of the last war, is the managing director of Qantas, the oldest air transport company in the world. When he returned to Australia after the last war he started a freight and passenger transport service with two small Gypsy Moths, flying 70 m.p.h. and taking two days for the trip from Charleville to Cloncurry (600 miles).

He called it Queensland and North Territory Air Services—hence the present name. To-day Qantas is a full partner, subsidised by the Australian Government, of the B.O.A.C., and till Singapore fell had 18-ton flying boats on the Sydney-Singapore-Southampton route.

Mr. Fysh, who is 47 but looks younger, keeps in constant touch with the latest technical developments. Recently he went up in a Mosquito with Maj. Geoffrey de Havilland, and, in his own words, "nearly blacked out," owing to the new light bomber's terrific speed. *June 24*

Gen. Montgomery at a Play

I do not think anyone would have recognised Gen. Montgomery as he stepped out of the car that took him to the Strand Theatre while he was in London if he had not been wearing his famous tank man's beret with its two badges.

Gen. Montgomery is not well known to Londoners, apart from

the many photographs of him that have been published, and the first thing that caught the attention of the crowd was the black beret.

There was a stunned silence for a moment before someone gasped incredulously, "No, it can't be!" and then the cheers started. Gen. Montgomery smiled and waved happily. He was looking remarkably fit and brown.

He appeared to enjoy the play, "Arsenic and Old Lace." It was perhaps typical of him that he did not talk much about it to the principals, but rather of the Desert, and of the pressing need for reading matter for the men there. *July 13*

Souvent Femme Varie

During firing by a mixed A.A. battery at a practice camp an Instructor of Gunnery was watching two girls setting angles, as ordered, on their predictor. The I.G. noticed that one of them was several degrees out, and going up to her told her that her inaccuracy was spoiling the shooting.

She looked him up and down for a moment, then she said, "My, but you are fussy!"

The I.G. retired, completely baffled. *July 13*

Last Word on Herrenvolk

A prominent Dane, addressing a recent meeting in Copenhagen, said: "I have only one thing to say. It is that if God had intended the Germans to rule the world I think He would also have endowed them with the capacity to do so." *July 14*

Latest Noel Coward Lyric

Mr. Noel Coward, who is doing a broadcast in the Forces programme at 9.20 p.m. on Monday, is announced by the B.B.C. to be singing one new song. The refrain runs:

"Don't let's be nasty to the Nazis,
Don't let's be beastly to the Huns."

He tried it out at the stage party after the last night of his recent season at the Haymarket Theatre, where it had a dramatically hilarious reception. *July 16*

Loyal Wykehamist

Sir Archibald Wavell's choice of title confirms the general assumption that he would follow the modern practice of assuming a peerage in his own name. As to the territorial designation, "of Cyrenaica and Winchester," I doubt if there have been any good guesses about the second of these place-names.

As far as I remember, no new peer has ever before paid his old school so fine a compliment as this. The only near parallel, I suppose, is that of the great son of Oxford who took Oxford and Asquith as his actual title.

As for "of Cyrenaica," it is precisely in line with the designation "of Megiddo" chosen by Sir Archibald Wavell's hero of the last war, Lord Allenby, and of the similar choices made by other great soldiers.

Bright Idea

I remember, by the way, that when the conferment of a peerage on Lord Allenby was announced, someone on his staff offered a bright suggestion.

This officer, mindful at once of the sobriquet "the Bull" which had become attached to Lord Allenby owing to his lung-power in moments of annoyance and of the Psalmist's reference to the roaring of certain "strong bulls," thought that "Allenby of Bashan" would be a good idea. *July 23*

Nelson's Sicilian Dukedom

The Dukedom of Brontë in Sicily, which a grateful King of Naples conferred upon Nelson, will soon be in Allied hands. Nelson's titles have had a strange history. He left no direct heir and after his brother's death his British titles passed to a nephew, Thomas Bolton. These honours still remain with the Bolton family, but Parliament stipulated that no member of it could succeed to them until he had changed his name to Nelson.

Involved Sicilian law made it impossible for Thomas Bolton to become Duke of Brontë. One of Nelson's nieces became Duchess of Brontë. At her death the title passed to her son, the first Viscount Bridport, and that title belongs to the present Lord Bridport, who is, appropriately enough, a naval officer.

The Dukedom of Brontë, incidentally, has played a curious part in English literature. A dour Northern Irishman who greatly admired Nelson changed his name from Patrick Brunty to Patrick Brontë. He was the father of Charlotte, Emily and Anne Brontë.

August 4

Catches at Lord's

Controversy about Leslie Compton's left-handed catch from Constantine when leaning over the Pavilion rails in the England v. Dominions match at Lord's reminds me of a catch I once saw at the University match.

E. P. Hewetson, the Oxford fast bowler, had gone in eighth or ninth wicket and, as usual, began to lay about him. Soon he made a terrific hit, and sent the ball soaring high over the bowler's head towards the Pavilion.

As the ball began to drop a member, who had been sitting on the Pavilion benches with his top-hat over his eyes, rose, put his hands together, and made an effortless catch. Amid laughter he nonchalantly flicked the ball to the Cambridge man by the railing—and sat down.

August 5

Australia in Two Days

Mr. F. G. Miles, the aircraft designer, who has put forward the idea of a great London base for both land aircraft and sea-planes near Cliffe, about four miles east of Gravesend, is convinced that in the post-war years civil transport 'planes of great size will be in operation.

He himself has designed an 80-ton, eight-engined machine capable of carrying 150 passengers at 350 miles an hour, he tells me. Even this huge aircraft has been eclipsed by an American designer, who has worked out one of 200 tons, with accommodation for 250 passengers.

Mr. Miles says these powerful aircraft of the future will be able to fly to Australia in 48 hours. They will make only three intermediate stops, and passengers will be able to sleep "aboard."

Also he foresees the development of entirely new types of engines of greater power and less weight than those in use to-day. One of these models, I understand, has already got beyond the blue-print stage.

August 6

Actor, Sailor

Mr. Alec Guinness, whose account of amphibious operations seen from "sea level" appears on this page to-day, was not paying his first visit to Italy when he took his landing-craft to the beaches of Sicily. In the early part of 1939 he played Hamlet in Rome during the Old Vic's Continental tour, repeating his London success in the part.

Mr. Guinness is now 29. After spending 18 months in an advertising agency he went on the stage in 1934, and before he embarked on a naval career he had played such parts as Henry V, Aguecheek, Lorenzo, and Bob Acres in "The Rivals."

As a rating, before taking his commission—he is now a lieutenant—he had voyaged to America, and was released by the Admiralty to appear for a month in the New York production of "Flare Path."

August 20

The Queen and Lyautey

There is a good story of the Queen in ' Call No Man Happy," M. André Maurois's recently published autobiography. When they were Duke and Duchess of York she and the King were being conducted by Marshal Lyautey round the Colonial Exhibition at Vincennes.

Tea was being taken at the lakeside. ' Monsieur le Maréchal," said the Queen, ' you are so powerful. You created the beautiful country of Morocco and you have made this fine exhibition. Would you do something for me?"

Surprised, the Marshall asked what he could do. The Queen then said that the sun was in her eyes—could the Marshall make it disappear? Before Lyautey could reply the sun went behind a cloud.

In a lowered voice, the Queen explained to M. Maurois, who was sitting next to her, "I saw the cloud coming." *September 1*

Arrested Bishop

Himmler's arrest of the Bishop of Munster is more than a trial of strength with the Roman Catholic Church. It is also a clear declaration by the newly-appointed national boss to the German people that henceforth they have no personal rights at all.

It is for these rights that Mgr. Count von Galen has been fighting from the pulpit of St. Lambert's Church since the early days of the war against what he calls "the enemy within," the Gestapo.

After one of his sermons Gestapo men were sent to arrest him. He invited them to take him through the streets in his episcopal robes. They declined and went away.

Later he was arrested. Soon, however, the Nazis took fright and released him. He was carried back to his residence shoulder-high.

Retort from the Pulpit

His courage and dynamic personality are part of the tradition of a family which has provided religious leaders for centuries. To these qualities he adds a sense of humour.

A Nazi interrupted one of his sermons, demanding: "What right has a celibate without wife and children to talk about the problems of youth and marriage?"

The bishop sternly retorted: "Never will I tolerate in this cathedral any reflection upon our beloved Fuehrer." *September 1*

Verity's Big Day

Hedley Verity, who has died of wounds received in the Sicilian campaign, told me during one of his last matches before the war that he looked back on Monday, June 25, 1934, as the outstanding day of his cricket career.

Overnight rain followed by sun made the Lord's wicket just right for him that day. The Australians were unable to cope with the way he made the ball come back and lift, and England beat them at Lord's for the first time in 38 years.

King George V was there to congratulate Verity on his feat of taking 14 wickets in a day and equalling Rhodes's 1904 performance of 15 wickets in a Test match. Rhodes was there, too, to see the remarkable bowling of his Yorkshire successor.

At the end of the match Verity needed police protection to escape the attentions of the crowd of 30,000 spectators. They stood in front of the Pavilion calling for him. Wyatt coaxed him on to the balcony, but he could not be persuaded to make a speech. *September 4*

Propaganda

Two Belgian workmen travelling in a train near Antwerp were arguing in undertones and one of them said aloud, "I'm absolutely fed up. I would rather work 12 hours a day for the Germans than two for my own people."

A German officer sitting near said, "Perhaps you would say that again—on the radio."

When the Belgian repeated his words before the microphone, the announcer was surprised, and asked quickly, "And what is your trade?"

"Grave-digger." *October 1*

Elizabeth v. Victoria

When Parliament reassembles the first bill to come before the House of Lords will be that including Princess Elizabeth on the Council of State which functions during the King's absence from this country. I wonder how many people know that but for an unforeseen hitch we might have been expecting her to ascend the throne one day as Queen Elizabeth III.

If Sir Walter Scott had had his way there would have been no Queen Victoria. He dined with the Duchess of Kent in 1828 and was presented to Princess Alexandrina Victoria of Kent, as the future Queen was then known officially. "I hope that they will change her name," said Sir Walter. Three years later King William IV asked Parliament to make suitable provision for the Princess who would undoubtedly succeed to the throne.

This gave Sir Matthew White and Sir Robert Inglis an opportunity for expressing the hope that the Princess would come to the throne as Queen Elizabeth II.

Their proposal was fairly popular, but there was one obstacle which could not be overcome. The 12-year-old Princess had decided views of her own. Her attitude to the great Tudor Sovereign was one of violent antipathy. *October 11*

Rye Celebrity

I had often seen Miss Radclyffe Hall, who has died at the age of 57, in the neighbourhood of Rye and Winchelsea.

I doubt whether the inhabitants of Rye took her literary claims as seriously as those of Henry James or of E. F. Benson—who lived in Lamb House, a stone's throw away from the old church, after Henry James's death, and rose to be Mayor of Rye.

She was, none the less, a serious and sensitive writer. "Adam's Breed," which she wrote some 17 years ago, is still widely read.

Her appearance was striking and decidedly masculine. Some years ago I was in the Flushing Inn in Rye when the widow of a Victorian celebrity entered the room. She caught sight of Miss Hall and, summoning the waiter in the lordliest manner, said: "Please ask that young man to remove his hat." *October 12*

A Notable Centenary

It was on Nov. 10, 1843, that two young booksellers, Daniel Macmillan and his younger brother Alexander, of Scottish peasant stock, published their first book and founded the world-famous house which still bears their name.

The centenary is celebrated by the publication of "The House of Macmillan," by Mr. Charles Morgan, one of the best of the younger generation of authors whose own books bear the Macmillan imprint.

It is a fine story he has to tell. Among the distinguished names that appear in it are Tennyson, Matthew Arnold, Thomas Hughes, Gladstone, John Morley, Pater, Lewis Carroll, Henry James, Hardy, Kipling and Yeats, to name only a few of the outstanding Macmillan authors in the last 100 years.

Bernard Shaw Rejections

Every publisher has a list of famous authors who have been turned down by the firm. One of Macmillan's rejections was Mr. Bernard Shaw, who sent them his first novel, "Immaturity," in January, 1880. The same fate met "The Irrational Knot" and "Cashel Byron's Profession." When, in 1885, Macmillan rejected "An Unsocial Socialist," the youthful writer's wrath was stirred, and Mr. Morgan is able to print the letter that George Bernard Shaw, of 36, Osnaburgh Street, N.W., sent in reply.

The last letter from G.B.S. is a long one sent on Sept. 11, 1943, to Mr. Daniel Macmillan. Magnanimously Mr. Shaw now considers that the publishers' reader of 50 years before thought more of his "jejune prentice work" than he did himself. *November 11*

Father of Lend-Lease?

A teacher in an East End school had been teaching a youthful class about Noah and his family. She asked a small boy for the name of Noah's eldest son.

"Spam," he said. "You win on points," she replied.

November 15

Princess Elizabeth, Horsewoman

Many were interested to read yesterday that Princess Elizabeth had ridden to hounds for the first time. It was when she was staying with her parents at Queen Mary's war-time home in the country, and the pack she went out with is one of the most famous in the country.

Owing to the war early-rising Londoners have had no opportunities, as they might otherwise have done, of seeing the Princess and her sister riding in the Park.

The people of Windsor are more fortunate, and for quite a number of years the two Princesses have been familiar figures on their ponies trotting or cantering in the Long Walk. In less strenuous days the King was frequently seen with them.

A good judge, both of a horse and its rider, who has always taken his morning exercise hacking in the lovely rides of Windsor Park described Princess Elizabeth to me as having good hands as well as a good seat. *November 23*

Referred to You

Unfortunate owners of much war-damaged property are being set some teasing problems in the new forms they may be receiving shortly.

From many prose-gems included I cull the following:

> Provided that provision may be made by regulations made by the Treasury for substituting in this subsection, for the references to the amounts respectively therein mentioned references to values ascertained by reference to such matters as may be specified in the regulations.

A friend suggests that the only thing to do is to employ ferrets.

November 23

Officially Hansard

For the first time since 1889 the name "Hansard" appeared yesterday on the cover of the official reports of both Lords and Commons. In spite of the official dropping of the old name more than half a century back, it has continued in regular use in Parliament and Whitehall.

Until a few months ago the official report frowned on the use of the old name in Parliament. When an M.P. spoke in debate of "Hansard" it was always changed to "Official Report."

Recently it has allowed tradition to override accuracy, and has left any reference to "Hansard" in the form the M.P. made it.

Now the name is to appear boldly on the cover in brackets after the main title "Parliamentary Debates," a step recommended by the Committee on Publications and Debates.

One M.P. who has noted the change with special interest is Sir Edward Campbell. He is the father-in-law of Mr. John Hansard, a direct descendant of the T. C. Hansard who, with William Cobbett, started the report 140 years ago. *November 26*

Subaltern Who Scored

The C.R.A. was watching a gunner subaltern doing a shoot. The subaltern was working out all his calculations on a small slide-rule with considerable speed and accuracy.

After observing him for a time with slight distaste, the C.R.A. suddenly snatched his slide-rule away. "Your slide-rule's been shot away. What are you going to do now?" he said.

Without a word the subaltern felt in his battle-dress pocket, produced another slide-rule and carried on. *December 1*

Correspondent's Travels

Mr. Marsland Gander, *Daily Telegraph* war correspondent, just back from North Africa, tells me his arrival with a colleague at Paddington created quite a stir.

The sight of the packages of bananas and oranges which they had brought home was too much for the porters, who crowded round and begged for some for their children. They got about half of the precious fruit.

Mr. Gander has been in 18 different countries during the past two years, and has covered 50,000 miles. He has been on operational cruises in six types of warships.

Where There is Plenty

This time the homeward journey impressed him with the amazing contrasts the war had brought in the distribution of commodities.

At Gibraltar there were silk stockings, oranges, and Spanish sherry in abundance.

The war seemed remote in Cairo. At night the main shopping centre was a blaze of light. He could have as many eggs as he wanted.

Shops are full of Swiss watches, sweets and silk clothing of every kind, all unrationed. He heard of one English film star who had spent £1,000 replenishing her wardrobe.

While he was in Algiers, shipwrecked Ensa stars were still going about in battle-dress, as clothes were as scarce as whisky.

Of all the places Mr. Gander has visited recently, Algiers struck him as the key spot for Anglo-American co-operation. This he attributes to Gen. Eisenhower's influence, which he says could be discerned down to the smallest detail. *December 24*

Creator of Peter Rabbit

How many of us, about this season of the year, used to look forward to possessing another of those delightful animal books of Beatrix Potter, whose death is announced.

I have known young families in which, Christmas after Christmas, no stocking was complete without one of the immortal series that began with "Peter Rabbit" some 40 years ago. They sold by millions in several languages.

The charming delicacy of Miss Potter's illustrations to the books led to her becoming for some years designer of Queen Mary's Christmas cards. *December 24*

Good Reason

A rather shabbily dressed man, wearing a much-frayed Old Etonian tie, was standing at a hotel bar. A youthful Etonian, after eyeing him for some time, went over and said, "Why are you wearing an Old Etonian tie?"

"Because I can't afford a new one," replied his elder, and resumed his drink. *December 29*

How Tito Got His Name

A good deal has been made known of the history of the remarkable Jugoslav partisan leader, Marshal Tito, whose real name is Josip Broz. There have been many statements and theories about how he got his nom de guerre, none of them satisfactory.

I am told that it is a combination of two Serbo-Croat words—"ti," meaning "thou," and "to," meaning "that." The Marshal has a habit, when giving instructions to subordinates, of saying, "Thou wilt do that."

That is the whole history of the name now internationally known. *December 30*

A Desert Scandal

It appears that Col. Whiteley, the chairman of the Croydon Bench, who a month ago told a girl witness wearing trousers that her garb was an "insult to the court," has many sympathisers in Cairo.

The French newspapers there have been commenting unfavourably on the wearing of slacks in public places by women members of Ensa concert parties. They are referred to as "garçonnes," which may be translated as "tomboys."

I may recall what took place in the remote Siwa oasis, in the Libyan Desert, in 1941. An Arab girl who had married a European advertised her westernisation by wearing beach pyjamas in public.

This so shocked oasis opinion that the Siwa elders approached the British political officer, asking him to exile the lady, on the ground that "her trousers were rendering Siwa the laughing stock of the whole Desert." *December 31*

1944

One event, of course, stands out above all others in 1944—D-Day, as the Allied invasion of North-West Europe was known. For many months Stalin had been trying to force the British and Americans to invade France and had frequently and bitterly complained that Russia alone was shouldering the burden of the war in Europe. This was not in fact true, for in June, 1944, Germany had 165 much-depleted divisions on the Eastern Front, while 131 divisions were held down or actively engaged by Allied forces elsewhere in Europe, and at least two-thirds of her air force and practically her entire naval strength were occupied by events far removed from the Eastern Front. The Allies were naturally unwilling to embark on the invasion of Europe until the success of the operation could be reasonably assured and it was not until June 6, 1944, that circumstances combined to make it possible. On that day 156,000 British, American and Canadian troops landed in Normandy under the supreme command of General Eisenhower, with General Montgomery in command of the land forces.

Events thereafter are too well known to need repeating here. Suffice it to say that the initial speed of the advance made it seem possible that its impetus would carry the Allies over the Rhine before the enemy could rally his forces and make a stand. But after the failure of the airborne troops at Arnhem to hold the bridge long enough for the main body to come to their support it became clear that both sides needed time to catch their breath. Then on December 16 Field-Marshal von Rundstedt launched a counter-offensive in the Ardennes with the object of driving the American First Army back across the Meuse and striking north to recapture Antwerp. The attempt failed but Anglo-American relations were not improved when General Montgomery was sent to cope with the situation. The Ardennes offensive later became known as the Battle of the Bulge.

The story of the Russian advance into Eastern Europe is largely a matter of dates and distances. Against the massive weight of the Russian steamroller the Germans had nothing to offer but the spendthrift courage of the doomed, as each country in its turn was liberated from one form of tyranny to find itself in the stranglehold of another. During the advance evidence of the atrocities committed by the Germans, particularly of the wholesale massacre of the Jews, accumulated rapidly. It also came to light that the Russians themselves had murdered some 12,000 Polish soldiers near Katyn in 1939. The details of this grisly affair have never been satisfactorily resolved but its immediate repercussions had cast an ominous shadow over the Teheran Conference between Churchill, Roosevelt and Stalin, in November, 1943.

A brief mention must be made of the Warsaw Rising of August, 1944, which gave the unhappy Poles a taste of things to come. As the Russians approached the city the Polish underground army rose against the Germans, but the Russian advance was inexplicably halted and Warsaw was left alone in her agony. After sixty days the city surrendered, by which time 15,000 men of the underground army had been killed, 200,000 civilians had been killed, wounded or simply vanished, and the city itself was in ruins. It is worth reminding oneself that it was to preserve the national integrity of Poland that Britain and France had gone to war five years earlier.

The year in Italy was marked by the Anzio landings and the battle for, and tragic destruction of, the monastery at Cassino. By the year's end the Allies were as far north as Ravenna but it had been hard going all the way.

Now to the Far East, where in Burma the Fourteenth Army, under the inspired leadership of General Slim, was on the offensive and by December, thanks to the decision of Lord Louis Mountbatten, the Supreme Commander in South-East Asia, to fight through the monsoon season, had crossed the Chindwin. One incident which stands out as perhaps the most heroic feat of arms of any single unit during the Second World War was the stand of a battalion of the Royal West Kents at Kohima, where they held off the Japanese for sixteen days. Four thousand Japanese were killed.

In the Pacific the Americans drew the net gradually tighter round Japan, establishing themselves first in the Marshall Islands, then in the Marianas and, at last, back in the Philippines.

At home 1944 was remembered not only as the year of D-Day but also as the year of the V-bombs. Before all the bases from which they were launched in North-West Europe had been overrun 22,000 people in and around London had lost their lives and 750,000 houses had been demolished or damaged.

1944

In America President Roosevelt was elected for a fourth term of office.

Peterborough's bête noire *of the year is undoubtedly Sir Richard Acland, founder of the left-wing Common Wealth Party, who comes in for several pastings. Puns are out this year but obituaries are definitely in, the passing being noted in more or less favourable terms of General Wingate, Lord Lonsdale, Rex Whistler, Dame Ethel Smyth and Sir Harry Oakes, as well as Lord Moyne whose encomium is reprinted here.*

Golden Miller Mystery

Golden Miller's startling failure in the 1935 Grand National, the year after he had won the great steeplechase, remains one of racing's unsolved mysteries. In his book, "The Life of Golden Miller," published to-day by Hutchinson, Mr. Basil Briscoe, who trained the horse, recalls that after the race he was examined by two veterinary surgeons.

They found nothing wrong. Consequently, Golden Miller ran again the next day in the Champion Chase. He unseated his jockey again—at the first fence this time.

"Miss Paget unfortunately blamed me for the incidents and considered her horse had not been properly trained," says Mr. Briscoe. "I felt that, under the circumstances, if those were her views, I could not possibly continue to train my old pal."

So ended his long association with The Miller and Miss Dorothy Paget.

"£500 Thrown Away"

Mr. Briscoe bought Golden Miller in 1930 as an unbroken three-year-old from Ireland. Describing the colt's arrival in England he says that he thought he had never thrown away £500 so easily. "He stood in the box with his head down. He had a coat on him like a bear and mud on him from head to tail."

Golden Miller, under Mr. Briscoe's care, became one of the most spectacular and popular steeplechasers of all time. He won the Grand National and five Cheltenham Gold Cups—a record.

He ran in 55 races and won 29, winning stakes when he was owned by Miss Paget amounting to £15,000. The Miller is now 17 and lives in peaceful retirement on an Essex stud farm. *January 6*

Cold-Store Mindedness

Prof. J. C. Drummond, Scientific Adviser to the Ministry of Food—he will be "Sir Jack" when the King has given him the accolade on his New Year's honour—belongs to the refrigerationist group of present-day food experts. He thinks that, for countries with a high standard of living, refrigeration and not dehydration will be the dietetic dictator of the future.

When I met him at lunch yesterday he told me that he looked to the time when every housewife would be "cold-store-minded." "I am trying to convince architects," he said, "that in post-war houses they must design for the refrigerator as inevitably as for the bathroom."

The type he contemplates is that now in vogue in America with compartments at different temperatures. While British scientists lead the world in the chemical research in foodstuffs, the United States, he says, is far ahead of us in putting knowledge into practice.

Gourmet on Vitamins

I gathered that we were particularly behindhand in the transport of frozen food by rail or road. By quick freezing and consistent preserving at minus 20 degrees centrigrade most foodstuffs can be kept indefinitely.

The Professor, who will return to his Chair of Bio-chemistry in London University after the war, talks of food with more authority than that of a mere scientist. A follower of M. André Simon, he is one of those members of the Wine and Food Society who have added to dietetic literature.

Before the war he collaborated in a book, "The Englishman's Food." In this, vitamins and proteins, while treated with respect, are not allowed to interfere with the just claims of the gourmet.

January 8

Fables of 1944

Time 4.45 a.m. The telephone rings.

"Are you Western 1164?"

"No, I am Western 1146."

"I'm so sorry you've been troubled."

"Not at all, my dear sir. I had to get up and answer the telephone anyway."

January 8

Rank and Wealth

Gen. Sir Frederick Pile, speaking at the Mansion House yesterday, told a story of two American soldiers who one night recently asked him where West Kensington was. The three found a cab and while he was telling the driver where to go the privates settled themselves firmly in the back.

After an interesting conversation they reached their destination, where the Americans said they were going to pay for the cab.

"Oh, no," said the General. "I am senior to you."

"Oh, yes," one of them replied, "but you don't get so much pay."

January 14

Final

A young soldier at a school for parachute troops approached his instructor after a lecture and asked, "Suppose the parachute doesn't open?"

"That," snapped the sergeant, "is called jumping to a conclusion."

January 15

Digits that Count

The captain in the Middle East who received a "standard text telegram" from his wife, whom he had not seen for two years, saying "Son born," had reason to be surprised.

On inquiry he found that the code number was 185 instead of 85. The cable should have read, "Receiving letters occasionally."

Addition or subtraction of the first digit might lead to even greater shocks. Cable 67 runs "My thoughts and prayers are ever with you." No. 167 consists of two words. They are "Twins born."

January 20

Jet Plane Collaborator

Group Capt. Whittle, the brilliant and modest R.A.F. scientist who invented the jet system with which the Gloster aircraft was equipped, would be the first to give a measure of credit to the designer of the aircraft itself. I learn that this was Mr. W. G. Carter, who was at one time the chief designer of both the old Sopwith Company and the Hawker Company.

The successful application of the jet principle to an aircraft is in itself an outstanding achievement. That all the flying of the prototype should have been accomplished without accident is a considerable tribute to those who designed, built and installed the unusual power plant.

To begin with, they had to produce a "pusher." Almost all other modern aircraft are "tractors." Pressures, weights and accelerations had to be balanced at all speeds.

I am told that the new system is proving even more successful than was expected, and offers great promise for the future of aviation. *January 24*

Liars All

Very few of those who tackled the problem I quoted from Sir Arthur Eddington's "New Pathways in Science" got to grips with it all. The question was:

> If A, B, C, D each speak the truth once in three times (independently), and A affirms that B denies that C declares that D is a liar, what is the probability that D was speaking the truth?

I gave Sir Arthur's answer, but nine out of 10 of my correspondents who wrote to me about it failed to see how the eminent mathematician reached his result. They argued that nothing A, B and C said affected the fact that the chances of D speaking the truth were 2 to 1 against.

Elusive Answer

Sir Arthur writes that it was many years after he first heard the problem that it occurred to him that it actually had an answer—and was an instructive example of what he calls the Exclusion Method. He adds:

> The reader will be in a better position to appreciate the enormous advantage of the exclusion method if he has first been driven wild by attempting to solve the problem without it.

His explanation of the problem is that

> The combinations inconsistent with 'A declares &c.' are truth-lie-truth-truth and truth-lie-lie-lie, which occur, respectively, twice and eight times out of 81 occasions. Excluding these D is left with 27—2 truths to 54—8 lies, so that the required probability is 25/71.

I suppose it is really quite simple. *January 24*

Mistaken Vocation

An officer back from Archangel tells a story of barter and exchange there which he swears is true.

A British merchant seaman went ashore with 10 cigarettes in his pocket. For these the Russians gave him 100 roubles.

With the money he bought 12 wine-glasses. These he took aboard a British merchantman, where the steward, very short of glasses, offered him two bottles of gin in exchange.

Tucking them under his arm, he boarded an American merchantman, which was absolutely dry, and swapped them for 6,000 cigarettes.

Ashore again he sold these to the Russians for 10,000 roubles. With the money he bought two fine skins, which he sold in London to a fur dealer for £100. *February 1*

Navy's Greek Prince

Tall, fair and good-looking, Prince Philip of Greece signalled his return to London by visiting the Distinguished Strangers' Gallery in the House of Commons yesterday. He is a lieutenant in the Royal Navy and was in H.M.S. Valiant at the Battle of Matapan.

A cousin of King George of the Hellenes, and close in succession to the Greek throne, he is also a cousin of our King and Lord Louis Mountbatten's nephew.

The Prince, who was in British naval uniform, looked across to another part of the Gallery where other naval officers of the United Nations—a party of Chinese officers—were watching the proceedings with close interest. *February 3*

A.P.H.'s Latest

A few days ago when Petty Off. A. P. Herbert was attending a charity function, he was asked for his autograph by a young girl. The senior burgess for Oxford University promptly extemporised the following in her book:

> Be good, sweet maid, and, if you can, be clever, Or better still, just leave it to the gods. The chances are you won't be either ever, So what's the odds?

I hear, by the way, that Mr. Alan Herbert will soon cease to bear his present rank. A commission awaits him.

The House of Commons and his friends everywhere may regret the removal of this distinguished member of the lower deck to the less picturesque atmosphere of the ward room. But Service considerations cannot yield to sentiment. *February 14*

New Moon?

A story is told in Cairo of Lt.-Gen. Sir Arthur Smith, the new G.O.C.-in-C. Persia and Irak, when he was on Lord Wavell's staff. Always punctilious on matters of discipline, he was in his car one day when he noticed that a soldier failed to salute him.

Pulling down the window he looked out and asked the man why he had omitted to do so. "I never salute through glass, sir," was the answer.

"What do you take me for?" replied Sir Arthur. "A new moon?"

February 15

Gladstone and Cassino

Had it not been for Gladstone and his English friends the monastery on Monte Cassino might have been a place of ruin and desolation many years ago.

Garibaldi intended to dissolve it, together with other monasteries. He evolved a great scheme for bringing all the books and treasures from Monte Cassino to Rome.

Gladstone, whom he had first met in Chiswick House—then the near-London home of the Duke of Devonshire—dissuaded him. Because of the weight of English sentiment the Italian Government decided that it would be wiser not to proceed with the dissolution of the Monte Cassino monastery.

Dean Stanley's Visit

Italian indifference to the history of the monastery had always puzzled Gladstone. When he heard that the actual tomb of St. Benedict was in poor condition, he headed a list of subscriptions from England so that it could be fully restored.

After Arthur Stanley became Dean of Westminster Gladstone persuaded him to go to Monte Cassino because Westminster Abbey, as a Benedictine foundation, was once a daughter-house.

It would have shocked Gladstone beyond measure that the monastery should ever have been turned into a fortress and so made a military target.

In peace time the centenary of St. Benedict's death would have been observed with some splendour. He died in 544, though the actual date is unknown.

Britain as well as other corners of Christendom has a direct and historic link with the foundation, for a former monk at Monte Cassino was St. Augustine, Canterbury's first Archbishop.

February 21

P.M.'s "Young Friend"

"A young friend of mine, an Oxford don," was how Mr. Churchill introduced his reference to Lt.-Col. Deakin, D.S.O., who entered Jugoslavia by parachute a year ago and spent eight months at Marshal Tito's headquarters.

In the preface to the last volume of his "Marlborough," finished in 1938, Mr. Churchill records how he had "been greatly assisted in the necessary researches by Mr. F. W. Deakin, of Wadham College, Oxford." In fact, they visited the Marlborough battlefields together.

At the outbreak of war Col. Deakin was an officer in Oxford's A.A. battery, which embraced the old Oxfordshire Yeomanry. Mr. Churchill once served in this unit as a subaltern.

About two years ago Col. Deakin went abroad, and for a time nothing was heard of him. Friends at Oxford gave him up as lost.

"Brilliant Scholar"

His mother, who lives at Aldbury Common, near Tring, told me last evening that she knew he had been away from Cairo on some "hush, hush" mission.

The Warden of Wadham describes him as "immensely energetic and forceful, short, red-haired and lively, and a brilliant scholar."

February 23

Boulestin Vignette

As a friend of Marcel Boulestin's I always regarded him as one of the happiest of men. Doris Lytton Toye's appreciation in the spring number of Wine and Food emphasises that his happiness was rooted in his philosophy. Montaigne was his master.

Before the last war Boulestin had a flourishing business in London as a decorator, with a sideline as a populariser of French post-impressionists.

After being demobilised from the French Army in 1919, he came back with two Dufy's, one Vlaminck, and one Modigliani in his luggage.

£12 Modigliani

Caught by the post-war slump, he sold the Modigliani, for which he had given £12, for £90—later it would have been worth several hundreds. When his fortunes were at their lowest, he reviewed his prospects.

Then realising, in Montaigne's phrase, "je n'ai rien de mien que moi," he "shook himself like a duck, had a good dinner at the Café Royal, went to a show, and slept well."

In the autumn of 1922 he had occasion to see a director of Heinemann's about an etching. As he was leaving, he said, for no especial reason, "You wouldn't be interested in a cookery book, would you?" "It's exactly what we want," was the reply.

That was how Marcel Boulestin began his career as the acknowledged gastronomic leader of London in the period between the wars.

March 11

Romantic—But True

American officers were puzzled by a French statement for reverse Lend-Lease accounts dealing with palm trees chopped down on one of the French Pacific islands to build air bases. "That's just twice the number of palm trees we chopped down," they complained.

The French reply, according to the story published in the Washington Post, was: "Don't you know that for every palm tree cut down another dies of a broken heart?"

The Encyclopaedia Britannica confirms this romantic view, stating that plants of the coconut palm are born in fleshy spadices, male and female on distinct plants.

March 15

Air War Story

I spent an interesting hour yesterday reading "Target: Germany," which is "the U.S. Army Air Forces' official story of the VIII Bomber Command's first year over Europe."

Brilliantly written and brilliantly illustrated, it is a remarkable 1s 6d worth of over 100 pages, with wonderful photographs, many of which are quite new to me.

In giving credit to those concerned with its production, I should also mention the publishers: H.M. Stationery Office.

Nor is it entirely devoid of light relief. Here is a story from Chapter 3, "Act 1, Scene 1":

> One of the first problems was to find a place where the Americans could hang their tin hats. This was solved eventually by the acquisition of an old abbey. The story has been told how the duty officer on the first night of occupancy, was startled to hear bells beginning to ring all over the building. Investigation proved that each bedroom had a prim little card, relic of schoolgirl days, that read: "Ring twice for mistress."

In earlier days I heard this story told of the Canadians. I will leave it with them to argue questions of copyright. *March 16*

His Own Librettist

Mr. T. S. Eliot had originally agreed to collaborate in Michael Tippett's new large-scale choral work, "A Child of our Time," which is having its first performance at the L.P.O.'s Adelphi Theatre concert to-morrow afternoon.

When our leading poet was shown the first draft of the libretto, he was so impressed that he advised Mr. Tippett to continue with the writing of it himself. Thus encouraged the young Cornish composer has followed the example of Wagner and Berlioz and been his own librettist.

The production of such a big composition in war-time is something of an achievement for everyone concerned, including the publishers, who have contributed a large percentage of their paper quota to provide the choir with printed copies of the work.

I am not surprised to hear that "A Child of our Time" is difficult. There have in consequence been many rehearsals.

To some of them, members of Morley College and the London Region Defence Choirs have come straight from raid "incidents."

Mr. Walter Goehr, who has made a name for himself recently for his handling of contemporary music, will conduct.

March 18

Modern Art in Paris

The news that a small painting by Degas realised £2,500 at an auction sale of pictures in Paris, seems to show that the French capital may still claim to be the world's artistic centre so far as modern and contemporary artists are concerned.

The average price per lot in this sale was in the neighbourhood of £500, an average that has been equalled at few London and New York sales in recent years.

A Frenchman who arrived in London during the last few days tells me that many successful art exhibitions have been held this winter in Paris. Georges-Braques has just finished a show at the Petit Palais. German and French buyers vied with each other to secure his latest works.

Dufy and Segonzac

Admirers of Raoul Dufy will be interested to know that he is working with his brother in the South of France. He says he has no political views at all—either domestic or international.

At the other extreme is Segonzac, some of whose paintings were a feature of the Fighting French exhibitions held a few months ago at the Suffolk Galleries. He is a leader of the Parisian group of young people supporting "the aged Marshal."

Picasso, my informant tells me, has been treated with great respect by the Germans, who have been anxious to buy his work. He is now painting in Switzerland. *March 22*

Tale of the Ducks

A story is being told in naval circles of the Army's "Dukws," amphibian transport vehicles known as "Ducks"—one of which is on view to the public in Trafalgar Square for the first time during London's Salute the Soldier week.

While leading on the water a string of some 40 "Dukws," an R.A.S.C. convoy commander was rather surprised to see a flotilla of destroyers to starboard making towards him. A signal flashed from the leading destroyer.

The convoy commander, fearing the worst, requested its translation. He was relieved to learn that the signal merely said, "Quack! Quack!" *March 27*

Communist Prince

M. Molotov's declaration that Russia does not seek any territorial expansion in Rumania and does not intend to interfere with the social system in that country has heartened some Rumanians in London.

The greatest obstacle in the way of Rumanian resistance to the Germans has hitherto been the fear of the small intellectual bourgeoisie that Russia's defeat of Germany would mean their ruin and even physical destruction.

Now the Russian declaration should go some way to reassuring them.

It will, however, be a slight disappointment to Rumania's self-appointed Communist dictator.

He is Prince Callimacki, a member of an old Rumanian aristocratic family and formerly one of the most cultured and intelligent dandies of Bucharest society. His parents disinherited him on his marrying, as they thought, unsuitably.

This action swung him over from dandyism and Proust to Marxist ideology, and a long-range bombardment of Bucharest from Moscow. *April 4*

Stowe's 21st

To-day Stowe School comes of age. It was founded on May 11, 1923, when the former palace of the Dukes of Buckingham and Chandos was converted into a public school.

Stowe's success—its members rose in its first six or seven years from 100 to 500—is very largely due to the personality of Mr. J. F. Roxburgh, who now celebrates his 21st birthday as headmaster of the school which he created.

A tall, good-looking, well-dressed Scot, he has a presence and a charm of manner which have awed refractory governors, delighted parents and won unstinted loyalty from the boys.

Mr. Roxburgh, an old Carthusian and Cambridge man, is a scholar and connoisseur of many things, including wine.

Mlle. Roxbur'

At the Sorbonne, where he took his classical Licencié-ès-Lettres in one year instead of the normal two, he achieved the almost incredible feat for a non-Frenchman of being second in the essay.

About this he tells a story against himself. Mr. Roxburgh's handwriting—a large, bold and flowing hand familiar to generations of old Stoics—misled the examiners, who launched into a eulogy of the performance of "cette Mlle. Roxbur'." *May 11*

The Uncivil Servant

After 50 years' experience of domestic service, Mr. Albert Thomas, now butler to the Principal of Brasenose College, Oxford, has written his autobiography. It is to be published on Monday with the punning title of "Wait and See."*

As a youngster he was third footman to the late Duke of Norfolk. Every summer the family used to drive in a four-in-hand through Wales. At one village the Duke stopped at a post office to send a telegram.

He waited at the counter while the girl "was busily engaged in talking to a pimply-faced grocer's assistant." Finally, losing patience, he asked for a telegraph form in, for him, an unusually sharp tone. The girl flicked one towards him and the Duke wrote out a message and handed it in. *April 12*

Mark Twain–Churchill Duo

A special print of the film "The Adventures of Mark Twain," which has just had its American première, is being sent to Mr. Churchill.

Over 40 years ago the hero of the picture once sat at dinner next to the present Prime Minister. The two got on so well that they decided to continue their conversation tête-à-tête in the smoking-room afterwards.

As they rejoined the other guests Sir William Harcourt observed that whichever of these two ardent conversationalists had managed to get in the first word was certain to have monopolised the remainder of the evening.

Turning to Mr. Churchill, he asked, "Did you enjoy yourself?" "Yes," was the enthusiastic reply. Mark Twain, when asked the same question, hesitated. Then he said, "I've had a good smoke."

April 13

*See 16 June 1944.

Jamais La Politesse

An elderly man gave up his seat in a crowded Tube train to a young woman, who accepted without a word of thanks.

"Une belle dame sans merci," he murmured, as he clung to a strap. *June 3*

Oldest Wine Merchants

The old firm of wine merchants in St. James's, dating from the 17th century—Berry Bros. and Co.—has recently made a short addition to its title, and is now known as Berry Bros. and Rudd Ltd.

After the death of Mr. Charles Berry, the formation of a private company was forced on the firm owing to the expansion of the business both at home and abroad.

The old style of Berry Bros. and Co. had already been registered by a Yorkshire firm. Though no conceivable confusion would arise between a cloth and a wine business, official regulations demanded a change in the familiar name Berry Bros. and Co.

Major H. R. Rudd, the present head of the firm, who has been a partner for a quarter of a century, tells me that when he added his name he was satisfied that so short an addition would not interfere with the style of the well-known labels.

Weighed Byron

For two centuries or more the business has passed through family connections. The name of Berry has been associated with it since the first years of the 19th century.

Early records suggest that the Pickering who gave his name to the little old-world court behind the shop was one of the partners. Business is still carried on under "the Sign of the Coffee Mill."

The great scales on which during 200 years customers, including Byron and Beau Brummell, have had their weights recorded once served to weigh sacks of coffee beans. These were sold, no doubt, to the coffee houses in St. James's Street. *June 15*

Domestics' Three Cs

"Waiting and Seeing," the recently published autobiography of Mr. Albert Thomas, the butler to the Principal of Brasenose College,

Oxford, caused him to be the chief guest at yesterday's Foyle lunch.

His thick, white eyebrows bristled with good humour when he quoted a don's advice to him on how to make his first public speech. "Make it like a lady's dress, Thomas, short enough to be interesting and long enough to cover the subject."

He thinks that girls will return to domestic service after the war so long as care is taken of the "three Cs"—comfort, consideration and 'commodation.

Mr. Thomas confessed that a recent advertisement in *The Daily Telegraph* offering £7 10s a week and all found for a couple—a cook and a butler-house-parlourman—appalled him.

A fair wage, in his opinion, is 1s an hour with a maximum of eight hours' work. *June 16*

Wrong Bird

A naval friend who recently took over the command at a West of England port was inspecting his W.R.N.S. unit. He asked one of them if she would catch him some fish in the harbour in her spare time.

"Sir," she replied, "I am a Wren, not a cormorant." *July 15*

Discovered Farrar

Sir Newman Flower, the chairman of Cassell and Co., writes to me about the invitation to the wedding of Dean Farrar's daughter with the future Bishop Montgomery, which I reproduced recently. This invitation referred to the Dean's "manie learned and wholesome books."

Cassells, Sir Newman claims, discovered Farrar. The firm wanted someone who would put Christ "over" as a real human being.

They decided that a director, with a keen human and religious sense, should wander about the country listening to Sunday evening sermons until he found the right man.

One Sunday evening he went into a church where Farrar, then unknown, was preaching. He heard the sermon—a sermon that made Christ "human."

Offer in a Vestry

After the service he waited till the congregation had gone. Then he went to the vestry and offered Farrar on the spot £500 and his expenses to Palestine for a Life of Christ.

The book was an enormous success. Everyone read it, from Queen Victoria downwards, and Farrar from that time was famous.

Sir Newman Flower tells me that his firm, though they had paid Farrar £500 for the copyright, also gave him a royalty—though under no obligation to do this.

July 15

Discovery of a Dean

Literary "success stories" have, I think, an interest of their own. A. and C. Black write to me courteously contesting the claim of Cassells, to which I referred lately, to have "discovered" Dean Farrar when, in 1870, they commissioned him to write his enormously successful "Life of Christ."

A. and C. Black write:

> We published "Eric, or Little by Little," in 1858, "Julian Home, or A Tale of College Life," in 1859, and "St. Winifred's or The World of School," in 1862. Each immediately became a best-seller and continued to sell many thousands of copies a year for over 50 years. Even to-day the sales have not ceased.

The Dean, they add, was in 1870 already known far and wide through these stories, had been appointed Chaplain to the Queen, and had published at least one volume of sermons.

Well Rewarded

Dean Farrar, by the way, was doubly fortunate in his publishers. Just as Cassells gave him a royalty, although they had bought the "Life" outright, so A. and C. Black—having purchased for a moderate sum the copyright of "Eric," the first book of a little-known Harrow master—gave Farrar above and beyond their legal obligations a half-profits agreement.

This brought him a substantial income to the end of his long life.

July 21

F.D.R.'s Running Mate

No American party Convention, met to name its candidates for the two chief national offices, has ever before been so much agitated over its choice of a Vice-Presidential nominee as the Democratic Convention that has selected Senator Harry Truman of Missouri.

He is an able politician with a sound party record, around whose personality no conflicts have raged.

Usually the nomination for this office is very much a cut-and-dried affair. No man normally has an ambition to run for an office that in itself confers little power or importance, and is in fact regarded as placing its holder on the political shelf.

Rare Contingency

The Democrats, however, had to bear in mind the one rare contingency in which a Vice-President becomes all-important. That is the death of the President, whose place is automatically taken by the Vice-President for the rest of the four-year term.

Mr. Roosevelt is in excellent health and spirits, but should he be re-elected, the strain of a fourth Presidential term would be an ordeal such as no American statesman has ever had to face.

In the circumstances, the Convention is to be regarded as having done its best to play safe. *July 24*

Cossack to Shah

Shah Riza Pahlevi, who has just died in exile in South Africa, was a remarkable man. This ex-Cossack trooper became Shah of Persia, and ascended the Peacock Throne (of which tawdry piece of Oriental furniture he was reputed to have sold most of the remaining genuine jewels) by a mixture of brutality and genius.

He was grandiose in his ideas. The wide "boulevards" of Teheran, with their macadam surfaces, their electric light—and the open drain running down each side—were one aspect of his taste for the modern and the Western. Others are the huge unfinished opera house and some fine modern governmental buildings.

He insisted on the unveiling of Persian women—who are, in consequence, with the exception of the Turkish, the most emancipated in Asia. He broke the power of the mullahs by refusing to allow religious headwear.

Progress, Plus Profit

Typically, his decree enforcing the wearing of European hats came into force overnight. It was then found that the Shah happened shortly before to have bought up cheap a huge stock of European hats, which he was prepared to allow his subjects to buy for a consideration.

Brigandage he put down by the simple expedient of hanging anyone who was found in the neighbourhood of a highway crime. He broke up the power of the tribes by transferring them to other parts of Persia.

Like many other autocrats, he started by conferring considerable benefits on his people, but got swollen-headed, and fell an easy victim to German bribery and flattery. This led to Anglo-American-Russian intervention and his downfall. *July 28*

A Fallen Star

The statement that Maurice Chevalier was killed by French patriots on Friday cannot yet be taken as fact, but one can only say with regret that at any rate his arrest would not be surprising.

Although reports about him after the fall of France were at first conflicting, it has long been accepted as true by his countrymen that he devoted himself and his talents to collaboration with the enemy.

It would be a miserable end for an artist who did his duty in arms in the last war and suffered captivity in a German prison camp.

Londoners have never forgotten the gaiety and charm of one of the most popular French stars that they ever applauded.

I remember well the enthusiasm with which he was greeted by a packed audience at an entertainment given to the troops at Drury Lane, at which the late Duke of Kent and the Duchess were present, in the month before the French collapse.

It was in the year before the war that he was given the Legion of Honour "for signal services to French propaganda in all countries." The irony of it! *August 29*

Picasso in Paris

Now that the fog of war has lifted from Paris, Pablo Picasso's war life proves, after all, to have been quite unadventurous.

Throughout the German occupation the most Parisian of Spanish artists lived in his studio in the Rue des Grands Augustins. Gestapo officials came and asked questions. They went away and he went on painting.

Although Picasso has always refused to take part in group exhibitions, he has promised to join the autumn Salon next month as a gesture of solidarity with his fellow-artists.

Many German soldiers called to look at the three or four hundred canvases the artist has painted since June, 1940.

One German officer noticed a sketch of Picasso's mural "Guernica," which depicts the Luftwaffe's destruction of that Basque town. "Did you do that?" he asked brusquely. "No," replied the artist, "you did." *September 25*

Lord Mayor's Critic

Sir Frank Newson-Smith, the Lord Mayor, speaking at yesterday's lunch of the Paviors' Company in the Mansion House, admitted that he was "very miserable" at the idea of his term of office coming to an end next month.

He said that he had enjoyed a most happy year. Then he proceeded to tell a story against himself.

One job he had this year was to look over a mental hospital. He was invited to go into a large hall and address the staff and some of the patients.

After he had been speaking for a few minutes an inmate in the front row suddenly got up and said, "What a lot of rot." As he walked out he kept on repeating the phrase.

Sir Frank took no notice, but afterwards the superintendent said to him: "I was very interested in that man who interrupted you. He has been here for ten years, and that is the first lucid moment he has had." *October 12*

Ex-Civil Servant Candidate

I wrote recently about war-time Civil Servants with Parliamentary ambitions. One of the most prominent of them is Mr. Harold Wilson, who has just resigned as Director of Economics and Statistics at the Ministry of Fuel and Power to become prospective Socialist candidate at Ormskirk.

He is, I hear, going to make his first speech there to-night in what promises to be a lively fight with the sitting member, Cmdr. King-Hall.

Incidentally, the rival general election candidates were colleagues at the Ministry of Fuel when Cmdr. King-Hall was running Major Lloyd George's fuel economy campaign. At 28 Mr. Wilson is looked on by Socialists as a coming President of the Board of Trade or Chancellor of the Exchequer.

Don at 21

He made his way by scholarships from an elementary school to Oxford, where besides appearing for the University in cross-country events he became a don at 21. A friend of Sir William Beveridge, Mr. Wilson is now a Fellow and Tutor in Economics at University College, Oxford.

At the start of the war he volunteered for the Army. The Government, however, preferred to use him first in the Ministry of Supply and later in the economics section of the War Cabinet secretariat and the Ministry of Labour.

At the Ministry of Fuel he held the rank of assistant secretary and produced the recent statistical digest of coal output, the most terrifying White Paper I have yet encountered. *October 14*

Rabbits

A lady of my acquaintance who breeds rabbits applied to the Ministry of Food for a licence to sell them.

In due course she received a reply from the Welsh fastness whence the Ministry conducts these operations, which ended up with this cryptic sentence:

> The question as to whether it is necessary for you to hold a licence to sell live rabbits depends upon the condition, i.e. live or dead, in which the rabbits for food are disposed of, and, if dead, whether you should be in possession of any licence in respect of the sales.

So what? *October 18*

Assassination of Lord Moyne in Cairo

Mr. Churchill came into the House yesterday just as questions had ended. He looked grave and sad. In his hand he had the notes for the noble and intimate eulogy of his dead friend which he was to deliver.

When he spoke of the "foul assassins" his eyes flashed. Rarely have two words of the Prime Minister held more of concentrated detestation.

On their arrival at Westminster yesterday morning some members, recalling that the House adjourned after Field-Marshal Sir Henry Wilson's assassination, half expected the same procedure.

In fact, by a coincidence the House did adjourn very early—but this was merely a coincidence.

Knew the Empire

When Lord Moyne succeeded dynamic Lord Lloyd at the Colonial Office the more orthodox permanent officials thought that the waters would not be so often ruffled.

To some extent they were right, for the tranquillity and thoughtfulness of Lord Moyne soon made themselves felt throughout the Department.

More than once a minor official would go home happy because he had received a chit in Lord Moyne's own large hand, written in blue pencil, commending something done or suggested.

Lord Moyne's knowledge of the Empire was great. Perhaps two things dominated his career at the Colonial Office—and incidentally they were prominent in his subsequent Middle East studies.

No Colour Bar

The first was his insistence—privately and publicly expressed scores of times—that if we preserved the colour bar we should lower ourselves to the level of the Herrenvolk conception. The second was his conviction that justice must be done to the Arabs in Palestine.

In this latter problem he was forced by first-hand study to adopt a line somewhat different from the views which he had been alleged to hold before taking office.

He was so honest, however, that he did not mind the criticism which came as a result of his analysis.

That Secret Tunnel

Lord Moyne was a shy and retiring administrator. On the other hand he was seldom startled out of his savoir faire. The only case on which I saw him a little put out of countenance was when a delegation of West Indian editors came to visit him at the Colonial Office.

Lord Moyne was pouring out tea for the delegation in the Secretary of State's big room from an enormous teapot. One member of the delegation—a coloured editor of great charm from one of the outer islands—tried to catch his eye.

The policy of his paper was inseparably wedded to the theory that Britain was about to be invaded by tunnel. He came up behind Lord Moyne and suddenly exclaimed, "Mr. Secretary, sir, you're sure going to lose this war. You're going to be attacked from below."

At this sudden revelation of enemy strategy Lord Moyne nearly dropped the teapot. *November 8*

Lean Times

A young officer who had escaped from an Italian prisoner-of-war camp to Switzerland cabled to his father: "Hope return home shortly; prepare fatted calf; anything you wish bring with me?"

The father cabled back: "Delighted hear news. Bring fatted calf." *November 23*

Cautious Cordell

Mr. Cordell Hull, who has just resigned the post of Secretary of State, always makes absolutely sure of his facts.

The story goes that during a long train journey Mr. Hull's travelling companion remarked, "That's a fine flock of sheep we're just passing. They've just been sheared."

The Secretary of State, after a pause for reflection, replied, "Well, on this side, anyway." *November 29*

R.L.S. Best-seller

Sir Newman Flower, the head of Cassell's, has been telling me about his firm's connection with Robert Louis Stevenson, who died 50 years ago to-morrow.

It seems that one day a long-haired, picturesque-looking individual entered Cassell's office with a pasted-up copy of a boy's serial he had written. It had a name which will not be found in any list of Stevenson's work.

About eight months later he turned up again to ask what they had decided about his MS. He was told that Cassell's had been doing their best to find him, as they wanted to make arrangements to publish it.

This was how "Treasure Island," the name finally chosen for the story, was given to the world.

Unpublished Letters

Sir Newman, who has been in Cassell's since 1906, became its chief in 1927. A little while later he explored the firm's vaults.

There he found a number of unpublished Stevenson letters. He describes them as rather remarkable, hinting as they do at a book which Stevenson contemplated writing but never did.

These letters, which are Sir Newman's property, are still unpublished. *December 2*

Penicillin Story

Sir Alexander Fleming, the revered Scottish professor who discovered penicillin, showed yesterday how the modern scientist can, on occasion, take risks not less real than those taken by Pasteur and Lister in their day.

At the first of the three Harben lectures at the Royal Institute of Public Health Sir Alexnader gave his audience a surprise which forcibly, if unintentionally, brought home to them the greatness of the lecturer.

Laconically in his Scots accent he described what he called his "first and most important patient." The man was suffering from meningitis and was brought in at a time when penicillin had not achieved recognition. Failure, even on a hopeless case, might have done its protagonist considerable harm.

Almost Well in 10 Days

"He was dying," said Professor Fleming, "and nothing would have effect. I got in touch with Professor Florey at Oxford and asked for a supply of penicillin. I didn't know then whether it would kill him or not; but he was dying anyway and the chance had to be taken, so we tried it."

The man was out of danger in less than a week and in 10 days was almost well again.

His recovery made such an impression on Sir Alexander that he brought penicillin to the notice of the Minister of Supply, who immediately called a meeting of everybody interested.

That was the beginning of the Penicillin Committee, which has done so much to help production in this country. *December 12*

1945

At last we come to the year when the fighting stopped and the peace should have begun, but few could see in the second half of 1945 much similarity to what they had known as "peacetime" before the fighting started.

As the war drew to its close things moved so rapidly that one can do little more here than list a few of the outstanding events. In North-West Europe the failure of the Ardennes offensive marked the end of any further serious opposition. On March 7 the Americans crossed the Rhine by the bridge at Remagen and a bridgehead was soon established. Once over the river they occupied the Ruhr, and, on April 26, joined hands with the Russians on the Elbe, while, further north, Montgomery was driving the shattered German right wing back towards Schleswig-Holstein. The death of Hitler was announced on May 1, his old friend Mussolini having been lynched in Milan three days earlier, one day before the unconditional surrender of the German armies in Italy. The final submission of the Third Reich came on May 7 when Dönitz, the naval Commander-in-Chief, momentarily assumed the supreme power and was allowed by the Allies to sign the act of unconditional surrender. The following day was celebrated as VE Day.

It is sadly true that as adversity had brought the Allies closer together so success increasingly tended to reveal their divergent points of view, as the Yalta Conference, held in February, demonstrated all too clearly. Roosevelt stood firmly by his belief in Stalin's integrity, a quality which the more percipient Churchill failed to observe, while Montgomery's relations with his American colleagues became increasingly strained. The situation was not improved by the death in April of President Roosevelt which left General Marshall in virtual control of American policy in Europe. Then in the General Election held in July the Labour Party was returned to power with a large majority and Mr. Clement Attlee became Prime Minister. So it was that Mr. Churchill attended the initial sessions of the Three-Power Conference held in Potsdam, while Mr. Attlee acted as British representative in the concluding stages. It was hardly a favourable atmosphere in which to draw up the map of post-war Europe

In Burma the Fourteenth Army crossed the Irrawaddy on February 14, occupied Mandalay at the end of March and, when

Rangoon fell on May 3, entailing as it did the practical liberation of all of Burma, they and their brilliant commander, General Slim, had every reason to feel proud of the achievements of the "Forgotten Army".

In the Pacific the American stranglehold on Japan closed in remorselessly, and the names of Okinawa and Iwo Jima were written forever on the pages of American history. As the inevitable approached Japanese resistance became increasingly fanatical, the utterly unreal attitude of the militarists in Tokyo being epitomized by the last voyage of the super-cruiser Yamato *which put to sea on April 6 with only enough fuel for the outward journey. The end, as everyone knows, came with dramatic finality when the Americans dropped two atom bombs on Hiroshima and Nagasaki on August 6 and 9. On the 14th Japan surrendered and the Second World War was officially over.*

The problems of the post-war world do not concern us here, the end of the war seeming a more appropriate moment to end this selection than the arbitrary landmark of a new year. Peterborough signs off, suitably enough for one who listed his recreations in Who's Who *as "anything highbrow", with a quotation from Alexander Pope. It may not be unreasonable to suggest, however, that he viewed the prospect of a post-war Socialist Britain with marked distaste and left his readers in little doubt that, in his view, Churchill had won the war and had been dishonourably cast aside in the hour of victory. After the election he ran a series of paragraphs under the heading "Socialist Sayings", of which a single example must suffice: "'There can be no question of our supporting the Government in its rearmament policy.' Mr. Attlee in the Labour Conference debate, October, 1936."*

Taught Princess Elizabeth

Mr. C. H. K. Marten, the only K.C.V.O. in the Honours List, has been Vice-Provost of Eton for 14 years.

When in 1896 he returned to Eton from Balliol College, Oxford, where he took a first in Modern History, he quickly won a great reputation as a vivid and inspiring teacher of history.

On his appointment to the Vice-Provostship, there appeared in the Eton College Chronicle a welcome in verse over the initials of the then headmaster, Dr. Cyril Alington, now Dean of Durham.

One of the stanzas runs:

On ev'ry theme that's topical, or project philanthropical,
This best of Lower Masters brings unfailingly to bear
A brain that's full of interest, a heart that won't begin to rest,
But claims in ev'ry trouble its most sympathetic share.

The concluding stanza begins:

Etonian historians, Edwardians, Victorians,
Will hail in Henry Marten the begetter of them all.

For more than three years Mr. Marten was Princess Elizabeth's tutor in history and constitutional law and, it is said, found her a most enthusiastic student. *January 2*

Story from Italy

On a narrow road a British gun had sunk to a not inconsiderable depth in the mud (a common occurrence) when a high-ranking officer came up and asked, "Are you stuck?"

From the interior of the tractor drawing the gun came the answer, "No, we're burying the —— thing." *January 4*

Mr. Churchill in French

According to Dr. Leslie Burgin, greatest linguist in the House of Commons, they prefer in France Mr. Churchill's speeches untranslated. Dr. Burgin discovered this when recently he gave French translations of them to various Government departments in Paris.

It was pointed out, for instance, that "la fin du commencement" had not the ring of "the end of the beginning."

I was discussing this with a French writer yesterday, who gave it as his opinion that the difficulty of adequately rendering Mr. Churchill's oratory into French arose from his using—at his intensest moments—words of an Anglo-Saxon or Teutonic rather than of a classical derivation.

In support he quoted the famous "I have nothing to offer but blood, toil, tears and sweat."

The four essential words in this sentence, he remarked, would sound comparatively flat when directly translated into their French equivalents. *January 5*

Presidential Reading

I was interested in President Roosevelt's rider to his statement that ice conditions would determine whether the next meeting of the Big Three would be held at the North or the South Pole. His rider was to the effect that, in any case, he intended to take "The English Spirit" with him.

Its author, A. L. Rowse, is a pure-bred Cornishman. On his father's side he comes of a family of tin miners, and as a boy he went to the local elementary and secondary schools.

For the most part, however, he was left to his own devices and such reading as could be obtained in a working-class home. History was his passion.

Imaginative Historian

A brilliant career at Oxford was crowned by an All Souls Fellowship. Now at 41 Mr. Rowse has an assured reputation as a writer and an imaginative historian.

Mr. Jonathan Cape, who published his "Spirit of English History," tells me that he also hopes to bring out the second volume of his autobiography. Mr. Rowse is now at work upon it and is calling it "A Cornishman at Oxford."

He has, incidentally, political ambitions and has twice stood as a Socialist for his home constituency, Penryn and Falmouth.

January 10

The Ten "Thes"

The Genealogical Office in Dublin, until recently the Ulster Office of Arms, is preparing a register of ancient Irish titles dating from the days of the Gaelic clan system. Already it has acknowledged 10 men who claimed to be the present holders of the titles.

These titles are distinguished by the use of the definite article "The." They are The MacDermot, The McGillycuddy of the Reeks, The O'Callaghan, The O'Conor Don, The O'Donoghue of the Glen, The O'Donovan, The O'Morchoe, The O'Neill, The Fox and The O'Toole.

Some appear to be cosmopolitans. The O'Callaghan is a Spanish don living in Madrid. The O'Toole is a French count with an address in Paris. The O'Neill lives in Lisbon.

One an M.C.

A descendant of the last King of Ireland, The O'Conor Don, is a Jesuit. The MacDermot, also known as the Prince of Coolavin, recently celebrated his 82nd birthday. Both of these live in Ireland.

The O'Donovan is Col. Morgan O'Donovan, M.C., who lives at Bideford, but keeps contact with Ireland. Dubliners have a story about him.

Finding that he had no admission ticket to an international Rugby match in Dublin, he secured the loan of a programme seller's cards and uniform and got in to cheer for Ireland.

Most picturesquely named of all, The McGillycuddy of the Reeks, called after the County Kerry mountains, was until recently an Irish Senator. He is at present in this country. *January 12*

Right Answer

The teacher at a kindergarten class in Germany said: "Now then children, if your father was the Fuehrer, what would you like to be?'

The first boy replied, "A Field-Marshal," the second "An Admiral," the third "An Air Commodore." The fourth boy, who was a Jew, in his turn replied, "An orphan." *January 19*

Gainsborough Celebrates

That stalwart racehorse, Gainsborough, whose progeny have won 474 races and £340,144 in stake money, has arrived to-day at the ripe old age of 30. He is celebrating the event in retirement at the Harewood Stud, Newbury.

Twenty-nine years ago Gainsborough entered the sale ring at

Newmarket a yearling with a 2,000 guineas reserve on him. He did not reach it, and the late Lady James Douglas, his breeder, decided to race him.

Two years later Gainsborough won the Two Thousand Guineas, the Derby and the St. Leger—one of the three winners of the famous Triple Crown in this century.

Solario and Hyperion are Gainsborough's most illustrious sons. Lord Derby could have sold Hyperion for £100,000 even in war-time.

January 24

Paris Occupation Story

What must surely be one of the most unusual stories of the German occupation of Paris reaches me by way of New York.

After four years in London a Frenchman returned apprehensively to his apartment in the Boulevard Malesherbes, which had been commandeered during his absence by a Prussian colonel of the Luftwaffe.

To the Frenchman's astonishment and relief, instead of the expected devastation, he found the place in good order, and all his rare books and pictures intact. Even his cook reported that the "sale Boche" had not only paid her salary, but had also appreciated her skill.

Berlin Recompense

The greatest surprise of all, however, was a note which awaited him in French:

> My Dear Monsieur,
> Although I've not had the pleasure of making your acquaintance, I feel as if I know you well through your taste in books, pictures and cooking—all admirable. I've enjoyed thoroughly the years of your life which they've enabled me to live.
>
> Now circumstances suggest that I begin a journey towards Berlin. I anticipate that you too may shortly be visiting Berlin. In such a case, may I suggest that you arrange to be quartered in my apartment near the Grunewald.
>
> To be sure it cannot equal the perfection of your own, but there are good books, a few interesting prints and comfortable furniture.

The German ended by saying that he hoped his bibelots would

recompense the Frenchman for this second unavoidable absence from the perfection of his own apartments. *February 2*

Oslo's Song To-day

A favourite song in Oslo is the revival of the melody of the Swedish composer, Ernst Rolf, "It goes better and better every day."

The Norwegian SS newspaper Germaneren comments, "It is incomprehensible how Norwegians can be so dead to common decency as to go around singing such words." *February 3*

"Mein Kampf" Quotation

I have already picked out one or two quotations from "Mein Kampf" which have a topical application. Here is one particularly appropriate to the present moment:

> The German people, as its history has so often proved, is prepared to go on fighting for phantoms till it is bled white.

One wonders whether the German people have ever really read Hitler's diffuse gospel of Nazidom. *February 7*

The Gladstone Baronetcy

The family baronetcy to which Gladstone's grandson, Capt. A. C. Gladstone, the famous Oxford oar of 40 years ago, has just succeeded has a remarkable history. When Sir Robert Peel's Ministry came to an end in 1846 he wanted to honour two men.

One was a youthful member of his administration—William Ewart Gladstone. The other was the ex-Cabinet Minister's father, John Gladstone.

The latter was a rugged Liverpool individualist who defended slave-trading, built a number of churches and flatly forbade his famous son ever to become a clergyman. With Queen Victoria's special approval, Sir Robert Peel made John Gladstone a baronet.

The young statesman was touched, but as he was only the fourth son, neither he nor anyone else imagined that the baronetcy would come his way. Now, almost a century later, it descends to his grandson. *February 21*

Europe's Future

"This Question of Populations" is a pamphlet by that many-sided man, Mr. Laurence Cadbury. Besides being an authority on this subject, he is a director of the Bank of England and chairman of Cadbury Brothers and of the Daily News Ltd.—also a big game hunter.

Having read this 24-page pamphlet, I should say that it contains as much matter for disturbing thought as a shelf-load of political works.

Mr. Cadbury's point is that the post-war settlement, if it is to be lasting, must be still workable and enforceable in, say, 1970. That, he says, will hardly be the case if population trends go on as they are going now.

The position is that the peoples of the North and West of Europe are tending to shrink in numbers while those of the South and East —poorer and less well equipped—are increasing.

If these trends continue, Mr. Cadbury holds, the peace may again be endangered. These tendencies have been pointed out before, but Mr. Cadbury's presentation of them is fresh and arresting.

The best hope he sees for the poor but increasing peoples lies in industrialisation, which raises living standards and tends to check expanding numbers. *February 26*

"Colonel Chris"

Now on leave is an unusually interesting officer of the war-time British Army. He is Christopher Montague Woodhouse, Lord Terrington's second son, who at 27 is a full colonel.

Just down from Oxford when the war began, he joined the Royal Artillery and in 1942 started on his extraordinary series of exploits in Greece.

For two years he and his men were the bugbear of the Germans. Richard Capell, in a despatch last November, told *Daily Telegraph* readers how "Col. Chris"—the Greeks cannot pronounce Woodhouse—was the most famous man in Greece.

> His name is a talisman, his prestige acknowledged through the whole country and himself personally known north, south, east and west.

Hertford Scholar

Col. Woodhouse, who incidentally is known as "Monty" by his friends, is to attend a forthcoming investiture to receive the D.S.O. and O.B.E. he won in Greece.

At Oxford he was one of the best classics of his year, winning both the Hertford and the Craven, so his prowess in war is equalled by his prowess in scholarship.

After the war he intends to pursue his studies for the Bar.

March 9

Conversation Piece

An old lady sitting alone in a railway compartment was joined by an American soldier who was chewing gum.

After some 20 minutes she looked at him over her spectacles, saying kindly, "You know, young man, I am rather deaf, and haven't heard a word you've been saying the whole time."

March 12

Heine—Prophet

In the prose works of Heine, who died in 1856, I came across this prophetic passage:

> Christianity has occasionally calmed the German love of war, but it cannot destroy that savage lust. Once the Cross, that restraining talisman, is broken, the old Norse fury will take command.
>
> The old gods will rise from forgotten ruins and rub the dust of a thousand years from their eyes. Thor will leap to life, and his hammer will bring down the cathedrals.
>
> When the crash comes it will come like nothing ever heard in history. A drama will be performed which will make the French Revolution seem like a pretty idyll.

No wonder Heine's books have been burned and banned by the Nazis.

March 20

Schedule—Skedule

Henry Fowler, of "Modern English Usage" fame, would have liked a story which Capt. Gammans, the member for Hornsey, has brought back from America and told at a lunch given by the Paint Manufacturers' Association yesterday.

Gen. Eisenhower and Field-Marshal Montgomery were discussing "English as she is spoke" here and across the Atlantic. "I guess there's nothing wrong with our English," said "Ike."

"Nonsense," said "Monty." "Yanks can't even pronounce the language. Can you tell me, 'Ike,' what excuse there can be for calling schedule 'skedule'?"

"Well," replied "Ike," "that was the way I was taught to say it at shool." *March 22*

Untough Toscanini

Toscanini—78 to-morrow—on the rostrum is the toughest of conductors, getting every ounce from the players under his baton. In private life he is the most untough of men.

Here is an incident which happened during one of his visits to London in the immediate pre-war years.

A young woman who had lost her newly born child listened on the wireless by her bed to the concert Toscanini was conducting.

The next day she was able to write to him to say how much it had cheered her up. She did not sign her name, putting at the top only the words, "From a West End nursing home."

A few days later her nurse asked her if she had by any chance written to Toscanini, whose secretary was on the telephone.

He had every West End nursing home rung up until he got the right one. Then he sent the young woman a signed photograph and a few words of thanks. *March 24*

Steve Earned £250,000

Only a few hours before Steve Donoghue died yesterday he and Hotspur were talking flat-racing prospects in a West End restaurant. Steve told my colleague that he had had some heart trouble and was about to see his doctor.

The little man, Hotspur tells me, was in a quiet mood. Nevertheless, wearing the smile which helped to make him one of the greatest idols sport has known, he willingly spent a good deal of his evening signing his autograph.

Steve Donoghue undoubtedly lived every moment of his life, but he was unlucky to be born a super-optimist as well as a wonderful horseman. The two things did not work out to his advantage in the long run.

In 25 years his jockey earnings were considerably more than £250,000. He could not, however, appreciate the value of money. It melted as fast as it arrived.

Gordon Richards's Tribute

Gordon Richards, who took the jockeys' crown from the old champion, never forgot the encouragement he received from Steve when he was at the bottom of the ladder.

"However popular he may have been with the public, he was still more popular with us in the weighing room. He helped the least, the last and the poorest of us," said Gordon at a gathering held in 1938 to commemorate Steve's retirement.

Most of the front-rank jockeys to-day certainly owe much to Donoghue's fatherly advice when they were struggling apprentices.

At the height of his career he never lost his modesty. "Come on, Steve!" was sweet music, but hero worship did not distort his brilliant judgment. *March 24*

Earl Lloyd-George's Homeland

Ty Newydd (the new House), where Lord Lloyd-George died, commands a lofty view of the sweeping Cardigan Bay, and from his bedroom window he had an uninterrupted view of the sea.

He bought Ty Newydd in 1941, and it was here, on 40 acres of land, that he was continuing the experiments in fruit-growing that he conducted at his farm at Churt—experiments that were already being watched with considerable interest by Welsh agriculturists.

From the farmhouse Lord Lloyd-George could have tossed a stone on to the cottage where he lived as a boy.

He had a simple, unaffected upbringing in the "two-up and two-down cottage" where his uncle carried on business as the village cobbler, and from which he went to the village school and acquired his love of Welsh hymns in the Baptist chapel at Criccieth.

Memorable Tributes

I have often thought of two remarkable tributes to Lord Lloyd-George by two of his outstanding contemporaries, who had formerly been his political opponents.

Lord Milner, speaking at a private dinner just after the Armistice, used these words which, I believe, have never been published before:

> If there is one person to whom more than to any other this great victory is due, it is to the man who now presides over the destinies of this nation. His methods are dubious and his manners are often intolerable, but he has a genius and an insight and an absolutely amazing courage which place him, in my opinion, high among the great rulers of our race, not even excluding the elder Pitt, who also had grave defects of character.

The second tribute fell almost involuntarily from the lips of Lord Balfour while he was assisting in an ovation to the hero of the hour. "The little beggar," he said, "deserves it all." Coming from "A.J.B.," that was worth more than any formal eulogy. *March 27*

A Lawrence Confession

There was a characteristic Lawrence passage in one of the five letters written by the author to his friend, Vyvyan Richards, and sold with a copy of the "Seven Pillars of Wisdom" at Sotheby's yesterday. Here it is:

> My bodyguard of fifty Arab tribesmen, picked riders from the young men of the deserts, are more splendid than a tulip garden, and we ride like lunatics, and with our Beduins pounce on unsuspecting Turks and destroy them in heaps; and it is all very gory and nasty after we close grips. I love the preparation and the journey and loathe the physical fighting.

These letters naturally stimulated the bidding. Lawrence's well-known book has been fetching less than it did at one time, but the copy sold yesterday went to £520. *March 29*

An Author's "Lines"

Sir Osbert Sitwell calls his autobiography, which has just been published, "Left Hand, Right Hand!" because, according to palmistry, the lines of the left hand are "incised unalterably at birth," the lines of the right hand are those we make ourselves.

In the first volume—there are to be four—the author is chiefly concerned with his ancestors and the "lines" he has inherited. Among the portraits is one of Lord Londesborough, his grandfather on his mother's side, a man of immense wealth, which he dissipated "in a thousand different directions."

When he inherited his fortune in 1861 he provided all the chief servants with cheque books so that they drew on the funds without worrying him.

This is Sir Osbert's somewhat startling description of his own father's manners: "about the time of Charles II, but with a touch, too, of the Meredithian baronet, Sir Willoughby Patterne or Sir Austin Feverel, clinging to them." *April 9*

Sombre Coincidence

A curious fact was pointed out to me yesterday in connection with President Roosevelt's death. This is that the Presidents who were elected, or re-elected, in 1840, 1860, 1880, 1900, 1920 and 1940 have all died in office.

President Harrison died in 1841, Abraham Lincoln, first elected in 1860, was assassinated during his second term. President Garfield, elected in 1880, died in his first year of office.

President McKinley, re-elected in 1900, was assassinated in September, 1901. President Harding, elected in 1920, died in August, 1923.

President Roosevelt, re-elected for his third term in 1940, has maintained this sombre record.* *April 14*

Priority

A British scientist was due to lecture in Washington. On arrival at Foynes he was off-loaded to make room for a staff colonel with a priority. As this meant he would not be able to arrive in time, he cancelled his lecture and returned home.

Later it transpired that the staff colonel had flown to Washington for the sole purpose of being present at the lecture. *April 19*

Old Ties with California

M. Molotov's visit to San Francisco will doubtless remind him that Russia had many ties with California in the early part of last century.

*President Kennedy, who was assassinated in 1963, was elected in 1960.

I have been reading Gertrude Atherton's book about the early days in the Spanish colony, "Golden Gate Country," which has recently been published in America.

In 1806 Nicolai Petrovich de Rezanov, High Chamberlain to Alexander I, landed with a half-starved crew. He came for food and found romance, falling in love with "Concha," the Governor's beautiful daughter, who was destined to become the most famous woman in the history of Old California.

They never married, for de Rezanov died on the way to Rome to get the consent of the Pope.

Before his death he passed on the news that the country abounded in otters. Shortly afterwards a hundred Russians were settled on the coast, and remained until the supply of otters, which they killed at the rate of 1,000 a month, was exhausted. *April 23*

Governing Germans

Maj.-Gen. Gerald Templer, who has succeeded Brig. Robbins in command of the Military Government organisation of Field-Marshal Montgomery's 21st Army Group, has assumed a very responsible task.

He becomes de facto governor and supreme arbiter of the lives and conditions of many millions of Germans resident in the wide areas of Germany that British troops have conquered.

By training a professional soldier, of stern character and a strict disciplinarian, Gen. Templer has taken over a job which, as the war draws to its end in Europe, will become of ever-increasing importance.

He started the war as Deputy Director of Military Intelligence under Gen. Mason-MacFarlane at Lord Gort's headquarters at Arras, and played an active part in "Macforce," the heterogeneous collection of units under that General's command in the retreat to Dunkirk.

At the Anzio Landing

After rapid promotion at home, becoming at 43 the youngest acting lieutenant-general in the Army, Gen. Templer persuaded the Army Council to allow him to leave his corps to lead a division in the field.

At the Anzio landing, where his division suffered heavy losses, he served with great distinction.

Later he was appointed to command the Sixth Armoured Division in Italy. While holding this post he was severely wounded when the chassis of a large Army lorry, which had hit a mine just behind him, fell on his jeep, crushing his back and causing severe injuries to his spine. He has made a miraculous recovery.

Colossal Task

While originally, as a soldier, he looked askance at what he considered to be a civilian job, a month's tour of his vast bailiwick in captured Germany has already made him an enthusiast for Military Government.

The General is keenly conscious of the colossal tasks that the reorganisation of Germany and the disposal of the countless hordes of displaced persons, now wandering loose through the Reich, involve. *April 27*

Great Rider's Escape

One of the few prisoners to get out alive from the notorious Nazi extermination camp at Mauthausen, near Linz, was, I hear, the well-known gentleman rider, Capt. Lebellin de Dionne, of the French 4th Hussars, who before the war won such well-known events as the Prix de Paris at Auteuil and the Coupe Mussolini at Rome.

Arrested in 1941 as a French resister, he spent three years in various camps. Finally, in February, 1945, he reached Mauthausen.

Within an hour of his arrival he and 400 other prisoners were paraded on the drill ground. Despite the bitter weather, with a temperature well below freezing-point, they were forced to strip naked.

S.S. troopers, armed with a tommy-gun in one hand and a hose in the other, then kept them waiting for three hours. By that time a dozen had dropped dead.

The whole party were then marched off to another courtyard, where they were lined up against a wall and kept standing for another seven hours in complete darkness without food and water. Here another hundred died.

Shammed Death

Treatment of this kind, with sadistic variations by the camp commander, a Major Bachmeyer, continued throughout the night.

By the next morning Capt. de Dionne, who had so far miraculously escaped injury, realised that extermination of the whole party was certain. In a desperate attempt to save his life he fell on top of a pile of corpses, shamming death.

Shortly afterwards his body was taken with others on a handcart to the crematory, where he managed to steal away, still naked, to reach his barrack. There, in the confusion of the night's massacre, his return passed unnoticed. Only 64 men survived the 18 hours of torture.

Capt. de Dionne is already on the road to complete recovery, and hopes after the war to do some racing in England. *May 7*

Paris Prices Rocketing

In common with all other objects of permanent value such as jewels, gold, stamps and pictures, books have rocketed in price in France to-day. With the British gold sovereign standing at 5,300 francs as against a normal paper exchange rate for the pound sterling of 200 francs, this is not surprising.

My colleague, Douglas Williams, who recently attended a book sale in Paris, sends me some interesting and almost incredible prices that were reached. For a 1782 copy of "Les Liaisons Dangereuses," which in 1934 sold for 585 francs—less than £3—41,000 francs or over £200, was eagerly bid. For a collected edition of the works of Joachim du Bellay, sold 10 years ago for 5,600 francs, or £28, 160,000 francs, or £800, was paid.

£1,200 for a Montaigne

A 17th century edition of Molière, which brought only 6,100 francs, or £30, in the thirties, fetched 125,000 francs, or £625. An early copy of Montaigne's Essays, priced at 6,500 francs, or £32, in 1934, went at the astonishing figure of 240,000 francs, or £1,200.

Even relatively modern authors realised fantastic prices. Thus, Claude Farrère's "La Bataille" sold for £250 and several novels by Anatole France for sums ranging from £100 to £175 apiece.

A 1925 edition of de Maupassant's "La Maison Tellier" went for £60. Two of Stendhal's novels, "Le Rouge et Le Noir" and "La Chartreuse de Parme," made the highest prices of all at £1,540 and £1,150 respectively. *May 8*

Opera Landmark?

Sadler's Wells is reopening to-night with the first performance of a new opera by Benjamin Britten, the young English composer. It is likely to be a landmark, I am assured, in British opera.

It is nearly 10 years since a new opera by a native composer was produced there. This was Vaughan Williams' "The Poisoned Kiss," which, as sometimes happens, had eulogistic Press notices, only to be forgotten.

The idea for "Peter Grimes" came to Mr. Britten after reading an article by Mr. E. M. Forster on George Crabbe. The composer, then in America, at once set out to find a copy of Crabbe's works, finally choosing the long poem, "The Borough," on which to base his libretto.

A chance meeting with Koussevitzky led to the great American conductor's commissioning the opera in memory of his wife. Practical difficulties, however, prevented its production in America.

June 7

Pour Encourager les Autres

Among the sprinkling of uniformed women present when men of the Second Army Headquarters held a D-Day anniversary sports meeting in Luneberg was Junior Commander Mary Churchill.

She was first to rise as a volunteer in the ladies egg-and-spoon race. To encourage the others, however, it became necessary to make it a mixed race, and Brig. H. E. Pyman, the Chief of Staff, then joined Miss Churchill.

Potatoes were used for eggs, and Miss Churchill split hers in half in her first feverish attempt to scoop it up. Then she collided with the Brigadier at full speed, dropping the halves on the grass. Eventually a major of signals won in a canter.

German children had infiltrated into the arena. They sat, wide-eyed, between the Tommies, who continue to obey orders by ignoring them.

June 8

Verbigerative Cheque

Gertrude Stein's virtuosity in what an American psychiatrist has called "verbigeration" has given the English reading world plenty of amusement.

Miss Stein is not the only humorist, however, who thinks fun is fun and business is business.

Her publisher, Bennet Cerf, in a Steinish mood, sent her a cheque made out for "two thousand thousand dollars dollars."

She lost no time in cabling him from France: "Cut out this nonsense and make out my cheque properly." *June 11*

Fallen in Italy

From the current number of the Poetry Review, I quote this epitaph:

> Beneath the olive and the vine
> They rest, whom War has spent.
> Surely their clay makes oil and wine
> A greater Sacrament.

The author is Maj. David Tennant, a great-nephew of Sir Charles Tennant and cousin to Lady Oxford and Asquith. *June 26*

Souvenirs from Bembridge

Evidence that the Germans intended to land in the Isle of Wight, had they been able, has been discovered by Lt.-Col. David Niven, the film actor, who is now attached to Shaef.

With his sisters Lt.-Col. Niven had a cottage at Bembridge for several years before the war. He has just sent a couple of photographs to Cmdr. R. M. Tabureau, the honorary secretary of the Bembridge Sailing Club.

One is an aerial view of Bembridge Harbour and the other of the beach off the Garland Club.

He writes:

> The enclosed might amuse you and the members. I found them in a book of possible invasion beaches among the effects of a German S.S. Battalion Commander in Stolberg. It made me feel quite homesick!

The pictures, I hear, have been hung in the Club's dining-room. *June 29*

False Economy

On one of the few occasions on which Gertrude Lawrence tried to be economical she nearly alienated Noel Coward for life. She reports the incident in her memoirs "A Star Danced," just published in the United States.

After writing "Private Lives"—Miss Lawrence says it was written especially for her—Mr. Coward sent the script to her in New York and expressed the hope that she would be able to appear in the play with him in London.

Miss Lawrence was eager to do so, but was under contract to André Charlot, so she dashed off a cable in reply, which she made brief in order to save money. "Play delightful. Nothing wrong that can't be fixed," it said.

What she wished to imply was that she was sure Charlot would release her, but to the playwright the message had only one meaning: an actress was presuming to criticise his work.

A Playwright Scorned

"Noel Coward was furious. The splutter of his wrath lighted up the Pacific across which he was then travelling," says Miss Lawrence. "Cable wires were scorched by scathing comments on my ability as critic and actress."

He was still indignant when he caught up with her at Capt. Molyneux's villa at Cap Dail, near Monte Carlo. Miss Lawrence maintains that Mr. Coward has not entirely forgiven her for that cable to this day. *July 23*

Stalin's Love Birds

I hear from Potsdam that in the personal suite attending Marshal Stalin at the Three-Power Conference was a pair of budgerigars. The love-birds lived in a large gilt cage near the Marshal's bedroom, and he used always to pay them a visit before breakfast.

While orderlies waited, napkin on arm, Stalin chirped to his budgerigars, and the budgerigars chirped back.

The birds, it appears, are his constant companions. He takes them with him wherever he goes.

According to my informant, Molotov alone of Stalin's entourage, is allowed to chirp at the budgerigars. No one else ventures to take this liberty. *August 4*

"Little Billee"

Frederick Walker, one of whose water colour drawings fetched 760 guineas at Christie's yesterday, is immortalised by George Du Maurier as Little Billee in "Trilby."

This young genius was a best seller in Victorian days. Since then his works in oils have often brought huge sums at auction. In the Red Cross sale, 1917, his famous "Plough" realised as much as 5,400 guineas and was forthwith presented to the Tate Gallery by the buyer, Lady Wernher.

Already the nation owned Walker's picture, "The Harbour of Refuge," given by Sir William Agnew in 1893. Two days before making this munificent gift, he had refused an offer of 10,000 guineas from the Duke of Westminster. *August 4*

Living Well

Douglas Williams, *The Daily Telegraph* War Correspondent who has been visiting American headquarters at Frankfurt, tells me he was much impressed by the way in which Gen. Eisenhower's staff are looked after.

Lunching at the snack bar, which is open for service all day, he paid four marks, or two shillings, for the following perfect hot-weather meal:

Cold meat plate—consisting of ham, sausage, roast lamb, tuna fish, pickle and salad—a tumbler of tomato juice and one of orange juice, apple pie with peach ice-cream, and a boiling hot cup of coffee with real cream.

After lunch he went to the American officers' "Naafi," and for 25 marks, or 12s 6d, received the following ration: 12 good cigars, 100 cigarettes, a tooth-brush, seven chocolate and candy bars, a large writing pad, a tin of peanuts, a tin of orange juice, three up-to-date American magazines, six boxes of matches, and a bottle of hair lotion.

And then, it may be suggested, he woke up. But no, it really happened. *August 8*

Lord Cherwell's Distinctions

Mr. Churchill's reference to Lord Cherwell's part in the discovery of the atomic bomb was well deserved. Lord Cherwell acted as liaison officer between the scientists and the War Cabinet, and was himself one of the members of the consultative committee which directed the whole enterprise.

His personal association with Mr. Churchill during the years of his Premiership made him known to the general public, but as Professor Lindemann he was already a distinguished figure at Oxford and among scientists. He and Mr. Churchill had been intimate friends for many years.

He is a man of great personality and outstanding parts, who combines eminence as a scientist with a general knowledge of the world. It was this combination of qualities which made him so useful to Mr. Churchill during the war.

He is also an aeronautical expert and in the last war distinguished himself as an experimental pilot. His favourite games are golf and tennis.

His work inevitably brought him into contact with Professor Einstein, whom he was able to help when he was a victim of Nazi oppression. *August 8*

French Scientists Help

Two French scientists who have played an important part in the research which resulted in the atomic bomb are the Duc de Broglie and Prince Louis de Broglie, two brothers who belong to one of the great historic houses of France.

It was for his work in verification of Prince Louis de Broglie's theory of the electron that Sir George Thomson received the Nobel Prize in 1937. The Prince was awarded the Nobel Prize in 1929.

Both brothers are Academicians. The Duc de Broglie was elected in 1934, Prince Louis in 1944, the first election to the Academy after the liberation of Paris.

Kernel of the Atom

The Duc de Broglie has been a frequent visitor to this country, and has been given honorary degrees at Oxford and Leeds.

In 1931, speaking of the possibility of getting at the "kernel of the atom" and breaking it, he said:

"To the over-anxious modern world I would say this: no such result can possibly be achieved for several generations, and this only if in the interim men have not succeeded in destroying themselves and in causing the suicide of Western civilisation."

As it turned out, it was the necessity to destroy which provided the impetus to achieve in a few years what de Broglie was certain would take so much longer.

Even so, his final warning holds good: "We scientists work for the betterment of mankind, not for its destruction. There is no hope for the future of science unless peace is assured." *August 8*

"Into Ruin Hurled"

The following lines from the "Essay on Man" have been sent me as a specimen of the prophetic genius of Alexander Pope:

Who sees with equal eye, as God of all,
A hero perish or a sparrow fall,
Atoms or systems into ruin hurled,
And now a bubble burst and now a world.

I suppose it is prophecy, in a sense, as neither Pope nor anyone else in the 18th century had any idea of the sort of atom that has just been exploded in Japan.

Pope's atom was just a tiny bit of something—like one of the specks of dust in a sunbeam. *August 10*

Index